Translating Style

A Literary Approach to Translation
A Translation Approach to Literature

Second Edition

Tim Parks

St. Jerome Publishing
Manchester, UK & Kinderhook (NY), USA

Published by

St. Jerome Publishing
2 Maple Road West, Brooklands
Manchester, M23 9HH, United Kingdom
Telephone +44 (0)161 973 9856
Fax +44 (0)161 905 3498
ken@stjeromepublising.com
http://www.stjerome.co.uk

InTrans Publications
P. O. Box 467
Kinderhook, NY 12106, USA
Telephone (518) 758-1755
Fax (518) 758-6702

ISBN 978-1905763-04-7 (pbk)

Typeset by
Delta Typesetters, Cairo, Egypt
Email: hilali1945@yahoo.co.uk

British Library Cataloguing in Publication Data
A catalogue record of this book is available from the British Library

Library of Congress Cataloging in Publication Data
Parks, Tim.
  Translating style : a literary approach to translation, a translation approach to literature / Tim Parks. -- 2nd ed.
      p. cm.
  Includes bibliographical references and index.
  ISBN 978-1-905763-04-7 (pbk. : alk. paper)
1. English fiction--Translations into Italian--History and criticism. 2. English fiction--20th century--History and criticism. 3. English language--Translating into Italian. 4. Modern-ism (Literature)--Great Britain. 5. English *fiction*--Appreciation--Italy. 6. Modernism (Literature)--Italy. 7. English language--Great Britain--Style. 8. Italian language--Style. I. Title.

PR137.I8P37 2007
458'.022--dc21
                                    2007020322

Translating Style

A Literary Approach to Translation, A Translation Approach to Literature

Second Edition

Tim Parks

Arising from a dissatisfaction with blandly general or abstrusely theoretical approaches to translation, this book sets out to show, through detailed and lively analysis, what it really means to translate literary style. Combining linguistic and lit crit approaches, it proceeds through a series of interconnected chapters to analyse translations of the works of D.H. Lawrence, Virginia Woolf, James Joyce, Samuel Beckett, Henry Green and Barbara Pym. Each chapter thus becomes an illuminating critical essay on the author concerned, showing how divergences between original and translation tend to be of a different kind for each author depending on the nature of his or her inspiration.

This new and *thoroughly revised edition* introduces a system of 'back translation' that now makes Tim Parks' highly-praised book reader friendly even for those with little or no Italian. An entirely new final chapter considers the profound effects that globalization and the search for an immediate international readership is having on both literary translation and literature itself.

Tim Parks was born in Manchester and studied at Cambridge and Harvard Universities. He presently runs a post-graduate course in translation at IULM university, Milan. He has written thirteen novels, the most recent being *Cleaver*, and three best selling accounts of life in provincial Italy as well as two collections of literary essays, *Hell and Back* and *The Fighter*. He is also the translator of Antonio Tabucchi, Italo Calvino, Alberto Moravia and Roberto Calasso and has twice won the prestigious John Florio prize and the Italo Calvino award for literary translation from Italian.

Praise for the first edition

This illuminating book should be read closely by anyone interested in the art of translation. Tim Parks belongs to that rarest breed of translator – one who also writes. He is a brilliantly idiosyncratic novelist who brings to the difficult task of translation a keen understanding of the way other novelists work.

Paul Bailey, *The Daily Telegraph*

A book ... for anyone with an interest in translation studies, whether they are studying, teaching or practising translation. But equally a book for literary critics, essential for anyone concerned with Modernist fiction, and of great value to those working in the field of stylistics. ... the reader is rewarded with unexpected and often brilliant insights. This is certainly one of the most interesting books on translation to appear recently.

Jean Boase-Beir, *The Translator*

... a stunningly successful essay on the nuts and bolts of translation, the most useful, from a translator's point of view, that I have ever come across. ... All Parks's examples are rewarding and stimulating, and (more surprisingly, perhaps) he has made the book so readable that I have read it anywhere and everywhere, in bed, on buses, in a hospital waiting room, even in the bath. It is that sort of book, approachable, exciting.

Isabel Quigley

Attractive and interesting.

Umberto Eco

Translating Style is the ideal book for anyone who loves great literature ... and who is fascinated by the mysterious ways in which writers exploit all the arcane qualities of literary language to expand our experience and our sensibilities. Bravo!

Peter Bondanella

Contents

Acknowledgements

The author and publisher are grateful for permission to reprint extracts as follows:

From Samuel Beckett:
Disjecta, Calder, 1983; *Murphy,* Picador, 1973; *Proust and Three Dialogues with Georges Duthuit,* Calder, 1987; *Watt,* Jupiter Books edition, Calder and Boyars, 1972. Used by permission of Calder Publications Ltd, London.
Murphy (1968). Used by permission of Editions de Minuit, Paris. Translation by Samuel Beckett.
Murphy, Sugarco Edizioni, Milan, 1967. Translation by Cesare Cristofolini.

From T.S. Eliot:
Excerpts from *The Waste Land,* in *Collected Poems 1909-1962,* copyright 1936, copyright 1964, 1963 by T.S. Eliot, reprinted by permission of Harcourt Brace & Company, and by permission of Faber and Faber Ltd., London.

From Henry Green:
Back; *Doting*; *Loving*; *Party Going.* Used by permission of Harvill Press, London.
Passioni, Einaudi, Turin, 1990. Translation by Stefania Bertola.
Partenza in gruppo, Adelphi, 2006. Translation by Carlo Bay.

From James Joyce:
The Dead; *A Portrait of the Artist as a Young Man*; *Ulysses.* Used by permission of the Estate of James Joyce. Copyright the Estate of James Joyce.
Dedalus, Adelphi, Milan, 1976. Translation by Cesare Pavese.
Gente di Dublino, Garzanti, Milan, 1976. Translation by Marco Papi and Emilio Tardini.
Ulisse, Oscar Mondadori, Milan, 1978. Translation by Giulio de Angelis.

From D.H. Lawrence:
Women in Love. Copyright 1920, 1922 by D.H. Lawrence, renewed 1948, 1950 by Frieda Lawrence. Used by permission of Viking Penguin, a division of Penguin Books USA Inc. and Laurence Pollinger Limited, London.
Donne innamorate, Rizzoli, Milan, 1989. Translation by Adriana dell'Orto. Used by permission of Rizzoli Corriere della Sera.

Author's Note to the New Edition

This is a completely revised edition of a book written ten years ago. As such it represents a radical attempt to extend the book's readership, to move it out of a niche and put it in the way of any reader interested in style, language and literature.

Why was this necessary? *Translating Style* was never an overly academic book. It was never jargon bound. I had wanted to show how the experience of translation can tell us a lot about literature, give us insights into the books we love that we will not pick up from regular criticism. And I wanted to suggest that an understanding of literary strategies is essential for the translator. The only way to do this, I thought, was by analysing extended examples of stylish writing, together with their corresponding translations. To draw in as many people as possible I chose authors and books that many readers would be familiar with: the great modernists in particular: Lawrence Joyce, Woolf, Beckett, plus two favourites of mine, Barbara Pym and Henry Green. The problem was that since I looked extensively at Italian translations of those books (Italian being my second language), readers with little or no Italian would feel left out. I resigned myself to the idea that, for better or worse, such a book could appeal only to a limited audience.

Yet again and again, over the years, people with no Italian at all told me they had read *Translating Style* and found it fascinating. If only, they said, they could get a slightly better sense of the transformations that had taken place in the Italian translation! This edition attempts to meet the needs of these readers, to demystify the Italian translations and hence to make my comments on the original English texts more persuasive.

How? Imperfectly no doubt, using back-translations and, occasionally, glosses. From the second chapter on, from the point that is where we begin to discuss the work of our six chosen authors, every passage of Italian translation is followed by a back-translation, which is to say by the same passage returned (back-translated) into English. This allows the reader to see what changes in diction, focusing, imagery and content have occurred in the Italian versions. These are not literal or word-for-word back-translations, but nor are they attempts to return the Italian to stylish English. They simply seek to show what the Italian reader is getting in terms of information and its arrangement. Where necessary, a word-for-word gloss is given of some key Italian phrases.

It will sound laboured perhaps, but the intention is always to have fun, to sharpen the mind through a reflection on how the reading experience is constructed. The translation, or for those with no Italian, the back-translation, serves as a sort of shadow text, or simply alternative, comparison with which will give us new insights into the English original.

Translating Style also has an underlying polemic that emerges in a final chapter written specifically for this edition. One of the effects of globalization has been that more literature – novels, plays and poetry – is translated than ever before. Often translations are published simultaneously with publication in the original language. Thus the community to whom a writer addresses his work is no longer specifically national, but international, multi-lingual. The last chapter considers the consequences of a situation where writers often work with eventual translation in mind and readers, particularly outside the English-speaking world, read most of their literature in translation. It is quite possible that this will change the way language is used in literature, and indeed the very content of the books we read.

1. Identifying an Original

For the last ten years or so I have been playing the game of inviting students to look at the same passage in English and Italian and to tell me which is the original and which the translation, a game that would later develop into a methodology, or almost. Here is the kind of text one inevitably starts with, because it is so easy. It is taken from a tourist guide.

> The clear poem of the surrounding landscape, where very sweet sunsets go down, the fertile land with long poplar-rows and slow streams of rivers and canals, the laborious and strong people of the vast agricultural and industrial zone (simple and persevering in their own traditions) form like a ring round the historical group of the city that the exemplary wisdom of the local administrations has opportunely respected.[1]

And the Italian:

> La limpida poesia del paesaggio circostante su cui scendono tramonti dolcissimi, la terra ubertosa con lunghi filari di pioppi e pigre correnti di fiumi e canali, la gente vigorosa e laboriosa della vasta zona agricola ed industriale (semplice e tenace nelle proprie tradizioni) fanno come da corona al gruppo storico della città che la saggezza esemplare delle amministrazioni locali ha opportunamente rispettato.

There is rarely a student who does not identify this as an Italian original in the space of a minute or so. And even the native English speaker with little or no Italian will immediately be aware that the English here is either a poor translation or a parody of some kind. Indeed, native English speakers have a tendency to burst out laughing when they hear the text read out loud. But can we say why exactly? And is there anything useful to be learnt from our reactions to a text like this?

Having shown students the passage I invite them to try to identify examples of lexical interference in the translation (for example false cognates, or collocations that are acceptable in Italian but not in English), then grammatical

---

[1] Multilingual tourist brochure published by Pelloni editori, Mantua. The text is undated, but believed to be about 1980.

interference (syntactical structures that are considered 'correct' and ordinary in Italian but not in English) and finally what I refer to as 'cultural interference' (elements that might be desirable in a passage of this kind in Italy, but not in an Anglo-Saxon culture).

What emerges from such an analysis when applied to this particular translation is that while there are many lexical and cultural 'problems', there is only one straight grammatical error in the English ('form like a ring'). So we are not talking about total incompetence on the part of the translator here. On the contrary, a large number of grammatical transformations have been successfully performed.

With regard to lexical interference, it is true that the false cognates ('laborious', 'zone', 'group') do their worst; nevertheless we soon appreciate that, like the grammar, they are not the main culprits in generating that growing hilarity that seizes the native English speaker as he reads through this text. The problem is rather more complicated.

Let us consider the collocation presented in the opening line:

The clear poem

La limpida poesia (*The clear/transparent/unruffled poem/poetry*)

Here we notice that while 'poem' is a true cognate of 'poesia' it is unusual to use the word figuratively in this way in English. The uncountable noun 'poetry', also a true cognate of 'poesia' (Italians use the same word for both the single 'poem' and the more generic 'poetry'), lends itself more easily to figurative use. Partly as a result of the difficulty with this leap into the figurative, and partly because the words 'limpido' and 'clear' only overlap for a limited part of their respective connotative ranges, the word 'clear' tends to be understood, before 'poem', as meaning 'easily comprehensible' rather than indicating, as does 'limpido', visual clarity, as in 'a clear day' or 'clear water'. As a result we have the impression that the writer has attempted a metaphor with lyric pretensions, but in the end made no real sense at all.

Only a little further on in the same opening sentence, the emphasizing of 'very' before 'sweet' to translate the Italian superlative 'dolcissimi' (*sweetest/very sweet*) in 'tramonti dolcissimi' (*sunsets very sweet*) is also a problem. One might just about accept 'sweet sunsets', though it is hardly recognizable either as common or poetic usage in English (alliteration helps us to accept it), but 'very sweet' draws too much attention to this adventurous collocation, seems rather prosaically to beg the question, 'ok, exactly how sweet can a sunset be?'

Then with splendid bathos those sunsets 'go down'. This, like the use of 'very', is by no means a grammatical error. True, the word 'sunset' already includes the idea of 'going down', so there is an element of redundancy here, but then so does the Italian 'tramonto' (*sunset*). Imagine a sentence of the variety, 'The sunset slowly subsided behind a horizon of soft hills'. Such a statement does not seem impossible, and the logic is exactly the same as 'very sweet sunsets go down'. No, the thing to notice here is simply that one can and one does say this in Italian, whereas one cannot say it in English (or not without being laughed at).

Similarly, while one can say 'tenace nelle proprie tradizioni' (*determined/ persevering in their own traditions*) in Italian, to say 'persevering in their own traditions' in English only begs the fascinating question, 'in whose traditions if not their own?'. The emphasizer 'own', like the previous 'very', is thus not only superfluous but distractingly so.

So far, then, comparison of the two passages does give us, if nothing else, a sense of the different spirit of these two languages, an awareness, that is, of how dangerous it can be to use emphasizers in English. Later on, even where the generous gesturing of the Italian translates easily into English (in terms of pure semantics) we cannot help feeling uneasy in the presence of words like 'vast' (to describe the agricultural area around Mantua), or expressions that insist on 'the exemplary wisdom of the local administrations'. And even without completing a word by word analysis of the whole passage, what has been said so far should be enough to prompt a first and obvious conclusion: that much of language has to do, not with the grammatical rules and transfor-mations we can learn in the classroom (though they are vital), but with what the people who speak the language consider normal and acceptable.

With this particular passage, then, we are aware of how much would have to change in an English translation, in order to achieve a reader reaction not too unlike that of an Italian reader of the original. The first line, for example, might have to go something like: 'The sharp lyricism of the surrounding countryside with its delicately hued sunsets ...'. We would have to aim, that is, for a style common to such texts as tourist brochures. And since this would remind us of the fact that the chief intention of this passage, indeed its *raison d'etre,* must be to encourage people to come to Mantua, one might begin to question whether some of the information in this passage could ever be rendered in the kind of lexis, syntax and register that the English use in tourist brochures.

Perhaps another way of putting this reflection would be to ask: does the English tourist really want to know about the 'vasta zona ... industriale' (*vast industrial area*) around the city? Will he believe that the 'local administra-tions' have acted with 'exemplary wisdom'? Certainly, as a translator one might become uneasy about writing such things. Hence a passage like this makes us aware of the need to translate, as it were, the general purpose or function of a text, rather than its exact semantic surface. This is a matter we shall have to return to.

For we still have not really answered the most interesting question of all. Why do native English speakers respond to this translation with laughter, or at least smiles? And, crucial for my purposes in this book, why do non-native speakers whose English is sufficiently advanced for them to appreciate that this is a poor translation not laugh?

The point here, perhaps, is that in its many departures from the kind of style one expects in a tourist guide (not to mention everyday English speech) the translation draws attention to itself as language rather than simply as content. In this regard it partakes of the arrogance of literature. That is, experience tells us that it is literature that usually assumes the right to deviate from more ordinary ways of saying things, to draw attention to itself as language. True, its deviations often then atrophy into the conventions of a recognizable poetic style, but it is a characteristic of the most dynamic literature to deviate even from these. Since a collocation like 'clear poem' certainly departs from more or less everything, it can be said to have something in common with literature. But of course we are happy (though not always initially so) for literature to offer such departures, because it often does so with what we sense is felicity: that is, we see an appropriateness between the deviation from standard forms of expression and the content of the text, and we sense a harmony between all the deviations taken together. The rhymed poem is the most extreme example:

> The fair breeze blew, the white foam flew,
> The furrow followed free;
> We were the first that ever burst
> Into that silent sea.[2]

But when a piece of writing assumes this right to deviate from standard forms, yet fails to deliver appropriateness and harmony, then we begin to laugh. We laugh at the gap between the ambitious gesture and the questionable achievement. Thus the Scottish poet William McGonagall gets an entry in *The Macmillan Encyclopedia* for his 'memorably bad poetry', much of which reads like a poor translation of a rhymed tourist guide:

---

[2] Samuel Taylor Coleridge, *The Ancient Mariner*.

Beautiful Railway Bridge of the silvery Tay!
That has caused the Emperor of Brazil to leave
His home far away, *incognito* in his dress,
And view thee ere he passed along *en route* to Inverness.[3]

The native English speaker laughs at the tourist brochure on Mantua because his sensibility to a common use of English, to the style of tourist guides and indeed to literary styles in general, makes him aware of the many amusingly inappropriate departures this passage makes from those forms, while nevertheless remaining comprehensible. Aping lyricism it plunges into absurdity. The foreigner does not laugh, or laughs less, because, although aware that there is much that is unusual and even 'wrong' with this English, his sensibility to the language is not such that he is acutely sensitive to its inappropriateness. Obviously we are in the area of subjective evaluation here, but the point I wish to establish is that it is extremely difficult to judge, in one's second language, the appropriateness or otherwise of a departure from ordinary forms of discourse. It is difficult to read the text, that is, with a finely developed sense of all the other texts which stand in relation to it and which give it, for the native reader, its full significance. Here, just to close the discussion is a possible translation of the piece, this time a little more aware of the sort of English that would ordinarily be used. Even those who have little Italian will be aware of how much has had to change, lexically, syntactically and 'culturally' to prevent the piece from seeming 'funny':

The lyrical beauty of the surrounding landscape with its soft-hued sunsets, the rich, arable fields bordered by poplar rows and gently flowing waterways, add a crowning aura to a city whose ancient centre has very sensibly been preserved intact. Meantime, within and without the town, the energetic, hard-working people of the busy North Italian plain carry on their simple, time-honoured traditions.

Proceeding from this opening example where original and translation are so easily and amusingly distinguishable, I might then go on to offer students a series of texts of the following variety.

GREAT MEALS IN MINUTES – Quick and Delicious.
The time-saver's cookbook. If you love good food but hate spending time preparing it, here's the cookbook you've been waiting for. GREAT

---

[3] William McGonagall, 'The Railway Bridge of the Silvery Tay', quoted from *Poetic Gems*, Duckworth, London, 1989.

MEALS IN MINUTES makes it possible for you to get in and out of
the kitchen in a snap – without resorting to those expensive and all-
too-familiar entrées.[4]

PIATTI PRONTI IN UN MINUTO. Una cucina rapida e squisita.
Il libro di cucina che vi farà risparmiare tempo. Se apprezzate la buona
cucina ma non avete il tempo per dedicarvi alla preparazione dei
cibi, ecco il libro che fa per voi. PIATTI PRONTI IN UN MINUTO
vi consentirà di entrare e uscire dalla cucina in un momento, senza
dover ricorrere alle pietanze surgelate, tanto costose quanto ormai sin
troppo comuni.

Here the uninitiated might be briefly confused as to which text is the original, since both English and Italian achieve a convincing register, deploying
the syntax and lexis typical of a junk-mail invitation to buy a cookbook. But
comparison of differences between the two rapidly points the way. These
might be listed as follows:

GREAT MEALS IN MINUTES

PIATTI PRONTI IN UN MINUTO – *DISHES READY IN A MINUTE*

The concept 'great' is absent in the Italian, while there is no concept in the
Italian absent in the English. Both texts include the kind of alliteration which
gives them that mnemonic quality useful in an expression that must function
as a title. If the text was translated into English from the Italian, is it likely
that a translator would have chosen to introduce the word 'great'? Hard to say.
Translating from the English, would there be any reason to eliminate some
reference to the very high quality of the food? Yes. An Italian audience might
be resistant to the notion that a meal produced in a few minutes could be 'great'.
The two cultures in question have rather different attitudes to cooking.

The phrases 'in minutes' and 'in un minuto' (*in a minute*), though semantically different, are standard forms in their respective languages for the same
concept, 'very quickly'. It is worth noting that while we are used to translators
making changes of this variety (where there are questions of standard forms)
there will be those who will object to changes that involve introducing or
eliminating a concept like 'great'.

---

[4] Promotional material for direct sales mailing, produced by Reader's Digest in the USA
and its subsidiary, Selezione dal Reader's Digest, in Italy. Again the material is undated,
but believed to be around 1988. Translation by Rita Baldassarre.

eliminate it. For one cannot reasonably assume, in Italy, that a large number of people 'hate' cooking, or, even assuming they do, that they are willing to admit as much.

The next divergence between the texts, 'the cookbook you've been waiting for' and 'il libro che fa per voi' (*the book that makes/is for you*) hardly helps us with the task of identification, since, as with 'in un minuto' and 'in minutes', both expressions have the same register and work well here in their respective languages, despite the evident difference in meaning. However, on reaching the last sentence, our growing suspicions that this must be an English original are amply confirmed.

> GREAT MEALS IN MINUTES makes it possible for you to get in and out of the kitchen in a snap – without resorting to those expensive and all-too-familiar entrées.

> PIATTI PRONTI IN UN MINUTO vi consentirà di entrare e uscire dalla cucina in un momento, senza dover ricorrere alle pietanze surgelate, tanto costose quanto ormai sin troppo comuni.
> (*DISHES READY IN A MINUTE will allow you to go in and out of the kitchen in a moment, without resorting to deep-frozen meals, as expensive by now as they are all too common*)

Here the very colloquial, unusual and appropriate, 'in a snap' is hardly matched, nor could have been inspired, by 'in un momento' (*in a moment*), while the last line shows the English referring to a cultural context (the use of recognizable deep-frozen entrées) which has to be explained in the Italian, whose readers are perhaps not familiar with such practices at all.

What conclusions can be drawn from all this? First that the text has been translated with a strong sense of purpose, or function. The translator strives to domesticate its content in order to arrive at the text's desired end (to sell the book). In this sense one might object that from a certain point of view, with the elimination of 'great' and 'hate', the text has not been 'translated' at all. For example, were this piece to appear in an American novel satirizing incongruous American attitudes to cooking, then an Italian translator with the task of communicating that incongruity in his own language would have been wise to maintain 'great' and 'hate'. No longer obliged to be faithful to the text's commercial function he would be eager to draw attention to its culture specific content.

Similarly, had our first piece about the attractions of Mantua appeared in an Italian novel ridiculing the kind of rhetoric to be found in Italian tourist

Quick and Delicious.

Una cucina rapida e squisita – *a cuisine/type of cooking [th*
and delicious

The concept 'cucina' (*type of cooking*) is absent (or only impl
lish. The presence of the word raises the register in the Italia
from the Italian, would an English translator have had any reas
the word? Perhaps yes, in the sense that the only word avai
here is 'cuisine', which seems too noble a concept for this ki
equally we can see why an Italian translator of an English
have wished to introduce the word. If he did not, he would I
masculine plural endings to the two adjectives 'rapido' and '
delicious) in order to have them agree with 'piatti' (*dishes*).
seem extremely primitive, stylistically, in Italian. Since both
might easily be the result of translation from the other, this d
very little about which text is the original.

The time-saver's cookbook.

Il libro di cucina che vi farà risparmiare tempo – *the boo*
that] will save you time

Here one can merely note that while it would take an inventi
lator to arrive at the compression of 'time-saver's', an Italiar
English expression has no alternative but to offer this entirely
Italian does not share with English the resource either of the
or the Anglo-Saxon genitive and is thus forced to introduc
'the book that will save you time.'

If you love good food but hate spending time preparing

Se apprezzate la buona cucina ma non avete il tempo
alla preparazione dei cibi
(*If you appreciate good cooking but don't have the tin*
preparing foods)

As with the title, the English, with its concept 'hate', seems
the Italian 'ma non avete tempo' (*but don't have time*). Agair
imagine an English translator introducing such a strong not
from the blander Italian, we can see every reason for an Ii

guides, then doubtless the English translator would have done well to avoid domesticating the register or eliminating expressions such as 'la saggezza esemplare delle amministrazioni locali' (*the exemplary wisdom of the local administrations*).

But even if such translations from hypothetical novels might seem more 'faithful,' they would be so only because of the translator's awareness of a different end function for his translation. The same could be said, for example, of a word for word translation, or gloss, of the variety undertaken in the classroom to explain to students the idioms and usages of the other language. Here one would indeed, and justifiably, write 'in one minute' for 'in un minuto' or 'over which very sweet sunsets go down' for 'su cui scendono tramonti dolcissimi'. But again function (in this case explication) would be paramount.

To conclude this part of our argument, we can say that given the profound differences between any two languages and cultures, the translator is forced to think hard about the function of the text, which is to say its author's intention. The translator's sensitivity to the language and context of the original leads to an assessment of its intentions, and it is to those that he then strives to be faithful.

Which brings us to literature… For if the function and intentions of the texts we have looked at so far, and indeed of almost every commercial or discursive text, are self-evident, the same cannot be said of literature. We can all agree that the intention of a technical manual is to explain something, the purpose of a contract to establish a series of terms and conditions, but can we feel so confident when considering a poem or a novel? Was it written to entertain, to make money, to offer an individual vision, to proselytize a particular metaphysic, to support a certain line of politics? Or all of these? Or out of pure vanity and megalomania? Critics, professors and indeed ordinary readers notoriously disagree as to the intentions of any particular author; interpretations are as many as they are diverse, so much so that the one characterizing quality of literature would appear to be its ability to have the reader aware of a range of possible but not definite or exclusive meanings. We might almost say that its intention is to avoid being seen to have a limited intention.

But how do literary texts achieve these effects? How far are they reflected in a translation? One way to approach this problem is to consider the generally accepted distinction between genre novels (or popular music, or popular painting) and works which are considered 'works of art'. We say a work is a genre novel when it adheres to a particular and well-known model, for example the detective story, exploiting the capacity of that form to generate an entertainment that is in no way thought-provoking, and yet, on its own terms, satisfying. In such cases, there is a clearly identifiable intention – uncomplicated entertainment. So long as a similar genre form exists in our own language we will experience no more than the ordinary difficulties in translating the work, and if our translation is as entertaining as the original we will feel our job has been well done. Conversely, we could say that a novel aspires to be literature when it departs from genre, when it declares its difference, and in so doing surprises and challenges.

There are many ways in which a work of literature can depart from genre, or, more generally, from the literature that has come before. Perhaps the subject matter is new, perhaps the function and trajectory of the plot has been altered, perhaps the traditional attitude towards chronology has been subverted, or different kinds of characters are introduced, or a different diction, or unusual syntax, or unusual combinations of, for example, lyrical elements (alliteration, rhyme) with an apparently inappropriate diction, etc. The intention of a work of literature, we might say, is to be found in the differences between itself and other literary texts.

One result of this is that passages taken from literary texts may often seem anomalous from the linguistic point of view, in that they frequently depart from ordinary manners of speech and writing. Interestingly enough, when the practice of inviting students to distinguish translated text from original text was still not much more than an amusing exercise for me, it was with a piece of literature that I first found almost the entire class getting it wrong. The group in question was made up of Italian teachers of English Literature following a British Council seminar. Hence these were intelligent, reasonably skilled and highly motivated readers. The passage was chosen, at random, from a novel recognized as literature of the highest order. The name of the character in the text is reduced to a B to prevent easy recognition of the original language.

> In a few minutes the train was running through the disgrace of outspread suburbia. Everybody in the carriage was on the alert, waiting to escape. At last they were under the huge arch of the station, in the tremendous shadow of the town. B shut himself together – he was in now.

> Di lì a qualche minuto il treno percorreva gli squallidi sobborghi della città. Tutti i passeggeri erano all'erta, in attesa di evadere dal convoglio. Finalmente entrarono sotto l'enorme arco della stazione, nell'ombra terribile e immensa della città. B si chiuse in se stesso: ormai era preso.

Of twenty students asked to consider this passage eighteen thought that the source language was Italian. When asked to explain why, they quickly identi-fied the four places where there are major differences between the two texts.

First, they felt that 'the disgrace of outspread suburbia' involved both an extravagance of diction ('disgrace') and an unusual and vague collocation ('outspread suburbia'). 'Gli squallidi sobborghi della città' (*the squalid sub-urbs of the town*), on the other hand, was the sort of statement one has heard a thousand times before.

Second, they were concerned that in the phrase 'Everybody in the carriage was on the alert, waiting to escape', the word 'escape' was insufficiently qualified. An object, direct or indirect, was required, they felt, after the verb. Otherwise, 'escape' from what? The Italian, 'evadere dal convoglio' (*'escape from the train'*), seemed clearer.

Third, they thought the expression 'B shut himself together' was grammati-cally anomalous and the most convincing demonstration that the English was at best an indifferent translation. 'B si chiuse in se stesso' (*B closed himself/with-drew into himself*), they pointed out, was perfectly ordinary Italian.

Finally, they thought that, like the use of the word 'escape', the expression 'he was in now' was insufficiently qualified. 'In' what? The Italian 'ormai era preso' (*by now he was taken/caught*) seemed clearer. The text, they felt, must be an Italian original. In fact it is taken from D.H. Lawrence's *Women in Love.*[5]

I have since repeated this experiment with numerous classes and the results are always the same. The passage thus confirms the conclusions we drew from the fact that non-native speakers, even those with high standards of English, tend not to laugh at poor English translations: they recognize departures from more ordinary forms of English (curious collocations, odd syntax) but find it difficult to decide, or rather to *feel*, if these are appropriate or ridiculous. In short, they can't distinguish with confidence between a poetic use of the language and a poor translation. This is especially true when the poetic usage is seen side by side with a translation in their own language that presents a series of entirely plausible, ordinary statements that might have come from any novel or newspaper.

But perhaps more interesting than these concerns (at least for our purposes) is the fact that, in this case, a group of students who had no special knowledge of Lawrence, *were* able, by comparing his English with a translation, to identify,

---

[5] The passage is taken from the chapter 'In the Train'. The name 'London' has been altered to 'suburbia' and Birkin has been shortened to 'B' in order to make the text less obvi-ously recognizable as an English original. The English quoted is from *Women in Love,* Penguin, London, 1982, p. 113. The Italian is taken from *Donne innamorate,* Rizzoli, Milan, 1989.

if not immediately to understand, those elements in the text which, as we shall
see in the following chapter, are *typical of Lawrence's style*, those strategies he
uses to fill even a small bridge passage like this with meaning. For it is fairly
easy to demonstrate that the four divergences or 'problems' that the students
identified are closely linked and serve to give the English passage a tighter
unity between style and content than is to be found in the translation.

Returning to the passage itself, let's look at the Italian version again together with a back-translation to see what impression it makes.

> Di lì a qualche minuto il treno percorreva gli squallidi sobborghi
> della città. Tutti i passeggeri erano all'erta, in attesa di evadere dal
> convoglio. Finalmente entrarono sotto l'enorme arco della stazione,
> nell'ombra terribile e immensa della città. B si chiuse in se stesso:
> ormai era preso.

> A few minutes later the train was going through the squalid suburbs
> of the town. All the passengers were alert, waiting to escape from the
> carriages. Finally they entered under the enormous arch of the station,
> into the terrible and immense shadow of the town. B withdrew into
> himself: by now he was caught.

So, B – or Birkin as we can now call him – arrives in town on the train. The
town is squalid and fearsome, as sensitive, liberal consciousness since the
industrial revolution has tended to find it, more a monster ('by now he was
caught') than a centre of civilization. Then everybody is in a hurry to be off
the train. Nothing surprising there. The only interesting thing is how the arrival in the city makes the protagonist withdraw into himself, presumably to
defend himself from a hostile environment. This is indeed a Lawrentian theme,
and some portentous adjectives are used to underline that hostility, but still
there is no real complexity. We merely have the orthodox view that the city is
difficult to deal with. There is nothing in the language which makes us pause
and reflect. All is transparent.

The importance of the four curiosities in the English text should now
become apparent. And here the first thing to note is that any unusual collocation or odd syntactical structure inevitably draws attention to itself, slows the
reader down, invites him to find meaning. While the Italian offers us such
entirely familiar expressions (and subtexts) as 'squallidi sobborghi' (*squalid
suburbs*) and 'si chiuse in se stesso' (*he withdrew into himself*), the English,
just by its curiosity, its extravagance, suggests something more complex,
suggests, above all, that ordinary expressions were not adequate for what
Lawrence wanted to say.

Of course this might be mere mannerism – idiosyncratic deviations from standard forms to no particular end – but it will be fairly easy to show that this is not the case with Lawrence, or at least not in this passage.

To begin at the beginning, the strong moral opprobrium implied by the word 'disgrace' is not directed at poverty or even ugliness, as is the case in the Italian. The concept 'squalid' is absent. If anything, the sense of shame has to do with the city's 'outspreadness', its being bigger than it ought to be, its expansion. The idea of spreading outwards from a centre is picked up a moment later, again negatively, in the expression 'the tremendous shadow of the town'. An undertone of malignant darkness in this process is clear enough. Those who have read *Women in Love* will be aware of Lawrence's constant condemnation of uniformity and amorphousness, his fear, not of poverty or squalor, but of sameness.

It is within the context of the city's unpleasant and formless extension that the two words 'escape' and 'in' should be read. For by not limiting the verb 'escape' in strict syntactical terms, (as in the Italian, 'escaped from the carriages'), Lawrence allows the word to take on portentous overtones. These people are eager to escape not just from the carriage, but in general, from the outspread city with all its disgraceful amorphousness, and from a related psychological unease perhaps.

The lack of qualification for the word 'in' has a similar effect, suggesting entry not just into the town but into some negative spiritual state. A deliberate lack of syntactical precision thus allows for wider interpretation, and indeed, one need only look at Lawrence's use of the words 'in' and 'out' in other parts of the novel to appreciate the associations he likes to attach to them and the importance of retaining them in translation. Just one example: when, towards the end of the novel, Birkin goes to visit the place where his friend Gerald has died in a snowstorm in the Alps, he sees that the local guides had driven stakes and ropes into the snow nearby. Had Gerald found these he might have followed them over the mountain ridge and down the other side into Italy, the south. 'What then?' Birkin reflects. 'Was it a way out? – It was only a way in again.'[6]

Women in Love is a novel about a group of people looking for alternatives from outdated and asphyxiating social conventions. This tiny bridge passage, with its half-realized metaphor of a city that is malignantly spreading outwards and with the weight it puts on words like 'escape' and 'in', serves to generate both an uneasiness (what does the author mean exactly?) and a pattern of images with which the novel as a whole pullulates.

---

[6] *Women in Love*, cit., p. 579.

Finally, it is in reaction to this oppressive atmosphere that Birkin 'shut himself together'. Clearly the Italian, 'si chiuse in se stesso' (*he closed/withdrew into himself*), is a rendering of one aspect of this curious statement. But there are other things going on here. The English expression seems to be the result of a collision between the common 'pulled himself together', with all its positive connotations of sensibly gathering up one's resources to face a challenge, and then some more negative idea of rejecting contact, shutting out others. The feeling is that Birkin's need to get up and face the oppressive world of the city determines a painful constriction of character as a form of necessary self-defence.

But leaving aside the question of exactly what any expression might mean, the important thing to grasp is the complexity and inner unity of the English, the way it hints at a possible metaphor, gives a weight to some words that goes beyond the immediate context, invites attention, begs questions. Regardless of any particular 'meaning', it is this fullness that is lost in the Italian, a fullness that can easily be assessed by comparing translation against original.

Backtracking a little, then, we can say that while it is essential for a translator to have a sense of the function of a text, its intentions, its context, this turns out to be a problem with literary works, which are famous for their complexity and ambivalence. Of course to a great extent such ambivalence can be created in ways which present no difficulty for a translator, through plot, character, imagery and so on. But unusual language use may also play an important part. In the literary text the choice of words and syntax will often combine or collide with the apparent meaning to generate that richness and, frequently, ambiguity, that we associate with literature and that would seem to be essential if a poem or novel is to offer a satisfying vision of life. In this sense, complexity, or ambivalence, can be seen as just one more way in which the literary text achieves its mimetic vocation: life is complicated. For our own practical purposes, we might say more crudely that in the literary text an awful lot of things can be happening at once, perhaps contradicting each other, perhaps qualifying each other; as a result the translator may find that it is not possible to express all of these complications simultaneously in his or her language.

The idea that drives the following chapters is that by looking at original and translation side by side and identifying those places where translation turned out to be especially difficult, we can arrive at a better appreciation of the original's qualities and, simultaneously of the two phenomena we call translation and literature.

2. Translating the 'Unhousedness' of *Women in Love*

In a statement as arrogant as it is stimulating, George Steiner, in *After Babel*, remarks: 'The principal division in the history of Western literature occurs between the early 1870s and the turn of the century. It divides a literature essentially housed in language from one for which language has become a prison'.[1] Developing his argument, Steiner claims: 'A classic literacy is defined by this "housedness" in language, by the assumption that, used with the requisite penetration and suppleness, available words and grammar will do the job'.[2] Concluding, he says of the situation post-1870: 'When literature seeks to break its public linguistic mould and become idiolect, when it seeks untranslatability, we have entered a new world of feeling'.[3] Important for our purposes here is Steiner's perception that idiolect is necessarily untranslatable.

Half a century after the date that Steiner proposes as a watershed, Lawrence found himself obliged to defend his idiosyncratic use of language in *Women in Love*, and in particular his incessant use of repetition. The reply, or at least part of it, is famous enough: ' ... every natural crisis in emotion or passion or understanding', writes Lawrence, 'comes from this pulsing, frictional to-and-fro which works up to culmination'.[4] But if we consider the reply as a whole we'll see that this appeal to the principle of mimesis is something of an afterthought, a sop. Immediately before this, and more belligerently, Lawrence defends his style thus: 'The only answer is that it is natural to the author'.[5]

The style is 'natural to the author'. That is sufficient justification. And if what is 'natural to the author' happens to lie outside the canons of a publicly accepted literary style, so much the worse for reader and critic. We can like or dislike the author's style, but we cannot ask him to change it, since that would involve his going against his nature.

Lawrence's position here would seem to confirm Steiner's intuition: the author is telling us that publicly approved literary language will no longer do for him. But given that any move towards private forms of expression is a move towards untranslatability (as we have already seen with an expression

---

[1] George Steiner, After Babel, Oxford University Press, 1975, p. 176.

[2] Ibid., p. 177.

[3] Ibid., p. 183.

[4] D.H. Lawrence, Foreword to *Women in Love*, Thomas Seltzer, 1920.

[5] Ibid.

like 'shut himself together'), what of the translator? Can Lawrence's stylistic idiosyncrasies be translated? Can one establish in another language the same and specifically 'Lawrentian' distance between individual voice and ordinary usage, a distance that contemporary critics certainly noted, otherwise they would not, almost unanimously, have complained of it.

Or, alternatively, is this a problem the translator can safely ignore? Perhaps these idiosyncrasies do not mean anything. Perhaps, given that Lawrence was so frequently criticized for his style, the translation may be better than the original to the extent that it eliminates individual tics and returns the text to a publicly approved style. Certainly the early Italian translator Vittorini frequently chose to 'improve on' what he felt was Lawrence's inelegance.[6]

Or, finally, is it possible that these idiosyncrasies, this insistence on individual voice, are part and parcel of one of the book's main themes? We have already seen, in our opening chapter, how one small and apparently insignificant passage from *Women in Love* is dense with notions of being 'in' or 'out', very much alert to the individual's need to adjust as he confronts society. Could it be that Lawrence's novel is about the whole problem of being, or not being, as Steiner puts it 'housed' in the language, where the language is seen as the all-pervading expression of social orthodoxy?

When we remember how scandalous critics found this novel, in terms both of subject-matter and style, it comes as something of a surprise to see how very tamely *Women in Love* begins.

> Ursula and Gudrun Brangwen sat one morning in the window-bay of their father's house in Beldover, working and talking. Ursula was stitching a piece of brightly coloured embroidery, and Gudrun was drawing upon a board which she held on her knee. They were mostly silent, talking as their thoughts strayed through their minds.
> 'Ursula,' said Gudrun, 'don't you really want to get married?' (p. 53)[7]

Two sisters, sewing, drawing, talking about marriage. We might well be back with Jane Austen. But Lawrence allows us this glimpse of a conventional world only to throw it into question. For to Gudrun's question as to whether her sister wants to get married, Ursula replies, 'I don't know ... It depends

---

[6] See Fondi Alberto Mondadori, Arnoldo Mondadori, Autori, Fascicolo Vittorini. Vittorini frequently requests permission to cut sections of Lawrence's prose with justifications such as: ' ... guastano la bellezza della narrazione ...' (they damage the beauty of the translation).

[7] All quotations from *Women in Love* are from the Penguin edition of 1982. Page numbers are indicated in brackets at the end of each quotation.

how you mean' (p. 53). Although this dialogue can present no problem for a translator, it is worth noting how, even at this early stage, the questioning of social conventions is presented as a questioning of semantics, of language. 'It depends how you mean.' Sure enough, a few lines later, we find the conventional moral understanding of a word being thrown wide open. Gudrun asks Ursula whether she has never felt 'fearfully tempted' to get married. And Ursula replies: 'Oh, if I were tempted, I'd marry like a shot. – I'm only tempted not to' (p. 54).

Chambers dictionary gives the meaning of 'tempt' as 'to put to trial, to test, to try or tend to persuade, especially to evil'. Is marriage an 'evil' to which one is 'fearfully tempted'? Surely not, or not in the conventional vision of marriage. But then is 'evil' such a bad thing anyway? Certainly the girls are excited as they go on to reflect how tempted they are 'not to'. They want to do what tempts them, it seems. Then Lawrence makes one of his portentous about-turns, adding a final comment to the discussion: 'In their hearts they were frightened' (p. 54). Melodramatic as this may seem, it has the advantage of recalling the earlier 'fearfully' ('fearfully tempted') which now, rather than being a mere emphasizer, is seen retrospectively to have real content. Temptation has to do with being outside convention and comes together with excitement and fear. This recovery of the dormant sense of 'fearfully' obviously puts the translator under pressure. Here is the whole exchange in English and Italian. Gudrun is following up Ursula's remark that she, Ursula, has turned down several good offers of marriage:

> 'Really! But weren't you fearfully tempted?'
> 'In the abstract but not in the concrete,' said Ursula. 'When it comes to the point, one isn't even tempied – Oh, if I were tempted, I'd marry like a shot. – I'm only tempted not to.' The faces of both sisters suddenly lit up with amusement.
> 'Isn't it an amazing thing,' cried Gudrun, 'how strong the temptation is, not to!' They both laughed, looking at each other. In their hearts they were frightened. (p. 54)

> 'Sul serio! Ma non eri tremendamente tentata?'
> 'In teoria, sì, non in pratica però,' disse Ursula. 'A ben pensarci, non è neppure una tentazione ... oh, se fossi tentata, mi sposerei in quattro e quattr'otto! Ma sono tentata solo a non farlo.' Sui volti delle due sorelle balenò un lampo di divertimento.
> 'Non trovi stupefacente,' esclamò Gudrun, 'che la tentazione a non

farlo sia così forte?!' Scoppiarono tutti e due a ridere, guardandosi.
Ma in fondo al cuore erano spaventate.' (p.20)[8]

Here is a back-translation to give the English reader an idea of the transformations that have occurred.

> 'Seriously! But weren't you tremendously tempted?'
> 'In theory, yes, not in practice though,' said Ursula. 'Thinking about
> it, it isn't even a temptation! Oh, if I were tempted, I'd marry in no
> time! But I am only tempted not to do it.' The faces of the two sisters
> lit up with a flash of amusement.
> 'Don't you find it amazing,' exclaimed Gudrun, 'that the temptation
> not to do it is so strong?!' They both burst out laughing, looking at
> each other. But deep in their hearts they were afraid.

The translator looks for and finds an emphasizer which is menacing, but all
the same the close parallel between 'fearful' and 'frightened' is not quite
there in 'tremendamente' (*tremendously*) and 'spaventate' (*afraid*). But if
I quote this passage in full it is to allow the reader to notice the effect of
the 'Ma' (*But*) introduced in Italian where there is no corresponding word
in English. ('Ma in fondo al cuore ...' *But in the bottom of the heart*). 'But'
suggests contradiction, something not in line with what has gone before.
The absence of the conjunction in Lawrence's original text implies that it is
normal, or at least not unusual, for people to laugh *and* be frightened at the
same time (simultaneous excitement and fear have already been established
as concomitant with temptation). Lawrence, that is, makes no concession to
our more conventional vision of things. The translation steps back from this
radical position, suggesting that it would be more normal for the girls to laugh
over this without being afraid.

Certainly there is nothing 'untranslatable' or even difficult here, but it is
interesting to see how these small slippages arise from a lack of sensibility to
the author's highly individual view point, which, as we will see, underlies the
text's larger problems. Two pages further on, for example, Lawrence is setting
up a first spatial metaphor to illustrate the dilemma of whether one chooses to
be inside or outside conventional society. Ursula has asked Gudrun why she
returned to her provincial home from a more artistic life in Chelsea. Gudrun
replies, significantly using a French expression, that perhaps her return was

---

[8] For the purposes of this analysis and all others in the chapter I draw on *Donne innamorate*,
Rizzoli, Milan, 1989, translation by Adriana dell'Orto. Page numbers are indicated in
brackets at the end of each quotation.

only '*reculer pour mieux sauter*' (Coming back the better to leap away again) (p. 56). Ever sceptical, Ursula asks where it is that one might jump to. And we have:

> 'Oh, it doesn't matter,' said Gudrun, somewhat superbly. 'If one jumps over the edge, one is bound to land somewhere.' (p. 56)

Somewhat surprisingly, the Italian translation, gives this as:

> 'Se si salta oltre una siepe, da qualche parte si dovrà pur cadere.'
> (p. 23)
> (*If you jump over/beyond a hedge, somewhere one must surely fall/land*)

One's first thought is that the translator might have mistaken 'edge' for 'hedge', but in the end I think not, though that does not mean that one word did not suggest the other. The translation of 'edge' into Italian is a serious problem, particularly coming as it does after a definite article ('the edge'), presumably an article of unique reference (there is no earlier mention of any 'edge'), implying that this is somehow that edge about which we all know.

The question is, is there any word in Italian which lends itself to such portentous figurative use, any word which suggests such a broad range of possible interpretation, both social and psychological? Il Nuovo Ragazzini bilingual dictionary explains 'edge' as follows: 'estremità *extremity*; margine *margin*; orlo *edge*; bordo *border* (of an object); spigolo *sharp edge*; sponda *edge* (in the sense of bank beside water)'. But, left unqualified, none of these possibilities would sound right after the verb 'saltare' (*jump*) ('se si salta l'orlo', *if you jump the edge*, sounds merely incompetent in Italian). No doubt aware of this, the translator decided to settle for a simple and less portentous metaphor.

In any event, what is curious and interesting with the choice of 'hedge' is the way the Italian seems more 'English' than the English, as if Gudrun were taking her metaphor from fox-hunting, the only situation in which I can imagine hedges being jumped. Unhappily, this sport is so emblematic of the conventions Gudrun wishes to escape as to suggest an irony and banality absent in the vaguer, more disturbing original, which simply asks, 'But what is beyond the edge? Where can you jump to?'.

One way or another, then, whether tempting or jumping, *Women in Love* is a book which seeks to disorientate, to have us share the disorientation of characters who ask of marriage 'It depends what you mean', characters determined to jump over the edge, even if they do not know what lies beyond it. Analysis of the paragraphs immediately following this conversation will suggest how much the Italian transformation of 'edge' into 'hedge' trivializes the original.

But before I quote this passage I would like to remark that it was first chosen for classroom use entirely at random, and for the simple reason that it amounted to an exact page in both English and Italian editions of the novel and thus saved me any complicated cutting and pasting before using the photocopier. I also want to add that all the above reflections on the opening pages of the novel were stimulated by comparison of the original and the translation of this randomly chosen passage. It may seem unprofessional to proceed in this fashion (and unwise to confess to having done so), but I want to insist on the way translation problems, even of passages that do not seem central, necessarily point to an author's strategies. But now to the passage itself. Having asked Gudrun why she came back from Chelsea to the provinces, Ursula now enquires about her sister's relationship with their father.

> 'And how do you find home, now you have come back to it?' she asked. Gudrun paused for some moments, coldly, before answering. Then, in a cold, truthful voice, she said:
> 'I find myself completely out of it.' 'And father?'
> Gudrun looked at Ursula, almost with resentment, as if brought to bay. 'I haven't thought about him: l've refrained,' she said coldly.
> 'Yes,' wavered Ursula, and the conversation was really at an end. The sisters found themselves confronted by a void, a terrifying chasm, as if they had looked over the edge.
> They worked on in silence for some time. Gudrun's cheek was flushed with repressed emotion. She resented its having been called into being.
> 'Shall we go out and look at that wedding?' she asked at length, in a voice that was too casual.
> 'Yes!' cried Ursula, too eagerly, throwing aside her sewing and leaping up, as if to escape something, thus betraying the tension of the situation, and causing a friction of dislike to go over Gudrun's nerves.
> As she went upstairs, Ursula was aware of the house, of her home round about her. And she loathed it, the sordid, too-familiar place! She was afraid at the depth of her feeling against the home, the milieu, the whole atmosphere and condition of this obsolete life. Her feeling frightened her.
> The two girls were soon walking swiftly down the main road of Beldover, a wide street, part shops, part dwelling houses, utterly formless and sordid, without poverty. Gudrun, new from her life in Chelsea and

Sussex, shrank cruelly from this amorphous ugliness of a small colliery town in the Midlands. Yet forward she went, through the whole sordid gamut of pettiness, the long, amorphous, gritty street. She was exposed to every stare, she passed on through a stretch of torment. It was strange that she should have chosen to come back and test the full effect of this shapeless, barren ugliness upon herself. Why had she wanted to submit herself to it, did she still want to submit herself to it, the insufferable torture of these ugly, meaningless people, this defaced countryside? She felt like a beetle toiling in the dust. She was filled with repulsion. (p. 57)

And the Italian:

'E che effetto ti fa la casa, ora che ci sei tornata?' domandò.
Gudrun tacque per qualche istante, freddamente, prima di rispondere. Poi in tono gelido e schietto disse:
'Mi sento completamente emarginata.'
'E papà?'
Gudrun guardò Ursula quasi con risentimento, come sulla difensiva. 'A lui non ho pensato, me ne sono astenuta,' disse con freddezza.
'Già,' fece Ursula, titubante; e la conversazione si concluse definitivamente. Le due sorelle si trovavano ad affrontare un vuoto, come se avessero guardato oltre l'orlo di un baratro pauroso.
Continuarono a lavorare in silenzio per un po', e le guance di Gudrun erano arrossate per l'emozione contenuta. Era irritata alla sola idea di averla provata.
'E se andassimo a dare un'occhiata a quel matrimonio?' domandò alla fine, in tono un po' troppo noncurante.
'Sì!' esclamò Ursula, con eccessiva veemenza, deponendo il ricamo e balzando in piedi come per sfuggire a qualcosa, in un modo che, rivelando la tensione che si era creata tra loro, dette sui nervi a Gudrun.
Mentre andava di sopra, Ursula prese coscienza del suo ambiente domestico, tutt'attorno a lei. E lo detestava, quel sordido luogo troppo familiare! Era impaurita dalla profondità del suo sentimento di avversione per la casa, l'ambiente, l'intera atmosfera e condizione di quella sua vita antiquata. I suoi sentimenti la spaventavano.
Di lì a poco le due ragazze camminavano in fretta lungo la strada principale di Beldover, una strada larga, fiancheggiata in parte da negozi, in parte da abitazioni, del tutto sordida e informe pur senza essere miserabile. Gudrun reduce dalla vita condotta a Chelsea e nel Sussex, rabbrividì ferita dalla bruttezza informe di quella cittadina mineraria

del Midlands. E tuttavia avanzava, lungo tutta quella sordida gamma di meschinità, nella lunga strada amorfa, ghiaiosa. Era esposta agli sguardi di tutti, percorreva quel tratto di strada come se affrontasse la tortura. Era strano che avesse deciso di tornare e di sperimentare appieno su di sé l'effetto di quell'informe, spoglia bruttezza. Perché aveva voluto sottoporvisi, perché voleva ancora sottoporsi all'insopportabile tortura di quella gente brutta, insensata, di quella campagna sfigurata? Si sentiva come uno scarafaggio che arrancasse nella polvere. Era colma di ripugnanza (p. 24).

Here is a back-translation:

'And what effect does the house have on you, now that you are back?' she asked.

Gudrun was silent for a few moments, coldly so, before answering. Then in an icy, blunt tone she said:

'I feel completely alienated,'

'And father?'

Gudrun looked at Ursula almost with resentment, as if on the defensive. 'I have not thought of him, I've abstained,' she said with coldness.

'Right,' said Ursula, hesitating; and the conversation was really over. The two sisters found themselves confronting a void, as if they had looked over the edge of a frightening precipice.

They went on working in silence for a little, and Gudrun's cheeks were flushed with controlled emotion. She was irritated at the mere idea of having felt it.

'What if we went to take a look at that marriage?' she asked at last, in a voice that was too careless.

'Yes!' cried Ursula, with excessive vehemence, putting down her embroidery and jumping to her feet as though to escape from something, in a way that, revealing the tension that had developed between them, got on Gudrun's nerves.

As she was going upstairs, Ursula became aware of her domestic milieu, all around her. And she detested it, that sordid, too-familiar place! She was frightened by the depth of her feeling of aversion towards the house, the milieu, the whole atmosphere and condition of that antiquated life. Her feelings scared her.

A little later the two girls were walking hurriedly along the main road of Beldover, a wide street, flanked partly by shops, partly by dwellings, entirely sordid and shapeless albeit without being poverty-stricken. Gudrun, back from the life she had led in Chelsea and Sussex, shivered wounded by the shapeless ugliness of that small mining town of the Midlands. And yet she advanced, along the whole sordid gamut of meanness, down the long, amorphous, gravelly street. She was exposed to the looks of everyone, she went down this length of the street as if she were facing torture. It was strange that she had decided to come back and experiment fully on herself the effect of that shapeless, bare ugliness. Why had she wanted to submit herself to it, why did she still want to submit herself to the unbearable torture of these ugly, senseless people, this disfigured landscape? She felt like a cockroach labouring in the dust. She was full of repugnance.

Perhaps it is worth noting that on presenting this material in class I tend to read the Italian, that is the students' native language, first, so as to establish and talk about the impressions they receive from the translation. Here, for example, the dramatic situation certainly conveys a sense of uneasiness generated by complex emotions. And, as in the train passage quoted in the previous chapter, uneasiness is heightened by the use of portentous imagery ('le due sorelle si trovavano ad affrontare un vuoto' – *the two sisters found themselves facing a void*; 'come se affrontasse la tortura' – *as if she were facing torture*). So the translation is by no means without its efficacy. But having said this, if you were to invite the Italian student, or a reader of the back-translation, to look for anything unusual in the language, any place where it departs from ordinary usage, it is unlikely that they would be able to do so. Perhaps the use of the verb 'astenersi' (*abstain*) to describe Gudrun's decision not to think of her father is a little unexpected. Usually one abstains from something one imagines one would enjoy, which hardly seems to be the case here. But apart from that what we have is a piece of conventional narrative prose, and a very, as they say, smooth translation.

It must be said that on reading the English, foreign students, even at high levels of competence, are not at first struck by a significant difference in tone. However, on close examination they quickly discover the many places where the texts part company. The challenge then is to assess exactly what has been changed or lost in the translation, to see, for example, if there is any relationship between these places where the texts diverge and the overall content of the passage. Will this tell us something about Lawrence's intentions, or at least about the style that he felt was 'natural to the author'?

The simple dialogue and attendant comment with which the passage begins would appear to offer no particular problems, if only because there is nothing out of the ordinary in the way the girls express themselves. The language does not draw attention to itself, except perhaps in the repetition involved in 'coldly' and 'cold', which the Italian chooses to translate as 'freddamente' (*coldly*) and then 'gelido' (*icy*). It is hard not to notice, however, the change of 'out of it', to 'emarginata' (*alienated* or literally *expelled beyond the margin*, a term used for underprivileged minorities).

'I find myself completely out of it.'

'Mi sento completamente emarginata.'
I feel completely alientated

Gudrun's reply here is clearly part of the book's frequent use of 'in' and 'out' to indicate a character's relation to society and conventions. 'Emarginata' (*alienated*), on the other hand, quite apart from being an anachronism in the mouth of a girl speaking around the time of the First World War, introduces other connotations and implications. Most of all, the word suggests, if only because of its passive form, some responsibility on society's part for having pushed the alienated person out. It thus makes society at once an attractive place to be (nobody wants to be pushed out), but cruel. Not only is this not evident in the English (Gudrun never expresses her desire to be part of the family, nor complains about being excluded), but these connotations obscure the spatial simplicity of the metaphor Lawrence is setting up for the novel's conflicts. Gudrun feels 'out of it'. It would have been perfectly possible to translate this with 'fuori' (*out/outside*).

However, it is 'as if brought to bay', in line 7, translated as 'come sulla difensiva' (*as if on the defensive*), which offers us the first place where the translator is simply obliged to depart from the original. As so often, and particularly when presenting his characters' unconscious minds, Lawrence is using an animal metaphor (another one will appear at the end of the passage). If nothing else, this heightens the sense of instinctiveness and fatality, of character as something more than just a 'social being', as Lawrence put it in his essay on Galsworthy. When tackled on the question of her relationship to her father, and thus to the conventions of home and family, Gudrun is like a hunted animal.

But 'brought to bay' has a very specific meaning: Chambers explains the expression as, 'the last stand of a hunted animal when it faces the hounds at close quarters'. The expression thus includes the ideas of the dead end, of dangerous proximity, of fear, but also of aggression (the hunted animal turns to fight). One way or another all these ideas will reappear at least once in this passage and many more times throughout the book, usually in reference to Gudrun. The translation, 'sulla difensiva' (*on the defensive*) cannot achieve the same complexity. But then no expression with a similar range of connotation is available in Italian.

In the next paragraph we note merely that the curious 'me ne sono astenuta' (*I have abstained from it*), with reference to Gudrun's decision not to think about her father, is a faithful rendering of the English 'refrained'. Later I hope to show how other elements in the text make this curious usage more explicable in the English than it is in the Italian.

But it is in the next two short paragraphs that a whole series of minor differences begin to suggest how much more complex and unusual the English text is than the Italian. Gudrun is upset about being asked about her position in the family, Ursula wavers and we hear that 'the conversation was really at an end'. This idea of a point beyond which one cannot proceed looks back to the expression 'brought to bay' two paragraphs before, and onwards to the words 'void', 'chasm' and 'edge', all used in the next sentence. Crucially, like the expression 'out of it', earlier on, and that 'edge' that Gudrun felt so confident about jumping beyond only a moment before, it is a spatial image. The Italian translation, 'e la conversazione si concluse definitivamente' (*and the conversation concluded definitively*), on the other hand, is temporal. It does not convey the notion of a limit in space and so drops the connection between the idea of impasse and those of danger and emptiness, an unknown beyond. Just as, in the brief passage about the train's arrival in London, Lawrence hints at what one might call a latent metaphor – the city as some kind of evil spreading outwards from the centre – here we have an underlying image of a barrier, a point beyond which it would be dangerous, if not impossible, to proceed. The image then rises to the surface, comes to consciousness as it were, in the next sentence:

> The sisters found themselves confronted by a void, a terrifying chasm, as if they had looked over the edge.

> Le due sorelle si trovavano ad affrontare un vuoto, come se avessero guardato oltre l'orlo di un baratro pauroso.
> *The two sisters found themselves facing a void, as if they had looked beyond the edge of a frightening precipice.*

Students will always point to this as one of the sentences which is syntactically different in the Italian – the word order has been rearranged – though they may find it difficult to decide whether this makes any difference to the meaning, whether Lawrence had any reason for the phrasing he chose, or whether the translator is just performing a necessary grammatical transformation.

On examination we see that both the English and the Italian sentences begin with a metaphor, 'The sisters found themselves confronted by a void', 'Le due sorelle si trovavano ad affrontare un vuoto' (*The two sisters found themselves facing a void*). The English continues by placing 'a terrifying chasm' in apposition to the void, ('a void, a terrifying chasm') then closes with a simile, 'as if they had looked over the edge'. The Italian avoids the use of apposition by moving the simile forward (' un vuoto, come se avessero' – *a void, as if they had*) and bringing in the 'terrifying chasm' ('baratro pauroso' – *frightening precipice*) at the end of the sentence as part of the simile, not the metaphor: 'come se avessero guardato oltre l'orlo di un baratro pauroso' (*as if they had looked beyond the edge of a frightening precipice*).

Why? Why not leave things as they were in the English? Presumably the translator (or perhaps an editor) was nervous about concluding the sentence with: 'come se avessero guardato oltre l'orlo' (*as if they had looked over the edge*); this for the very same reason that earlier the translator baulked at the possibility of writing 'se si salta l'orlo' (*if you jump the edge*). In Italian the word 'orlo' would seem stranded and awkward if left unqualified at the end of the sentence. Italian does not do this kind of thing. Readers would demand to know: the edge of what?

Yet turning back to the original it becomes clear now that there is something equally odd (if not equally awkward) about the English, something syntactically not quite right. By shifting from metaphor into simile, Lawrence has, grammatically at least, detached 'the edge' from the preceding 'void' and 'chasm', with the result that the definite article before 'edge' becomes, once again, as in Gudrun's earlier use of the word, an article of unique reference, rather than, in strictly grammatical terms, referring back to the 'void'.

> The sisters found themselves confronted by a void, a terrifying chasm,
> as if they had looked over the edge.

The trick will be clearer if we change the content of the simile. Imagine, for example,

> The sisters found themselves confronted by a void, a terrifying chasm,
> as if they had lost their way in a land of nightmare.

We can now see that, detached as it is from the void through this switch from metaphor to simile, Lawrence's 'the edge' now comes to mean, as in the earlier passage, 'that edge about which we all know and of which there is only one'. Of course, coming as it does so hard on the heels of the preceding metaphor, the reader vaguely feels that 'the edge' *does* refer back to the void and the chasm, and this anaphoric attraction masks the extraordinary nature of the sentence. But the reader is also aware that the word is taking on a portentousness beyond the immediate context of the conversation. In shifting 'baratro pauroso' (*frightening precipice*) to the end of the sentence so that it explains 'orlo' (*edge*), which then becomes nothing more than the edge of the fearful gap in their conversation, the translation achieves a syntactical smoothness lacking in the English, but loses some of its powerful uneasiness and ignores the game Lawrence is playing of bringing the reader sharply up against one kind of end or another: 'edge' must fall, unexpectedly and dangerously, at the end of the sentence, the end of the paragraph. Perhaps the best way to clinch this argument is to put Lawrence's original English side by side with a version using exactly the same diction but following the syntactical organization of the Italian.

> The sisters found themselves confronted by a void, a terrifying chasm, as if they had looked over the edge.

> The sisters found themselves confronted by a void, as if they had looked over the edge of a terrifying chasm.

Before going on to look at the rest of the passage, it is worth noting that what happens with the word 'edge' here has much in common with the placing of 'escape' at the end of a sentence in the passage examined in the previous chapter:

> Everybody in the carriage was on the alert, waiting to escape.

> Tutti i passeggeri erano all'erta, in attesa di evadere dal convoglio.
> *All the passengers were alert, waiting to escape from the train.*

The English phrasing allows the word 'escape' to escape the limitations of the context. The more 'housed' Italian confines it safely in its immediate reference. In any event, the point that needs to be made here is not so much that these sentences, taken separately, have been translated badly, let alone incorrectly, but that attention to divergences between text and translation points us both to Lawrence's habit of setting up underlying spatial images and to the way he gives power to these images through the deployment of unusual phrasing and syntax. It is these aspects of the original that the translation is not able to reproduce.

The next paragraph gives us:

> They worked on in silence for some time. Gudrun's cheek was flushed with repressed emotion. She resented its having been called into being.

> Continuarono a lavorare in silenzio per un po', e le guance di Gudrun erano arrossate per l'emozione contenuta. Era irritata alla sola idea di averla provata.
> *They continued to work in silence for a little, and Gudrun's cheeks were flushed because of the contained/controlled emotion. She was irritated at the mere idea of having felt it.*

Apart from the decision to change the, in psychological terms, precise word 'repressed' (particularly significant when used as early as 1916) to the more banal 'contenuta' (*contained/controlled*), the most striking thing here is the very complex psychology and syntax of 'She resented its having been called into being'. Close attention to the difference between this and the Italian 'Era irritata alla sola idea di averla provata' (*she was irritated at the mere idea of having felt it*), shows us how subtle Lawrence's characterization is and how easily that subtlety is lost.

Gudrun is not simply (or not even) annoyed that she has experienced the unpleasant emotion of realizing how far she feels outside her family, she is annoyed with Ursula for having made her experience that feeling, indeed for having generated that consciousness. The word 'resentment' has already been used once in the passage to suggest Gudrun's anger with her sister for cornering her over her attitude to her father. The loss in the Italian, which here omits this resentment and its object, is thus considerable, and not merely a matter of content and information, for the very contortion and compression of Lawrence's syntax is an important factor in conveying the passage's dramatic tension. Again, this need not necessarily be seen as a criticism of the translator, since in order to get the same complexity as the English one would have to expand the phrase quite considerably, perhaps making it over-explicit (I have yet to find the Italian translator who can offer a satisfactory solution for 'she resented its having been called into being').

The two sisters having reached this impasse, we now have another simple dialogue, where Gudrun tries to get out of the hole they have got into by suggesting they head off to see a wedding in the town, an invitation that Ursula accepts. But even this simple exchange sparks off trouble.

'Shall we go out and look at that wedding?' she asked at length, in a voice that was too casual.

'Yes!' cried Ursula, too eagerly, throwing aside her sewing and leaping up, as if to escape something, thus betraying the tension of the situation, and causing a friction of dislike to go over Gudrun's nerves.

'E se andassimo a dare un'occhiata a quel matrimonio?' domandò alla fine, in tono un po' troppo noncurante.

'Sì!' esclamò Ursula, con eccessiva veemenza, deponendo il ricamo e balzando in piedi come per sfuggire a qualcosa, in un modo che, rivelando la tensione che si era creata tra loro, dette sui nervi a Gudrun.

What if we went to take a look at that wedding?' she asked at last, in a tone [that was] a bit too careless.

'Yes!' exclaimed Ursula, with excessive vehemence/excitement, laying down the embroidery and jumping to her feet as though to escape something, in a way that, revealing the tension that had been created between them, got on Gudrun's nerves.

Gudrun is 'too casual' (she tries to cover up, to repress), Ursula responds 'too eagerly', 'betraying' the tension between them. The differences between original and translation are small here, but significant in their way. By opting for 'un po' troppo noncurante' (*a little too careless*) and 'con eccessiva veemenza' (*with excessive vehemence/excitement*) the Italian loses the blatant parallelism of the English (a conventional tool of characterization), then sacrifices the attendant intensity of 'throwing aside her sewing' for a tamer 'deponendo il ricamo' (*laying down the embroidery*)

More significantly, in choosing 'rivelando' (*revealing*) to translate 'betraying' (the exact Italian translation would be 'tradendo'), part of Lawrence's meaning and of the underlying drama in the passage is lost. Gudrun's irritation with Ursula has to do with the fact that her sister continually betrays the complicity in repression, the agreement not to talk about difficult things, that Gudrun expects and on which so many social exchanges are based. In this sense it is Ursula who shows herself to be the more unconventional of the two. Too candid for her sister's liking, too willing to admit that all is not well, she finally causes 'a friction of dislike to go over Gudrun's nerves'.

The translation of this extraordinary expression into the entirely commonplace 'dette sui nervi' (*got on her nerves*) is something that every student will notice, though when asked to produce an acceptable translation themselves everybody will appreciate the difficulty involved. Perhaps the most we can say here is that the idea of a fight at close quarters implied by 'brought to bay' has now become 'friction', unpleasant contact. Nobody is more adept than Lawrence at developing a syntax of uneasiness and conflict. It is this mood within the very structure of the sentences that is lost in translation.

The next paragraph leaves drama behind to concentrate on Ursula's point of view, her relationship with her home. Like Gudrun's, it is a profoundly unhappy one, with the difference that, while afraid of her feelings, Ursula does not appear to be attempting to repress them or to 'refrain' from thinking about them. Apart from one or two of the merest quibbles, the paragraph offers very little in the way of divergence between translation and original, partly because, reading carefully, we discover that there is nothing out of the ordinary in either the syntax or imagery of the original English. It is at this point that one appreciates how Lawrence is reserving his most contorted syntax for Gudrun, something that the next paragraph will amply confirm. In failing to distinguish between more and less complex syntactical phrasing, the translation risks losing an important instrument of characterization. With Ursula prose flows easily, with Gudrun it does not.

The next paragraph is the longest. It begins descriptively with a picture of the town through which the girls walk, but then concentrates on Gudrun's point of view and, more particularly, on the question, why has she returned to a place she does not like? Divergences between translation and original are of various kinds, as is inevitable in a complex piece of prose like this, but I will concentrate only on those that students will invariably point to even if they cannot explain.

The first comes at the end of the first sentence.

> The two girls were soon walking swiftly down the main road of Beldover, a wide street, part shops, part dwelling houses, utterly formless and sordid, without poverty.

The whole drift of the earlier part of this sentence is towards some conclusion that confirms the squalid and, we suspect, poverty-stricken nature of the town. Thus the surprise and abruptness of Lawrence's conclusion, 'without poverty', is clearly intended to make a point. It is not lack of money which makes this place sordid, he appears to be telling us. It is something else, something that has to do with those repeated words, 'formless', 'amorphous', 'shapeless'. Although there is nothing that would prevent the Italian from achieving a similar abruptness, it is interesting that the translator softens the remark here by introducing the concessionary 'pur' (*albeit*).

> Di lì a poco le due ragazze camminavano in fretta lungo la strada.

principale di Beldover, una strada larga, fiancheggiata in parte da negozi, in parte da abitazioni, del tutto sordida e informe pur senza essere miserabile.

A little later the two girls were walking hurriedly along the main road of Beldover, a wide street, flanked partly by shops, partly by dwellings, entirely sordid and shapeless albeit without being poverty-stricken.

The surprise of the English and the force of the point Lawrence is making is lost in what now appears to be merely a nuanced observation of the kind we might find in any number of novels. At moments like this it appears that rather than comparing the resources of one language and another, we are comparing a radical and individual voice, a voice 'unhoused' in social convention if we like, with the voice of a translator who is entirely at home with received ideas and habits of mind. In the first voice anything can happen, in the second very little will be allowed to happen.

But it is the next sentence that produces the most extraordinary collocation of the whole passage and perhaps the most serious (this time inevitable) loss in the Italian.

Gudrun, new from her life in Chelsea and Sussex, shrank cruelly from this amorphous ugliness of a small colliery town in the Midlands.

Gudrun reduce dalla vita condotta a Chelsea e nel Sussex, rabbrividì ferita dalla bruttezza informe di quella cittadina mineraria del Midlands.

Gudrun, returned from the life she had conducted in Chelsea and Sussex, shivered wounded by the shapeless ugliness of that small mining town of the Midlands.

The curious thing about the English is the paradoxical nature of 'shrank cruelly'. That Gudrun shrank implies that she is afraid, hurt, sensitive, but the adverb 'cruelly' suggests that Gudrun herself is causing pain. Of course on one level we read the adverb 'cruelly' as merely an emphasizer, as in the once common collocation 'cruelly cold', but on another we cannot help feeling, uneasily, that this adverb is telling us something about Gudrun's character, about this woman who determinedly ('yet forward she went') comes back to 'test the full effect of this shapeless, barren ugliness upon herself'. That is, the apparent contradiction of 'shrank cruelly' takes us to the heart of a contradiction, a conflict in Gudrun's character: her uneasy relationship (attraction/rejection) with every area of conventional social and family life. The Italian 'rabbrividì ferita' (*she shivered wounded*) merely suggests that Gudrun is a sensitive and vulnerable girl. Perhaps more importantly, not being a paradoxical and provocative juxtaposition, as 'shrank cruelly' clearly is, it does not draw the reader's attention to Gudrun's psychological complexity. Lawrence's use of 'cruelly' here is not dissimilar to the affects achieved with 'fearfully' in the expression 'fearfully tempted' examined earlier. In both cases the translator is placed in difficulty by the ambivalence of an emphasizer whose usually dormant semantic content is brought into antithetical play.

At this point it is worth going back and remembering the expression 'brought to bay'. Like 'shrank cruelly', it suggests both fear and aggression. We also found that 'refrained', in the way Lawrence uses it, suggested some confusion as to whether Gudrun's thinking about her relationship with her family was a pain or a pleasure. In short, in this first chapter (we are on the fifth page of the novel) Lawrence is already establishing that profound contradiction in Gudrun's character that will lead her to both love and destroy her partner Gerald. Almost every time she is referred to, some quirk of grammar or imagery is used to underline the enigma that she is both afraid and belligerent, drawn to those things that pain her. Again, we must remember that 'fearfully tempted' was her expression, not the narrator's.

The rest of the paragraph brings this character trait to the surface as Gudrun becomes aware, at least up to a point, of her own masochism in returning. And as it comes to the surface, rather than remaining hidden in syntactical contortions and oxymoronic collocations, this quality begins to emerge in the Italian too, though it is interesting that even here there are one or two changes that, to risk a joke, take the edge out of the English. One notices, for example, how the translation chooses to transform the statement, 'she passed on through a stretch of torment', into a simile, 'percorreva quel tratto di strada come se affrontasse la tortura', (*she went down this length of the street as if she were facing torture*) thus losing the force of the idea that this truly *is* a torture for Gudrun. (One observes in passing that the punning compression of 'stretch of torment' was impossible in the Italian.)

Another word that loses its complexity in the translation is 'barren'. In English the word contains the twin ideas of desolate and infertile (desolate because infertile). The most common modern use would be desolate, and thus the translator is right to choose the word 'spoglia' (*bare/stripped*). But given Lawrence's frequent use of biblical language (of which more later), the word is surely chosen to look forward to the barrenness of Gudrun's relationship with Gerald.

Approaching the end of this paragraph, one might ask whether 'meaningless people' is really the same as 'gente insensata' (senseless people)? One suspects not. Lawrence does not tell us that the local people are 'senza senno' (*without sense/discrimination*), as the *Novissimo dizionario della lingua italiana* defines the Italian word, but that their lives are without meaning. They are one with the amorphous townscape (which is also the 'disgrace of outspread London'). They mean nothing. They can be ignored, and will be throughout this novel. They are not, that is, among that elite – Ursula, Gudrun, Birkin, Gerald – whom Lawrence had chosen to write about because, as he put it in a letter to Catherine Carswell, they were 'the flower of an epoch's achievement', and it was 'only through such people that one could discover whither the general run of mankind ... was tending'.[9] On a number of occasions one feels the translator has as much trouble with Lawrence's political ideas as with his syntax.

The paragraph ends with another animal image, Gudrun 'felt like a beetle toiling in the dust', this time rendered perfectly satisfactorily in the Italian. But it is only in the English that one can appreciate the similarity with the earlier animal image of 'brought to bay'. In both cases Gudrun is represented as being doggedly determined in a desperate situation. Typically, it is difficult to decide whether the 'repulsion' she is described as feeling as the paragraph closes is directed towards herself or to the situation, or both.

Perhaps the most severe criticism levelled at Lawrence with regard to *Women in Love* was that the characterization was insufficiently distinct and likewise the experiences in love of the two central couples, Ursula and Birkin, Gudrun and Gerald. More or less all critics of the period agreed on this. A comment from John Middleton Murry sums up the feeling.

> *Women in Love* is five hundred pages of passionate vehemence, wave after wave of turgid, exasperated writing impelled towards some distant and invisible end; the persistent underground beating of some dark and inaccessible sea in an underworld whose inhabitants are known by this alone, that they writhe continually, like the damned, in a frenzy of sexual awareness of one another. Their creator believes that he can distinguish the writhing of one from the writhing of another ... to him they are utterly and profoundly different; to us they are all the same.[10]

---

[9] Lawrence, quoted by Catherine Carswell in *The Savage Pilgrimage*, Chatto, 1932, p. 68.

[10] John Middleton Murry: 'The Nostalgia of Mr D.H. Lawrence', *Nation and Athenaeum*, 13 August 1921.

In short, Lawrence is accused of precisely the amorphousness that he everywhere abhors. The curious thing here is that our own analysis of the opening
pages, and in particular our consideration of where the Italian translation of the
book is forced to part company with the English, not only suggest very clear
distinctions between Ursula and Gudrun, but also a connection between those
distinctions and the novel's central theme of the relationship of individual to
society and above all social mores vis-à-vis love and marriage. Gudrun seems
at once fascinated and repulsed by conventional marriage, as she has likewise
been drawn back to a home town she abhors. Ursula seems more calmly and
maturely to have rejected convention, even if she does not yet know quite
what else might be available for her elsewhere. With these ideas in mind, we
can now look for confirmation of our discoveries by comparing some more
carefully selected passages with their translation. Here, for example, is the
moment when Ursula and Gudrun see Gerald brutally forcing his horse to
stand still close to a passing goods train. The horseman is digging in his spurs
to compel the horse to overcome its instinct to flee.

> 'And she's bleeding! – She's bleeding!' cried Ursula, frantic with
> opposition and hatred of Gerald. She alone understood him perfectly,
> in pure opposition.
> Gudrun looked and saw the trickles of blood on the sides of the mare,
> and she turned white. And then on the very wound the bright spurs
> came down, pressing relentlessly. The world reeled and passed into
> nothingness for Gudrun, she could not know any more. (p. 170)

The Italian gives the passage thus:

> 'E sanguina! Sanguina!' gridò Ursula, folle di contrarietà e di odio
> verso Gerald. In pura antitesi, era lei stessa la prima a comprenderlo
> perfettamente.
> Gudrun guardò e vide i rivoli di sangue che colavano lungo i fianchi
> della giumenta, e sbiancò in volto. E poi, proprio in corrispondenza
> della carne viva, calarono i lucenti speroni, affondando spietatamente.
> Il mondo vacillò e trapassò nel nulla per Gudrun, che perse comple-
> tamente il senso della realtà. (p. 166)

And the back-translation:

> 'And she's bleeding! She's bleeding!' shouted Ursula mad with op-
> position and hatred towards Gerald. In pure antithesis, she was the first
> to understand him perfectly.

> Gudrun looked and saw the trickles of blood that were running down the mare's flanks, and her face went white. And then, right in correspondence with the wounded flesh the bright spurs came down, sinking in ruthlessly. The world wobbled and passed into nothing for Gudrun, who completely lost her sense of reality.

There is little need to engage in meticulous analysis to appreciate what happens here. The translator is completely at ease with standard description, effective, if a little slack when dealing with Ursula's psychology ('prima a comprenderlo' – *first to understand him* – for 'she alone understood' is incorrect, in that it suggests that her sister would later understand Gerald, which, alas, she never does). The problem is Gudrun. For once again the most complex phrasing is reserved for Gudrun and, as in the long passage examined previously, the Italian explains away the original with an expression at once reductive and trivial.

> The world reeled and passed into nothingness for Gudrun, she could not know any more.

> Il mondo vacillò e trapassò nel nulla per Gudrun, che perse comple-tamente il senso della realtà.
> *The world wobbled and passed into nothing for Gudrun, who com-pletely lost her sense of reality*

It is precisely in its inability to follow the English, however, that the translation makes us aware of the original's complexity and semantic vagueness. What does it mean that the world 'passed into nothingness'? And, even more pro-vocatively, what does it mean to say that 'she could not know any more'. The Italian expression 'perse completamente il senso della realtà' (*lost completely the sense of the reality*) is an entirely ordinary way of suggesting that someone loses his or her sense of proportion, of objectivity, falls into obsession. It would not be inappropriate to describe someone falling into love, or hate, though it does impose a rather limited non-Lawrentian vision of what 'reality' might be (what could be more frighteningly real than obsession?).

But then, is Gudrun falling in love or into obsession here? The English 'she could not know any more' is such an obscure expression, and all the more so because 'any more' could be interpreted in terms of time, or as the object of the verb 'know'. Does Lawrence simply mean that Gudrun can bear no more of this business with the blood or the spurs? If so, why did he not make it clear? Or is he inviting us to think in terms of Gudrun's deeper psychology?

Once again, he avoids putting neat limits on his prose (and evading limits is what this novel is about). Once again we have a sentence that creates a sense of disorientation, precisely the disorientation of transgressing limits, or, as in 'brought to bay', of finding oneself thrust against them. We can turn now to another moment in the book, another difficult challenge for the translator, to get a better idea of what Lawrence intended here.

Gerald invites the sisters to a party on the lake below his house. Gudrun and Ursula cross the lake and there, separated from her sister, Gudrun meets Gerald and promptly, inexplicably, slaps him across the face. But this does not deter him. Nor does it liberate Gudrun from her fascination for him. They kiss. Rowing back across the lake together in what is now deep twilight they hear a commotion. Two people are drowning. Gerald orders for all lights to be put out and dives into the dark water to look for the drowning pair. Gudrun waits, after a few moments Gerald surfaces from the water and grabs the boat. And we have this:

> He was not like a man for her, he was an incarnation, a great phase of life. She saw him press the water out of his face, and look at the bandage on his hand. And she knew it was all no good, and that she would never go beyond him, he was the final approximation of life to her. (p. 249)

> Per lei non era un uomo, era un'incarnazione, una fase solenne della vita. Lo vide tergersi l'acqua dal viso e controllare la fasciatura alla mano. E comprese che non era un buon segno, e che non le sarebbe più riuscito di sorprenderlo: Gerald per lei era l'offerta suprema che la vita le faceva. (p. 265)

And the back-translation:

> For her he was not a man, he was an incarnation, a solemn phase of life. She saw him wipe the water from his face and check the bandage on his hand. And she understood that it was not a good sign and that never again would she be able to surprise him: Gerald for her was the supreme gift that life gave her.

Perhaps this time we can simply list the differences:

> He was not like a man for her.
> Per lei non era un uomo – *For her he was not a man*

The English uses 'like', the Italian does not. Here one feels this is a necessary transformation. Otherwise the Italian would sound nonsensical.

> a great phase of life

> una fase solenne della vita – *a solemn phase of life*

Are 'great' and 'solemn' semantically equivalent (always assuming we know what Lawrence is talking about)? One suspects slightly religious overtones and positive connotations in 'solemn', absent in 'great'.

> press the water out of his face

> tergersi l'acqua dal viso

One is struck by the precision and force of the image in English, the Italian is somewhat weaker and offers a more common expression but is semantically more or less equivalent. The translator rarely has any difficulty with physical description when it does not take on figurative overtones.

> And she knew it was all no good

> E comprese che non era un buon segno
> *And she understood that it was not a good sign*

The Italian is unnecessarily weak here. It would surely have been possible to get closer to the desperation of the English ('E comprese che era del tutto inutile', perhaps – And she understood that it was quite pointless). But it is worth noting that the translator's lapses correspond to moments of maximum ambivalence in the original. Does this remark refer to the chance of saving those drowning in the water? Or to Gudrun's relationship with Gerald? Or to everything? The Italian suggests the first, the English is more ambivalent and prepares us for the rest of the sentence, which confirms that it is her own problems Gudrun is concerned with. She is not thinking of the drama in the water at all!

> she would never go beyond him

> non le sarebbe più riuscito di sorprenderlo
> *never again would she be able to surprise him*

So great is the distance between original and translation here that one wonders how and with what compass it was travelled. But our first reflection must be that once again it was the semantic vagueness of the original that prompted the translator's flight. What does 'she would never go beyond him' mean? Can we write the exact equivalent in Italian, that is: 'non gli sarebbe mai andata oltre' (word for word: *not to him would she ever go beyond*)? Can we write something, that is, whose meaning remains obscure to us? The translator decides not and, looking for something that can be contained within the limits of the context, something that will not be linguistically 'unhoused', decides, I suspect, to interpret this arcane phrase in relation to Gudrun's earlier action of slapping Gerald round the face. That really did surprise him. Then she was on top. Now she appreciates that she will never be able to do it again. She is in his thrall. Thus the translator's version, though those who know the book will be aware that this is not true. Gudrun does manage to surprise Gerald on numerous occasions.

Returning to the English, the point is surely that we have another spatial image of an obstacle and a postulated 'beyond'. This time, however, it is Gerald who is the obstacle and Gudrun is no longer confident that she can jump the edge and get beyond. Gerald, for Gudrun, is what the psychologists now like to refer to as a 'limit experience'. There is nothing on the other side of Gerald for her. The meaning of the earlier 'she could know no more' now becomes clearer. Gudrun simply cannot digest Gerald, cannot put him behind her and go on to experience something else. Her development was arrested by the image of this man digging his spurs into the bloody horse. No knowledge will ever mean more than this. If this is the situation, her hitting Gerald first and then her never being able to go beyond him are both manifestations of the same blocked psychological condition (he is a limit she thrusts against), and not, as the Italian suggests, two contrasting moments in Gudrun's development. If we grasp what the Italian is losing here in it's difficulty in presenting Gudrun's state of mind, then we will have got some sense of Lawrence's complexity and also his consistency as he sets up his characters and plot.

> he was the final approximation of life to her

> Gerald per lei era l'offerta suprema che la vita le faceva
> *Gerald for her was the supreme gift that life made her*

There are times when it seems easier to understand Lawrence by considering what he is *not* saying, than by establishing what he is. The Italian translation offers considerable scope for this approach, a sort of conventional paraphrase which shows us just how original Lawrence is. Once again here the elusiveness of the original prompts some well-intentioned interpretation on the part of the translator that shifts the tone of the book towards her more conventional vision. 'offerta suprema' (*supreme gift/offer*) carries decidedly positive connotations, suggests a benevolent, perhaps even Christian view of a world where life offers the individual wonderful opportunities.

While you can see how the translator might have arrived at this version, the English is much more threatening. 'Final', especially in the dramatic context of searching the lake for two drowning youngsters, has overtones of death. ' ... final approximation' might suggest that this is the last time life is going to get close to her (in the sense of 'final nearing/approach'), or that this is as close as she and life are going to get. Whichever way you look at it, there is a menacing feeling of limitation here (she will get no closer than this, nor this close ever again), it is something that dogs Gudrun and her relationship with Gerald from beginning to end. All this is missed in the Italian, not because such things are unsayable in that language, far from it, but because Lawrence chooses to express himself in a style that is itself a pushing against limits, breaking the barriers of normal syntax and semantics. Even assuming the translator had appreciated all that is going on in the English, to recreate this effect and generate the same range of connotation would require a very considerable act of creativity.

A few lines later in this same scene, Lawrence indulges in his most easily identifiable stylistic technique, repetition:

> Again there was a splash, and he was gone under. Gudrun sat, sick at heart, frightened of the great, level surface of the water, so heavy and deadly. She was so alone, with the level, unliving field of the water stretching beneath her. It was not a good isolation, it was a terrible, cold separation of suspense. She was suspended upon the surface of the insidious reality until such time as she also should disappear beneath it. (p. 249)

The barrier this time is the surface of the water. Its affinity with death is all too obvious. Gerald passes through it. Gudrun remains on this side, aware that any going beyond for her will mean the end. In terms of the drama and psychology of the scene, Gudrun is so locked into her own obsessions (stressed by all the melancholy repetition) that she cannot even feel concern for the two people drowning. The Italian is as follows:

Si udì lo sciacquio di un altro tuffo, e Gerald sparì in acqua. Gudrun sedeva immobile, abbattuta, impaurita nella grande, piatta superficie del lago, così greve e mortale. Si sentiva così sola, con la piatta, morta distesa dell'acqua che si allungava sotto di lei. Non era un isolamento piacevole, era una terribile, gelida separazione di attesa ansiosa. Gudrun era come sospesa sulla superficie dell'insidiosa realtà, come in attesa del momento in cui anche a lei sarebbe toccato sparire al di sotto. (p. 265)

One heard the splash of another dive, and Gerald disappeared in the water. Gudrun sat motionless, downhearted, frightened in the great, flat surface of the lake, so heavy and deadly. She felt so alone, with the flat, dead expanse of water that stretched beneath her. It wasn't a pleasant isolation, it was a terrible, icy separation of anxious waiting. Gudrun was as if suspended on the surface of this insidious reality, as if waiting for the moment when she too would have to disappear beneath.

An analysis of the differences here gives us:

and he was gone under

e Gerald sparì in acqua
and Gerald disappeared in the water

The use of the verb 'to be' as auxiliary gives the expression an old-fashioned and portentous ring, reinforced by the fact that the expression 'to go under' can mean to succumb and by inference to die. Again Lawrence allows his verb to take on wider connotations by avoiding a delimiting object. The differences in the Italian are obvious enough.

Gudrun sat, sick at heart, frightened of the great, level surface of the water, so heavy and deadly.

Gudrun sedeva immobile, abbattuta, impaurita nella grande, piatta superficie del lago, così greve e mortale.
Gudrun sat motionless, downhearted/depressed, frightened in the great, flat surface of the lake, so heavy and mortal/deadly

Even the simplest expressions can cause complications. Here the translator chooses not to write the simple 'stava seduta' (*sat/was sitting*), feeling perhaps that it is information without any emotional or dramatic import. She thus introduces 'immobile', perhaps thinking of one of Lawrence's favourite words, 'motionless'. Here the idea is in harmony with the stillness of the lake and offers some alliteration with 'impaurita' (*frightened/scared*). It thus seems a good idea. What most students will notice, though, is the switch from 'frightened of' to 'impaurita in' (*frightened in*). In the Italian Gudrun's fear is thus understood as having to do with the drowning accident, or with her relationship with Gerald, whereas in Lawrence's original it is more instinctive. She is afraid of the water. Why? We already know that she can swim, because she has done so only an hour or so before.

The water is described as 'level', 'heavy', 'deadly', and then again in the next sentence as 'level' and 'unliving'. Particularly ambivalent is 'deadly', which can mean as an adjective 'causing death' or as an adverb 'in a manner resembling death'. The Italian is effective here, finding exactly the same range of possibilities in 'mortale'. But why the insistence on 'level' which seems somewhat strange when translated as the Italian 'piatto' (*flat*)? Death, we recall, is traditionally described as 'the great leveller'. Gudrun is frightened of the water in so far as it represents her mortality, which is, as it were, one with Gerald as swimmer and diver; he is the final experience she can expect from life. Coming up against the limit of Gerald is also an encounter with her own limitations, indeed with the very idea of limitation. Hence it is an approach to the 'unliving'. Definition by negatives is, of course, another way of playing with the idea of limitations. It is difficult to imagine an Italian equivalent for the disturbing 'unliving'.

It was not a good isolation

Non era un isolamento piacevole
It was not a pleasant isolation

Another definition by negatives. Leaving aside the difficulties with finding a suitable equivalent of 'good' here (the ordinary Italian 'buono' will just not do), one can appreciate the enormous distance between that and 'piacevole' (*pleasant/ pleasing*). Once again, Lawrence's text is open to far wider moral and figurative interpretation. The Italian limits us to a consideration of Gudrun's comfort, physical or mental as the case may be.

it was a terrible, cold separation of suspense. She was suspended upon the surface of the insidious reality until such time as she also should disappear beneath it.

era una terribile, gelida separazione di attesa ansiosa. Gudrun era
come sospesa sulla superficie dell'insidiosa realtà, come in attesa del
momento in cui anche a lei sarebbe toccato sparire al di sotto.

*it was a terrible, icy separation of anxious waiting. Gudrun was as
if suspended on the surface of the insidious reality, as if waiting for
the moment when she too would have to disappear beneath.*

The cohesion of the English is evident enough. Lawrence increases suspense
vis-à-vis the drowning accident by concentrating on Gudrun's sense that her
fascination with Gerald has somehow suspended her from reality. Beyond
that suspense is only death. Despite the unnecessary 'come' (*as if*) in 'come
sospesa' (*as if suspended*) the translation seeks cohesion by repeating 'attesa'
(*wait/waiting*) and then, with the repetition of 'sparire' (disappear), the earlier
use of the same verb ('Gerald sparì sotto' – *Gerald disappeared beneath*) is
retrospectively given some of the weight that 'Gerald was gone under' had
had in the English. One can't help admiring the translation here, while at the
same time it makes us aware of the extraordinary density and allusiveness that
Lawrence's English maintains page after page.

To return to the content of the passage, it appears that contact with Gerald
has a way of generating heightened consciousness in Gudrun, together with
a frightening awareness of her own mortality. Again this is in line with the
description of her in the opening pages as someone attracted to what damages
her. As a last comment on the way Lawrence deploys unusual syntax to explore
Gudrun's predicament, and the way the problem of translation exposes this,
here are a few lines from shortly after the couple's first love-making two hundred pages later. Gerald has fallen happily asleep. Gudrun is not so lucky.

But Gudrun lay wide awake, destroyed into perfect consciousness.
She lay motionless, with wide eyes staring motionless into the darkness, while he was sunk away in sleep, his arms around her. (p. 430)

The inner unity of Lawrence's text, its recovery of the idiomatic 'wide' of
'wide awake' in the description of her 'wide eyes', then the insistent oppressive monotony of the repeated 'ess's, (consciousness, motionless, darkness)
is remarkable and bound to cause problems. But there are more interesting
difficulties on the syntactical and semantic levels.' Here is the Italian.

Ma Gudrun rimase desta, dilaniata, in uno stato di lucidità perfetta.
Giacque immobile, con gli occhi sgranati a fissare immobili il buio
mentre lui, sprofondato nel sonno, la teneva abbracciata. (p. 499)

> But Gudrun remained awake, torn apart, in a state of perfect lucidity.
> She lay motionless, with eyes wide open staring motionless at the dark
> while he, sunk in sleep, held her in his arms.

Immediately noticeable is the translation of 'destroyed into perfect consciousness' as 'dilaniata, in uno stato di lucidità perfetta' (*torn apart, in a state of
perfect lucidity*). As in previous examples, Lawrence adopts an unusual syntax
to achieve disturbing compression and juxtaposition. Usually when something
is destroyed it is destroyed and that is that. There is no further state. Here the
use of 'into' transforms 'destroy' into a verb of transformation, transgressing
conventional limits.

The next surprise is that what Gudrun is destroyed/transformed 'into'
is something traditionally thought of as positive in Western tradition, 'consciousness', but here the state is rendered negative by coming as the result of
a process of destruction. Placing the adjective 'perfect' before consciousness
only emphasizes this unusual juxtaposition. In the space of a few words Lawrence both evokes a state of mind that most will recognize (the unpleasantness
of a hyperconscious insomnia), thus giving the description authenticity, and
refers us to his own theories as to the damaging nature of a consciousness
divorced from emotions and animal nature. In uncoupling the participle
'dilaniata' (torn apart) from 'uno stato di lucidità perfetta' (*a state of perfect
lucidity*) the Italian loses much of this complexity, while it is also clear that
'consciousness' means more than 'lucidity'. The problem of course is that the
Italian 'coscienza' (*consciousness/conscience*) has connotations which would
be inappropriate here (a guilty conscience is not Gudrun's problem), while
again 'consapevolezza' (awareness) lacks connotations that are required. Most
of all, while Lawrence's text is markedly distant from any kind of standard discourse and gains much of its meaning from that distance, the Italian, although
its content does transmit the drama, is stylistically ordinary.

Looking at the last line of this passage, one notes again how Lawrence uses
metaphor to gesture, quite subtly, towards the portentous. Here the limits of
back-translation and gloss are all too evident. Gerald is 'sunk away in sleep,
his arms around her'. The metaphor 'sunk away' is not a common expression
in English to describe a sleeper and, recalling the earlier passage about the lake
and the drownings, the fact that his arms are 'around her' becomes menacing,
as if he were dragging her down underwater (the couple who drowned did
so partly because the non-swimming girl clutched her arms round her lover).
'Sprofondata' (*sunk*) translates 'sunk away' perfectly, but in this case it is *an
absolutely standard way* of saying deeply asleep in Italian, and so calls no
attention to itself and does not so readily recall water or drowning. As a result

the final 'la teneva abbracciata' (*he held her in his arms*) seems more tender than frightening.

So much for Gudrun. At almost every turn Lawrence's descriptions of her, his insistence, through twisted syntax, on her complex psychology and complex predicament with Gerald, cause problems for the translation, problems that help us to appreciate the original. But what of Ursula? I suggested earlier that the language was less prone to complexity in its descriptions of her. How does Lawrence establish her difference from Gudrun, distinguish her relationship with Birkin from that of her sister with Gerald? Here is a passage immediately after Ursula and Birkin's rapturous embrace in the backroom of a country inn. We need hardly discuss, as others have, whether some form of fellatio has taken place.

> After a lapse of stillness, after the rivers of strange dark fluid richness had passed over her, flooding, carrying away her mind and flooding down her spine and down her knees, past her feet, a strange flood, sweeping away everything and leaving her an essential new being, she was left quite free, she was free in complete ease, her complete self. So she rose, stilly and blithe, smiling at him. He stood before her, glimmering, so awfully real, that her heart almost stopped beating. He stood there in his strange, whole body, that had its marvellous fountains, like the bodies of the sons of God who were in the beginning. There were strange fountains of his body, more mysterious and potent than any she had imagined or known, more satisfying, ah, finally, mystically-physically satisfying. She had thought there was no source deeper than the phallic source. And now, behold, from the smitten rock of the man's body, from the strange marvellous flanks and thighs, deeper, further in mystery than the phallic source, came the floods of ineffable darkness and ineffable riches.
>
> They were glad, and they could forget perfectly. They laughed, and went to the meal provided. There was a venison pasty, of all things, a large broad-faced cut ham, eggs and cresses and red beet-root, and medlars and apple-tart, and tea.
>
> 'What good things!' she cried with pleasure. 'How noble it looks! Shall I pour out the tea?'
>
> She was usually nervous and uncertain at performing these public duties, such as giving tea. But today she forgot, she was at her ease, entirely forgetting to have misgivings. The tea-pot poured beautifully from a proud slender spout. Her eyes were warm with smiles as she gave him his tea. She had learned at last to be still and perfect. (pp. 396-7)

It is clear that the tone here is different from those of the previous passages. There is a drawing on biblical diction which juxtaposes provocatively with whatever sexual experience has taken place and likewise with the pub meal the pair then sit down to. Italian does not have such a recognizably biblical diction. But this was probably the least of the translator's worries as she dealt with this text.

> Dopo una pausa di immobile silenzio, dopo che i fiumi della strana, oscura, fluida ricchezza l'ebbero sommersa, inondandola, offuscandole la mente e dilagando lungo la sua spina dorsale e giù, fino alle ginocchia, defluendo dai piedi, uno strano flusso che spazzava via ogni cosa e faceva di lei un essere sostanzialmente nuovo, si ritrovò libera, libera e totalmente a suo agio, totalmente se stessa. Così, si rialzò, quieta e serena, sorridendogli. Birkin era ritto di fronte a lei, baluginante, così terribilmente reale, che il cuore di Ursula quasi smise di battere. Lui se ne stava lì nel suo strano corpo intatto, che possedeva le sue prodigiose sorgenti, come i corpi dei figli di Dio che erano al principio della creazione. C'erano strane sorgenti nel suo corpo, più misteriose e potenti di quanto Ursula avesse mai immaginato o saputo, più appaganti, ah, insomma, appaganti in senso mistico e fisico. Ursula aveva creduto che non esistesse fonte più profonda della fonte fallica. E ora, ecco, dalla roccia percossa del corpo dell'uomo, dagli strani, prodigiosi fianchi e dalle cosce, più profondi, più addentro al mistero di quanto fosse la fonte fallica, prorompevano i flutti dell'oscurità ineffabile e dell'ineffabile ricchezza.
>
> Erano contenti, immersi in un perfetto oblio, e ridendo si accostarono alla tavola apparecchiata per loro. C'era, figurarsi, un pasticcio di selvaggina, e poi grosse fette di prosciutto e uova e crescione e barbabietole, e ancora, nespole e crostata di mele, e il tè.
>
> 'Quante cose buone!' esclamò Ursula gioiosa. 'Che imponenza! ... Verso il tè? ...'
>
> Di solito era nervosa e insicura nello svolgimento di compiti pubblici, come servire il tè. Ma quel giorno scordò ogni cosa, era a suo agio, del tutto dimentica di essere incline all'apprensione. La teiera versava con precisione da uno snello beccuccio orgoglioso. Gli occhi di Ursula si accendevano di caldi sorrisi mentre gli tendeva la tazza di tè. Finalmente aveva imparato a farlo con mano ferma e con perfetta compostezza. (p. 455)

After a pause of motionless silence, after the rivers of the strange, dark, fluid richness had submerged her, flooded her, blurring her mind

and flooding along her spine and down, as far as her knees, flowing out
from her feet, a strange flow that swept away everything and made of
her a substantially new being, she found herself free, free and totally
at her ease, totally herself. In this way, she stood up again, calm and
serene, smiling at him. Birkin was standing up straight in front of her,
glimmering, so terribly real, that Ursula's heart almost stopped beating. He stood there in his strange, unblemished body, that possessed
its prodigious wellsprings, like the bodies of the sons of God who
were at the beginning of creation. There were strange springs in his
body, more mysterious and powerful than Ursula had ever imagined
or known, more satisfying, ah, in short, satisfying in a mystical and
physical sense. Ursula had believed that there was no source deeper
than the phallic source, and now, here it was, from the struck rock of
the body of man, from the strange, prodigious, hips and thighs, deeper,
more central to the mystery than the phallic source, out burst the floods
of ineffable darkness and ineffable richness.

They were happy, immersed in a perfect forgetfulness, and laughing
they came to the table prepared for them. There was, just imagine, a
game pie, and then thick slices of ham and eggs and watercress and
beetroot, and again, medlars and apple pie and tea.

'How many good things!' exclaimed Ursula with joy. 'How impres-
sive!... Shall I pour the tea? ...'

Usually she was nervous and insecure carrying out these public du-
ties, like serving tea. But today she forgot everything, she was at ease,
entirely forgetting that she was inclined to be apprehensive. The teapot
poured with precision from a proud slender spout. Ursula's eyes lit
up with warm smiles while she offered him the cup of tea. Finally she
had learned to do it with a firm hand and perfect composure.

The passage begins with a description of an after-sex experience exactly opposite to Gudrun's, a positive dissolving of everyday consciousness. The first
sentence alone provides us with all sorts of divergences between translation
and original.

After a lapse of stillness

Dopo una pausa di immobile silenzio
After a pause of motionless silence

Lawrence creates richness through ellipsis and compression. The word 'lapse'
usually refers either to time, to suggest a period when nothing important

happens, or to consciousness, generally in a negative sense, to suggest a loss of awareness. It can also refer, significantly enough, to a falling away from some orthodox dogma. Here, however, the word is not qualified or limited. All we discover is what fills the lapse (whether of time or consciousness, or both): stillness. When it comes to putting 'lapse' into Italian we find that there is no straightforward equivalent. Bilingual dictionaries offer translations such as 'errore' (*error*), 'sbaglio' (*mistake*), 'fallo' (*fault/slip*), 'caduta' (*fall*), and most significantly of all 'dimenticanza' (*forgetting*); [11] the translator in this case chooses the more limited word 'pausa' (*pause/break*) to give the immediate sense of a lapse of time and captures the semantic range of 'stillness' in 'immobile silenzio' (*motionless silence*). But the sense of a lapse of consciousness, a freedom from painful self-consciousness, which is what this whole text is about (and what sets it in contrast to the previous text after Gudrun and Gerald make love), is lost, and with it the associated strangeness of Lawrence's phrasing.

> after the rivers of strange dark fluid richness had passed over her, flooding, carrying away her mind and flooding down her spine and down her knees, past her feet, a strange flood, sweeping away everything

> dopo che i fiumi della strana, oscura, fluida ricchezza l'ebbero sommersa, inondandola, offuscandole la mente e dilagando lungo la sua spina dorsale e giù, fino alle ginocchia, defluendo dai piedi, uno strano flusso che spazzava via ogni cosa

> after the rivers of the strange, dark, fluid richness had submerged her, flooded her, blurring her mind and flooding along her spine and down, as far as her knees, flowing out from her feet, a strange flow that swept away every thing

In his extended essay *Apocalypse*, Lawrence attributes a positive moral value to figurative language, to the extent that it fights against the amorphousness and, as he sees it, emotionlessness of contemporary society.[12] His use of idiosyncratic phrasing aimed at leaving his work as open as possible to figurative interpretation has been observed throughout. Here we have a declared, extended metaphor to describe Ursula's positive experience of being emptied of consciousness, renewed by pleasure. The Italian translation differs in its use of 'l'ebbero sommersa' (*had submerged her*) for 'had passed over her' and

---

[11] *Il nuovo Ragazzini*, Zanichelli, Bologna, 1984.
[12] See, for example, Chapter viii.

then 'offuscandole la mente' (*blurred her mind*) for 'carrying away her mind'. 'sommersa' (*submerged*) is in line with the extended metaphor to the extent that it refers to fluids, but it has negative connotations that 'passed over her' does not. It suggests that Ursula remains in some sense submerged, drowned perhaps. More seriously, 'offuscandole la mente' moves us away from images of flooding and water, and again has negative connotations. It leaves her with a 'mente offuscata' (*blurred mind*) rather than carrying away her mind altogether. Finally 'defiuendo dai piedi' (*flowing out from her feet*) is another slight distortion of Lawrence's metaphor which has the 'fluid richness' flowing over and past Ursula, not through her. Here comparison draws our attention to Lawrence's consistency, the translation's tendency to substitute ease for precision (though here one feels the two could well have been reconciled).

Precision is also a crucial matter in the next part of the sentence.

> leaving her an essential new being

> e faceva di lei un essere sostanzialmente nuovo
> *and made of her a substantially new being*

In the English the flood sweeps Ursula's mind away and leaves her 'an essential new being'. It does not, as in the Italian, 'make her' that. The distinction is important to the extent that what Lawrence seeks to describe here is his much quoted notion of a deeper self which requires to be liberated from the wrong kind of consciousness, not made or created by some sex experience. In any event, the adjective 'essential' is being used in its primary sense of 'relating to, constituting, or containing, the essence'.[13] The translation with the adverb 'sostanzialmente' (*substantially*) which could either mean, banally 'to a great degree' or, absurdly one has to feel, 'with regard to substance' only shows us how precise Lawrence is being and how difficult to follow.

> she was left quite free, she was free in complete ease, her complete self.

> si ritrovò libera, libera e totalmente a suo agio, totalmente se stessa.
> *she found herself free and totally at her ease, totally herself*

---

[13] The definition is taken from *Chambers English Dictionary*, Cambridge University Press, 1988. The difference between translation and original here points us to Lawrence's concept of character as that which lies below temporary 'allotropic states'. Cf. *The Letters of D.H. Lawrence*, vol. 2, ed. George J. Zytaruk and James T. Boulton, Cambridge University Press, 1981, pp. 182-4.

As so often the Italian gives a standard expression, 'totalmente a suo agio' (*totally at ease*), for Lawrence's very different 'in complete ease'. One usually says 'at ease', or 'completely at ease', to the extent that 'in ease' seems bizarre, and 'completely in ease' almost unimaginable. Here one appreciates Lawrence's astuteness in masking his curious use of the preposition by interposing 'complete' (in complete ease). Nevertheless, we do have a sense of something unusual going on in a way we do not with the Italian.

The same can again be said of the difference between the curious 'her complete self' and the translation 'totalmente se stessa' (*totally herself*). This is certainly difficult. Where English has expressions like 'my better self' or 'my worst self', Italian, not having a noun 'self' to which various complements can be attached, uses 'la parte migliore di me' (*the better part of me*), 'la parte peggiore di me' (*the worse part of me*). The translator can hardly write 'la parte completa di sé' (*the complete part of me*)!

But rather than dwelling on possible alternatives in Italian, the thing to grasp is how all the translator's changes, whether forced or not, are in the same direction, towards more conventional, commonplace concepts than those generated in the English. In diverging from ordinary usage here, Lawrence insists that the experiences he is talking about require thought, and what's more deserve to be thought about in new ways. Again expressions like 'in complete ease' and 'her complete self' get their meaning through their provocative distance from the conventional. Without wishing to be unkind, the Italian reads like the kind of text Lawrence was eager to escape from.

So she rose, stilly and blithe, smiling at him.

Così, si rialzò, quieta e serena, sorridendogli.
In this way, she stood up again, calm and serene, smiling at him

'Stilly' and 'blithe' are wilfully poetic, if not archaic, in any event appropriate for Ursula as 'essential being'. 'Stilly' also picks up on the 'stillness' that opens the paragraph. It is difficult to imagine how the Italian could reflect this change of register.

He stood before her, glimmering, so awfully real, that her heart almost stopped beating.

Birkin era ritto di fronte a lei, baluginante, così terribilmente reale, che il cuore di Ursula quasi smise di battere.
Birkin was standing up straight in front of her, glimmering, so terribly real, that Ursula's heart almost stopped beating.

There seems little stopping Lawrence at this point. Now that we are dealing with an essential being one must be attentive to the primary, or at least older, sense of every word. Here 'awfully' surely has a great deal more awe in it than the 'terror' suggested by 'terribilmente' (*terribly*). As with fearfully' and 'cruelly' in previous examples, one must never treat emphasizers as merely such.

> his strange, whole body ... like the bodies of the sons of God who were in the beginning

> suo strano corpo intatto ... come i corpi dei figli di Dio che erano al principio della creazione
> *his strange, unblemished body ... like the bodies of the sons of God who were at the beginning of creation*

The references to biblical diction and similarly archaic syntax ('who were in the beginning') will be all too obvious to the native English reader. Lawrence is trying to give his language the same 'swept clean' essential nature as his characters. Chambers gives the archaic meaning of 'whole' as 'restored to health, healed'. It is not a meaning Italian can deliver with 'intatto' (*intact/ unsullied/unblemished*). In the same way the Italian has to be more explicit with its reference to the creation.

> mystically-physically satisfying

> appaganti in senso mistico e fisico
> *satisfying in a mystical and physical sense*

The English suggests a typically Lawrentian equivalence between, or convergence of, the mystical and the physical. This is what this passage and a great deal of Lawrence's writing is about, that physical and mystical must not be separated in obedience to the Cartesian scheme of things. The Italian adds them together but keeps them distinct.

> And now, behold, from the smitten rock of the man's body

> E ora, ecco, dalla roccia percossa del corpo dell'uomo
> *And now, here it was, from the struck rock of the body of man*

One notes in passing here the range of archaisms available in English, which the Italian has to translate with common contemporary expressions. 'Ecco' means behold of course, but since it is in everyday colloquial use in Italian it carries no weight and would ordinarily be understood the way we understand *voilà* in French. Likewise the English 'smitten rock' can only take us back to Moses, bringing in a flood (or gush…) of perplexing connotations, which would require at least a page or two to follow up (Moses sinned in smiting the rock, but God performed the miracle of producing water anyway – so is sex a sin that nevertheless prompts a miracle?). Such associations are not readily signalled in a language whose translations of the Bible are not so well-established and never had an important influence on Italian literary style. It's worth remembering that as recently as the 1860s a man was condemned to death in Rome for reading the Bible in Italian rather than Latin.

from the strange, marvellous flanks

dagli strani, prodigiosi fianchi
from the strange, prodigious hips

Lawrence prefers the animal 'flanks' to the human 'hips', as is his way, particularly when talking about our essential nature. The translator does not have alternatives to choose from. Italian makes no distinctions between humans and animals here.

came the floods of ineffable darkness and ineffable richness

prorompevano i flutti dell'oscurità ineffabile e dell'ineffabile ricchezza
burst out the floods of ineffable darkness and ineffable richness

Apart from the greater emphasis of the Italian verb, there is no divergence in the translation here, but I quote the line to show how at the climax of this part of the text, Lawrence makes explicit the unconventional linking of darkness and riches, already suggested at the beginning of the passage by the 'dark fluid richness' and again by the unusual suggestion that a lapse of consciousness is to be seen positively. To the extent to which the translation is able to deliver this kind of content when Lawrence makes it explicit, it does of course give the sense of the book, if not always the richness and consistency with which the idea is presented.

They were glad, and they could forget perfectly

> Erano contenti, immersi in un perfetto oblio
> *They were happy, immersed in a perfect forgetfulness*

This sentence offers the passage's most obvious contrast to Gudrun's experience of being 'destroyed into perfect consciousness'. The Italian chooses to repeat 'immersi' (*immersed*) looking for a link with the imagery of the previous paragraph, though we recall that the fluid richness had actually passed and gone in the English version; Ursula is no longer 'immersed'. '... in un perfetto oblio' (*in a perfect forgetfulness*) does not actually make it clear whether the couple are forgetting or forgotten. However, regardless of the exact meaning of the Italian, the crucial difference is its ducking away from the unusual English expression 'they could forget perfectly'. One sometimes talks of 'being able to forget', in the sense of forgetting an unhappy love, or an insult or crime. But one rarely uses the past tense of 'can' with 'forget' since this suggests not the achievement of a single act of forgetting (as in 'finally she *was able* to forget the whole nightmare') but an ability (as in 'when I was young I could swim very well'). The only occasion on which one might use 'could' with 'forget' is when we are suggesting that we have been put in a position where we are able to do something (I decided to take my exams early so that I could then forget about my studies). But this hardly seems the case here, and in any event to follow 'forget', not with an object of what one forgot, but with the adverb 'perfectly' is bizarre, especially given that 'perfectly' usually has positive connotations and 'forget' negative. Thus Lawrence insists on the special nature of his character's experience while again disorientating his reader by suggesting unconventional attitudes to the value of forgetfulness (as previously and conversely with the value of consciousness). Looking at the English one is brought up sharp and obliged to ask oneself what it might mean to 'forget perfectly'. The Italian is happy to remain in 'un perfetto oblio' (a perfect oblivion/forgetting) as far as this is concerned.

> They laughed, and went to the meal provided.

> e ridendo si accostarono alla tavola apparecchiata per loro.
> *and laughing they came to the table prepared for them.*

After the long periods of the previous paragraphs, Lawrence's short simple sentences are clearly intended to express ease. The Italian links the sentences. One also wonders whether the allusions to the Twenty-third Psalm with its 'still waters' and its 'thou preparest a table before me' is so clear in the Italian.

There was a venison pasty, of all things, a large broad-faced cut ham, eggs and cresses and red beet-root, and medlars and apple-tart, and tea.

C'era, figurarsi, un pasticcio di selvaggina, e poi grosse fette di prosciutto e uova e crescione e barbabietole, e ancora, nespole e crostata di mele, e il tè.
There was, just imagine, a game pie, and then thick slices of ham and eggs and watercress and beetroot, and again, medlars and apple pie and tea.

Middleton Murry found this sentence extremely hard to take. He writes: 'Why in the name of darkness, "a venison pasty, of all things"? Is a venison pasty more incongruous with this beatitude than a large ham?'.[14] Aside from the possible pun venison/venial, perhaps the answer to this is to be seen in the 'essential' meaning that Lawrence has been giving to much of his vocabulary in this piece. Could 'of all things' be referring us to creation here, in the sense 'of all things created' 'in the beginning'? Certainly the expression is followed by a very long list. The collocation 'all things' recurs frequently in the Bible, as any glance at a Bible concordance will suggest, and usually refers to God's largesse. The first use is when God blesses Noah after the flood (significantly enough): 'Every moving thing that liveth shall be meat for you; even as the green herb have I given you all things'.[15] One could hardly expect the Italian to pick up on this; ' ... figurarsi (*just imagine*) is merely effusive, translating very well the idiomatic sense of 'of all things', which is the sense that Middleton Murry was complaining about.

The notion that Lawrence is referring to creation, or creation after the flood, will seem a little less far fetched when we remember that Ursula now exclaims: 'What good things!' The Italian chooses to translate by stressing quantity rather than quality: 'Quante cose buone!' (*How many good things*!).

Which brings us to our final paragraph, where once again Lawrence keeps his text open to wider interpretation while the Italian limits it to the immediate tea-party context. Ursula, it seems, is usually nervous when obliged to assume a social role, like pouring tea. But not today.

But today she forgot, she was at her ease, entirely forgetting to have misgivings.

---

[14] Middleton Murry in Colin Clarke, *'The Rainbow' and 'Women in Love': A Selection of Critical Essays*, Macmillan, London, 1969, p. 71.
[15] Genesis 9.3, *The Bible*, Authorized Version.

> Ma quel giorno scordò ogni cosa, era a suo agio, del tutto dimentica
> di essere incline all'apprensione.
> *But today she forgot everything, she was at ease, entirely forgetting*
> *that she was inclined to be apprehensive.*

The Italian introduces an object for 'forget'. True it is a catch-all object (ogni cosa – *everything*), but it removes the strangeness of finding a verb like this left open. The repetition is lost by first using scordò (*she forgot*) and then 'dimentica' (*forgetful/forgetting*), but most of all the odd semantics of the last part of the sentence are altered. In the English she forgets 'to have misgivings'. The phrasing gives us the impression that normally Ursula 'remembers to have misgivings', as if the habit of being ill at ease in certain situations were somehow wilful. It is as if one were to say that someone forgot to have a bad dream. By introducing 'dimentica di essere incline' (*forgetting to be inclined*) the Italian returns the expression to conventional discourse (someone forgot that they were inclined to having bad dreams).

> The tea-pot poured beautifully from a proud slender spout.

> La teiera versava con precisione da uno snello beccuccio orgoglioso.
> *The teapot poured with precision from a proud slender spout*

Again an adverb which has to be taken seriously, particularly given the phallic image that follows. One wonders if 'con precisione' (*with precision*) was really the right choice for 'beautifully' in this wonderful moment of forgetfulness.

> Her eyes were warm with smiles as she gave him his tea. She had
> learned at last to be still and perfect.

> Gli occhi di Ursula si accendevano di caldi sorrisi mentre gli tendeva
> la tazza di tè. Finalmente aveva imparato a farlo con mano ferma e con
> perfetta compostezza.
> *Ursula's eyes lit up with warm smiles while she offered him the cup*
> *of tea. Finally she had learned to do it with a firm hand and perfect*
> *composure.*

With all that has been said so far, there is little need to comment on the licence the Italian takes in nailing the English down to its tea-time context in this last sentence. In defence of the translator, her difficulties do point us to the unusual nature of the English. A child may learn to 'sit still' or 'stand still', but clearly to learn to 'be still' suggests a deeper psychological development. And this is nothing compared with the idea of learning 'to be perfect' (presumably meant in its primary sense of 'complete', her 'complete self'). The translator decides to stick with pouring tea. How very English. In the translation one is limited to the feeling that a revelationary sexual encounter will make you a better hostess.

To analyse only a handful of passages in a book almost six hundred pages long is to scratch the surface. All the same, our comparisons of translation and original have brought out a pattern of stylistic techniques clearly integrated with the novel's desire to explore the limits of social convention through the experiences of four well-defined characters. One important and legitimate objection remains to be considered: that any analysis of this variety is dogged by the suspicion that the pieces considered *could have been translated better* and that in that case comparison would not have yielded all it has.

Two things can be said to counter this anxiety. First, and most practically, I have throughout this book sought out what I felt was the best available translation of the originals under consideration. There is no attempt to find translations which are wide of the mark. On the contrary. Second, and more importantly, there is much in the passages quoted from Lawrence's original that even the best translation would be unable to follow exactly. It might strive to compensate, but it would always be forced to diverge. So whatever the outcome, the struggle to get the text into Italian would draw attention to the style's peculiarities. For it is noticeable that where the English remains within the confines of ordinary usage, where it is happily 'housed' in common English, the translator has no difficulty. Where it begins to declare its independence, to establish a distance between itself and more ordinary ways of saying things, then it becomes hard indeed, and this precisely because it is an English 'housedness' that Lawrence is struggling with, it is English syntax that he subverts, not Italian. How can one suggest the unconventional nature of 'shut himself together', 'in complete ease' or 'destroyed into perfect consciousness' in another language? These expressions depend for their effect on the syntax, semantics, lexis and idioms of English. One cannot simply respond with an Italian that is merely and perhaps randomly unconventional. For again Lawrence's trick is to subvert without becoming incomprehensible or unattractive, without even disturbing the text's fluency. He is finding loopholes in the language, rather than taking a sledgehammer to it. He is looking for places where *English lends itself to subversion*. And such loopholes may not occur in the same places in the translator's language.

Here we can say that the translation problem alerts us to a deep irony in Lawrence's work: that however much he, or any other author, moves away from convention, it is always in relation to convention, to what is left behind that is, that his gesture is understood. You can't speak without using the language, even if you've decided to 'misuse' it, and ironically you can only subvert the language in ways it allows itself to be subverted. In short, when you jump over the edge, wherever you may land you can only define your position in relation to where you were before. It is a theme that recurs constantly in *Women in Love*. The centre and measure of things remains with convention and society and standard language use.

In conclusion, then, we can say that a text which seeks to escape a classical 'housedness' in language is a text which unavoidably draws attention to and starts to be about that language (and associated conventions) from which it is fleeing. It is this element of Lawrence's text which is lost, and for the most part inevitably, in an Italian that seems all too at home with itself and the conventional patterns of mind it enshrines.

As a final reflection, and in anticipation of the following chapters we might say this: those theorists who have (rightly I believe) considered style as an organized and interrelated series of deviations from a norm have always run into trouble when it came to establishing what that norm was, for of course every language has many forms of usage depending on which groups are using the language and in what circumstances. This book then is rather cheekily, but I hope practically, proposing that if we take a translation into any major European language of the style in question and then translate it back into English, we will have something as near to 'standard use' as we are likely to find. The translation is a normalizing grid against which the deviations of the original can be read.

3. Translating the Evocative Spirit in James Joyce

One of the advantages of beginning such a series of analyses with D.H. Lawrence is that, for all his notoriety, he is considered by most non-English-speaking readers to be a fairly traditional novelist in terms of style, perhaps because their first acquaintance with him came through translations of the variety considered in the previous chapter. They are thus unprepared for the linguistic density and contorted richness of his writing and rapidly appreciate that the smoothly written translation is achieved at the expense of the interesting and significant idiosyncrasies of the original.

With Joyce the situation is radically different. Such is Joyce's reputation for avant-garde writing that foreign readers expect the linguistic games to be so many as to be impossible to translate, the translator thus being relieved of any responsibility for having failed to re-create the complexity of the original and the critic reduced merely to remarking on this fact.

Having said this, however, it will quickly be evident that Joyce's early prose, in *Dubliners,* is more traditional, less problematic, and above all less provocatively idiosyncratic than Lawrence's. So what can be learnt from comparing English with Italian here, and will such a comparison throw any light on the kind of problems presented by Joyce's later writing? Here is the last page and a half of *The Dead.* I offer the material paragraph by paragraph. We come in at the point where, having told the sad story of the death of her young boyfriend of many years ago, Gabriel's wife falls asleep, leaving her husband to reflect on the emotions of the evening:

First the English:

> She was fast asleep.
> Gabriel, leaning on his elbow, looked for a few moments unresentfully on her tangled hair and half-open mouth, listening to her deep-drawn breath. So she had had that romance in her life: a man had died for her sake. It hardly pained him now to think how poor a part he, her husband, had played in her life. He watched her while she slept as though he and she had never lived together as man and wife. His curious eyes rested long upon her face and on her hair: and, as he thought of what she must have been then, in that time of her first girlish beauty, a strange friendly

pity for her entered his soul. He did not like to say even to himself that
her face was no longer beautiful but he knew that it was no longer the
face for which Michael Furey had braved death.[1]

And the Italian:

> Era profondamente addormentata.
>
> Gabriel, appoggiato su un gomito, guardò per alcuni minuti, senza
> rancore, i suoi capelli scarmigliati e la bocca dischiusa, e ascoltò il
> suo respiro profondo. Nella sua vita, dunque, c'era stata un'avventura,
> un uomo era morto per lei. Ora non gli dava quasi più pena pensare a
> quanta poca parte lui, suo marito, aveva avuto nella sua vita. La os-
> servava mentre dormiva, come se lui e lei non avessero mai vissuto
> insieme come marito e moglie. I suoi occhi curiosi si fermarono a
> lungo sul volto e sui capelli di lei, e nel pensare a quella che doveva
> esser stata allora, al tempo della sua prima bellezza d'adolescente, si
> sentì pervadere da una strana, fraterna compassione per lei. Non gli
> piaceva ammetterlo nemmeno con se stesso, che quel volto non era più
> così bello, tuttavia sapeva che non era più il volto per il quale Michael
> Furey aveva affrontato la morte.[2]

And a back-translation:

> She was deeply asleep.
>
> Gabriel, leaning on an elbow, looked for a few minutes, without
> rancour, at her tousled hair and open mouth, and listened to her deep
> breathing. In her life, then, there had been an affair, a man had died
> for her. Now it hardly upset him any more to think how small a part
> he, her husband, had had in her life. He watched her while she slept,
> as if he and she had never lived together as man and wife. His curi-
> ous eyes rested for a long time on her face and hair, and thinking of
> what she must have been like then, in the time of her first adolescent
> beauty, he felt filled with a strange, brotherly compassion for her. He
> didn't like to admit even to himself, that that face was no longer so
> beautiful, yet he knew that it was no longer the face for which Michael
> Furey had faced death.

---

[1] The paragraphs analysed from *The Dead* are taken from *Dubliners,* corrected text with an
explanatory note by Robert Scholes. Jonathan Cape, London, 1967, pp. 253-6.
[2] The Italian translation of the paragraphs analysed is taken from *Gente di Dublino,* Garzanti,
Milan, 1976. Translation by Marco Papi and Emilio Tadini, pp. 211-13.

At a first reading one notes only three or four places where the translation is obviously 'not the same' as the English, where a divergence, that is, might have something to tell us about the original. These are:

> deep-drawn breath
> il suo respiro profondo
> (*her deep breathing*)

> So she had had that romance in her life
> Nella sua vita, dunque, c'era stata un'avventura
> (*In her life, then, there had been an affair/adventure*)

> girlish beauty
> bellezza d'adolescente
> (*adolescent beauty*)

> a strange, friendly pity for her entered his soul
> si sentì pervadere da una strana, fraterna compassione per lei
> (*he felt filled by a strange, brotherly compassion for her*)

> beautiful
> così bello
> (*so nice/good-looking/beautiful*)

It is a thin crop. The recognizably 'poetic' deviation involved in turning 'deeply drawn' into a single compound adjective 'deep-drawn' is impossible in romance languages and students will find it hard to believe that any serious loss is involved in the correct and not unattractive 'il suo respiro profondo' (*her deep breathing*); readers should remember that the back-translation only conveys the semantics of the Italian, not how it sounds to an Italian ear.

Likewise the translation of 'romance' as 'avventura' (*affair/adventure*) is the result of a real problem of semantic segmentation. Italian just does not have such a strong and at the same time innocent word as the English 'romance'. Obliged to choose between 'passione' (*passion*), 'storia' (*affair*), 'amore' (*love*) and 'avventura' (*affair*, with a lighter sense than 'storia'), the translator is forced to interpret the nature of that relationship and in so doing certainly shifts the tone a little, but it is hard to see how this could have been avoided (perhaps the word 'amore' might have been preferable to the potentially squalid 'avventura' – *affair*).

'Girlish beauty' again presents a problem of semantic segmentation.

'Bellezza bambinesca' or 'fanciullesca' (*girlish beauty*) would suggest too young a girl. 'Bellezza di ragazza' (*beauty of a girl*) does not seem to refer us to the question of youth. Quite reasonably the translator chooses 'bellezza d'adolescente' (*adolescent beauty*), again accepting a shift in tone from the lyrical to the prosaic.

Only the phrase 'si sentì pervadere da una strana, fraterna compassione per lei' (*he felt filled by a strange, brotherly compassion for her*) seems to contain some significant semantic differences, as 'fraterna' (*brotherly/fraternal*) is substituted for 'friendly' and then the word 'soul' is eliminated. On reflection, one can appreciate the thinking behind the first of these shifts. The point of the word 'friendly' here is the way it suggests a non-sexual relationship, thus contrasting Gabriel's feelings now with his passion of some pages before in the story when he was eager to make love to his wife. 'Fraterna' (*brotherly*) does the same job admirably, while achieving a solemnity that 'amichevole' (*friendly*) lacks in Italian. But the translation's second departure is more problematic. The idea of pity 'entering the soul' is curious in English and clearly intentional, and one wonders if the word 'anima' (*soul*) could not have been introduced in some way. After all, this is the first word in the passage that at once significantly raises the level of diction and at the same time introduces the notion of death and, possibly, life after death, important issues in a story entitled *The Dead.*

But has this look at the translation helped us to understand the original in any way? And is there any relationship between these small divergences, as there clearly was when we looked at passages from Lawrence? At first glance, it would seem not. Perhaps all we can say is that in each case there is a slight loss of lyricism. 'Deep-drawn' is a typically poetical device, 'romance' and 'girlish' are lyrical words par excellence (the same could hardly be said of words like 'avventura' – *affair* – and 'adolescente' – *adolescent*), while 'soul' is very much the stuff of religious reflection or romantic poetry.

Having established this tenuous link – a question of register – we might ask, what are the other stylistic devices typical of lyrical writing and are they present in this text? The techniques we most commonly associate with lyricism are rhythm and rhyme, alliteration and assonance, and a preference, perhaps, for archaic word orders and diction. With this in mind, and returning now to the English, we quickly appreciate that this paragraph abounds in alliteration and in sentences with an unmistakable rhythm. The first sentence of the main paragraph, for example, has three clauses all beginning with verbs starting with ' l ', while the choice of 'deep-drawn', rather than 'deeply drawn', is now seen to be necessary for the sombrely accented, onomatopoeic rhythm at the end of the sentence:

> Gabriel, *l*eaning on his elbow, *l*ooked for a few moments unre-
> sentfully on her tangled hair and half-open mouth, *l*istening to her
> deep-drawn breath.

The third sentence, 'It hardly pained him now ...', is a *tour de force* of p's and
h's packed into an iambic metric which breaks down at 'he, her husband' to
end on a note as limp and poignant as the observation being made.

> It *h*ardly *p*ained him now to think *h*ow *p*oor a *p*art *h*e, *h*er *h*usband,
> *h*ad *p*layed in *h*er life.

On considering how this rhythm and above all the eloquent spareness it conveys has been established, it does not take long to recognize that it is achieved
through a remarkable predominance of monosyllabic words.

Turning back to the Italian now, we have a fuller sense of the transformation that has taken place. Although an attractive spareness and simplicity is
maintained throughout, Italian does not have the resource of an Anglo-Saxon
vocabulary with its huge stock of monosyllables, while in general, of course,
it is miserably difficult to establish a rhythmical style while maintaining the
same content and register as the original. So in the first sentence of the main
paragraph the alliteration is lost and likewise the sombre effect of the last
three heavy stresses in 'deep-drawn breath'. A certain dramatic abruptness is
also lost from the very direct 'So she had had that romance in her life'. The
Italian word order, 'Nella sua vita, dunque, c'era stata un'avventura' (*In her
life, then, there had been an affair*), is more elaborate, and again, there is no
chance of those sad monosyllables. Only in the sentence 'It hardly pained ...'
does the Italian lend itself to Joyce's alliteration and rhythm, and here the
translator cleverly reproduces the effects of the original:

> Ora non gli dava quasi *p*iù *p*ena *p*ensare a quanta *p*oca *p*arte lui, suo
> marito, aveva avuto nella sua vita.

Here back-translation cannot hope to indicate what has been achieved, since
the qualities we are talking about are rhythm and alliteration. And thinking in
terms of rhythm, one may now appreciate the prominence given to the word
'soul' in Joyce's original, coming, as it does, at the end of a long and beautifully rhythmical sentence:

> His curious eyes rested long upon her face and on her hair; and, as
> he thought of what she must have been then, in that time of her first
> girlish beauty, a strange, friendly pity for her entered his soul.

Clearly the word 'soul' is preparing us for the two heavy spondaic monosyllables which will end the paragraph, 'braved death'. And here again one notes in passing the slight and inevitable loss in poetic register from 'braved' to the more commonplace Italian 'affrontato' (*faced*).

This short passage, then, offers a delicate play between Gabriel's sad but simple reflections and the subtly rhythmical alliterative prose they are framed in. There is none of the robust complexity we found in Lawrence, none of the suggestion of difficult and controversial ideas that we will have to struggle to grasp. So that what appears to be slipping away in the translation of this text is not some intellectual content, but the musicality and exactness of register that give the passage its evocative power. Quite simply we might say that although the translation is excellent, the Italian is slightly less pleasurable and less moving.

Is there any point, having arrived at this forlorn conclusion, in a further detailed analysis of the next page or so that makes up the famous conclusion of *The Dead?* Will it just mean the discovery of more of the same? We shall see. Here, in any event, is the next paragraph, which follows the movement of Gabriel's eyes and mind as he continues to reflect on the evening:

> Perhaps she had not told him all the story. His eyes moved to the chair over which she had thrown some of her clothes. A petticoat string dangled to the floor. One boot stood upright, its limp upper fallen down: the fellow of it lay upon its side. He wondered at his riot of emotions of an hour before. From what had it proceeded? From his aunts' supper, from his own foolish speech, from the wine and dancing, the merry-making when saying good-night in the hall, the pleasure of the walk along the river in the snow. Poor Aunt Julia! She, too, would soon be a shade with the shade of Patrick Morkan and his horse. He had caught that haggard look upon her face for a moment when she was singing *Arrayed for the Bridal.* Soon, perhaps, he would be sitting in that same drawing-room, dressed in black, his silk hat on his knees. The blinds would be drawn down and Aunt Kate would be sitting beside him, crying and blowing her nose and telling him how Julia had died. He would cast about in his mind for some words that might console her and would find only lame and useless ones. Yes, yes: that would happen very soon.

And the Italian:

> Forse lei non gli aveva raccontato tutto. I suoi occhi si spostarono sulla sedia, dove lei aveva gettato alcuni dei suoi indumenti. Il laccio di

una sottoveste che penzolava a terra, uno stivale diritto, con il gambale afflosciato, accanto al compagno rovesciato su un fianco. Era stupito da quel tumulto di emozioni che aveva provato un'ora prima. Da dove aveva avuto origine? Dalla cena in casa delle zie, dal suo discorso insulso, dal vino e dalle danze, dall'allegria degli ultimi congedi nell'atrio, dal piacere di quella passeggiata lungo il fiume, nella neve. Povera zia Julia! Anche lei, ben presto sarebbe stata un'ombra, come l'ombra di Patrick Morkan e del suo cavallo. Per un attimo aveva scorto sul suo volto quell'espressione spettrale mentre cantava *Abbigliata per le nozze*. Ben presto, forse, si sarebbe trovato a sedere in quello stesso salotto, vestito a lutto, il cappello a tuba sulle ginocchia. Gli scuri sarebbero stati abbassati, e zia Kate, seduta in lacrime accanto a lui, soffiandosi il naso, gli avrebbe raccontato come era morta zia Julia. Lui avrebbe frugato nella mente per trovare qualche parola di consolazione, e avrebbe trovato soltanto parole trite e inutili. Sì, si sarebbe accaduto molto presto.

And a back-translation:

Perhaps she had not told him everything. His eyes moved to the seat where she had thrown some of her clothes. The lace of a petticoat dangled to the ground, one boot upright with its upper sagging, beside its companion pushed over on one side. He was amazed by the tumult of emotions that he had felt an hour earlier. Where had it come from? From the dinner in his aunts' house, from his silly speech, from the wine and the dancing, from the jollity of the last goodbyes in the hall, from the pleasure of that walk along the river, in the snow. Poor Aunt Julia! She too would soon be a shade, like the shade of Patrick Morkan and his horse. For a moment he had recognised on her face that ghostly expression while she was singing, *Arrayed for the Bridal*. Soon, perhaps, he would find himself sitting in that same drawing room, dressed in mourning, his top hat on his knees. The blinds would be lowered, and Aunt Kate, sitting beside him in tears, blowing her nose, would tell him how Aunt Julia had died. He would look around in his mind to find some words of consolation, and would only find trite, vain words. Yes, yes, it would happen very soon.

The first and most obvious difference to note here is that in the Italian the third and fourth sentences of the English have been rolled together. This involves the small sacrifice, perhaps not strictly necessary, of that spareness and appropriate limpness that characterizes the English.

> A petticoat string dangled to the floor. One boot stood upright, its limp upper fallen down: the fellow of it lay upon its side.

> Il laccio di una sottoveste che penzolava a terra, uno stivale diritto, con il gambale afflosciato, accanto al compagno rovesciato su un fianco.

> The lace of a petticoat dangled to the ground, one boot upright with its upper sagging, beside its companion pushed over on one side/flank.

Another difference here is the introduction of two elements that are not in the English. In describing the boots, Joyce says that, "One boot stood upright ...: the fellow of it lay upon its side', while the translation, as part of its search for a more fluid and articulated prose, links the clauses to give us, 'uno stivale diritto ... *accanto* al compagno *rovesciato* su un fianco' (*one boot upright ...* **beside** *its companion* **pushed over** *on one side*).

The problem with these tiny additions is that they draw our attention away from the delicate parallel Joyce is setting up between the two boots and the man and wife. Here one must remember the context. Only an hour before, Gabriel had been in a state of arousal, eager to make love to his wife. But on returning to the hotel, she tells him how some music at the party reminded her of Michael Furey, a boy whom she once loved and who died for her. Gabriel's arousal is understandably lost. His wife has cried herself to sleep, he is sitting up in the bed, watching her, wondering if Michael Furey was ever actually her lover.

It is not difficult to intuit, then, in the details that his eye picks up as these ideas cross his mind – her clothes, a petticoat string, her boots – both his sexual jealousy and his frustration over their own failure to make love. His disappointment is evident in the short, limp sentences, and most particularly in the description of the boots. Gabriel himself is the boot that 'stood upright' but with 'its limp upper fallen down'. His wife is the fellow that 'lay upon its side'. In joining the two clauses together with the word 'accanto' (*beside*) the translator suggests a togetherness that is not there in the English with its two starkly separate monosyllabic verbs ('one boot stood ... the fellow of it lay'). Only later will Joyce tell us that Gabriel 'lay down beside his wife'. Indeed the verb 'lay' will appear twice in the next paragraph to describe the positions of man and wife. Here the word's melancholy passivity serves to explain the surprise of Gabriel's next turn of mind ('He wondered at his riot of emotions of an hour before'). The translation of 'lay' as 'rovesciato' (*pushed over*), with its suggestion of something having been violently knocked down, seems inappropriate, since, while it might be applied to the boot, it could hardly be applied to the wife, thus spoiling the hinted analogy. 'Rovesciarla sul letto' (*push her over on the bed*), an expression which, with all its vigorous sexual implications, would be standard Italian, is exactly what Gabriel has *not* done, and what perhaps – for she may not have told him all the story – Michael Furey did.

Obviously one could insist too much on these tiny divergences. The translation, after all, is attractive. But if nothing else they draw our attention to the delicacy and precision of Joyce's prose here, the dispatch with which he sets up this image of the boots, whose purpose once again is to evoke the scene and, with it, Gabriel's state of mind, his dwindling sexual excitement, as he takes in that scene.

Pausing for a moment at this point, we can say that, as with Lawrence, the problem for the translator when faced with a text like this is not merely the linguistic one of rendering what the original words appear to say, but the problem of interpretation, or rather the question: to what range of interpretation does the original leave itself open? And then consequently and perhaps even more problematically: to which of the many things the original appears to be saying should the translator give precedence? While the passages looked at from Lawrence were certainly more difficult linguistically, in *The Dead* there is the real danger of the translator simply not noticing what is going on, so subliminally does Joyce operate.

But even assuming the translator notices everything, there will still be the problem of rendering it. The verb 'lay', for example, will occur five times in the last one and a half pages of the story and in a way that ties together the supine couple in their bedroom, the falling snow outside and the dead Michael Furey in his grave. Even if the translator did notice this, it is doubtful whether a single verb could be made to do the same job in Italian.

To continue: Gabriel's wondering about his emotions of an hour before leads him to a recapitulation of the evening as a whole and this in turn prompts him to reflect on the imminent death of Aunt Julia. Here we have the introduction of a new word for the dead, 'shade', bringing with it the vision of a different kind of after-life than that suggested earlier by the word 'soul'. Although 'ombra' translates 'shade' perfectly well in the Italian, the contrast with the earlier word 'soul' and the shift to a bleaker, pagan vision of death is absent, since the Italian did not translate 'soul.'

Towards the end of the paragraph, we have the description of the imagined scene with Aunt Kate in mourning for Aunt Julia. Here comparison of the two languages and in particular the different syntactical structure in the translation of the sentence beginning, 'The blinds would be drawn down ...' attracts our attention to the way Joyce uses repetition of the auxiliary 'would' and of the present participle form 'ing' to achieve an intense, oppressive and, partly thanks to the absence of punctuation, breathless rhythm.

> The blinds would be drawn down and Aunt Kate would be sitting beside him, crying and blowing her nose and telling him how Julia had died.

> Gli scuri sarebbero stati abbassati, e zia Kate, seduta in lacrime accanto a lui, soffiandosi il naso, gli avrebbe raccontato come era morta zia Julia.

> The blinds would be lowered, and Aunt Kate, sitting beside him in tears, blowing her nose, would tell him how Aunt Julia had died.

In rearranging the sentence with a relative clause ('seduta in lacrime accanto a lui' – *seated in tears beside him*) the Italian offers a more conventionally polished prose, but loses some of the intensity. It seems here that the translator is presenting us with something observed in the translation of Lawrence: a perhaps unconscious refusal to trust the stylistic traits of the original, a tendency to write what is traditionally thought of as good prose (and the Italian, if not the back-translation, *is* good prose), rather than what is suggested by the text. For, although the repetitive use of progressives is something that Italian generally avoids, nevertheless it would surely have been possible at least to write, 'e zia Kate sarebbe stata seduta accanto a lui, e avrebbe pianto' (*and Aunt Kate would be sitting beside him and would cry*). That is, it would have been possible to introduce the same breathlessness, albeit at the risk of writing a less elegant Italian.

If one quotes this apparently banal divergence (before going on, I hope, to more interesting ones), it is in order to show that when we talk about Joyce's powers of evocation we are not talking about something static, but about a dynamic attempt to capture shifting states of mind (later to flower in the stream of consciousness). As a result, the rhythms of the prose are constantly changing, from the bewildered but poised sadness of the first paragraph, the limp melancholy that opens the second, to the sudden excitement of revelation here: 'Yes, yes: that would happen very soon.' The translation, then, does not so much lose the rhythm of the original, as *the movement expressed through changes in rhythm.* In fact Gabriel's excitement here brings us directly to the changes of tone that occur in the next and then last paragraphs, where other, less subtle movements in rhythm occur.

The air of the room chilled his shoulders. He stretched himself cautiously along under the sheets and lay down beside his wife. One by one they were all becoming shades. Better pass boldly into that other world, in the full glory of some passion, than fade and wither dismally with age. He thought of how she who lay beside him had locked in her heart for so many years that image of her lover's eyes when he had told her that he did not wish to live.

Il freddo della stanza lo fece rabbrividire. Con cautela, si infilò sotto le coperte, a fianco della moglie. Uno alla volta, tutti sarebbero diventati ombre. Meglio passare nell'altro mondo con animo forte, nel pieno di una passione, piuttosto che svanire e avvizzire malinconicamente con gli anni. Pensò a quella donna che gli giaceva a fianco, che per tanti anni aveva tenuto chiuso nel suo cuore il ricordo degli occhi del suo innamorato mentre le diceva che non desiderava vivere.

The cold of the room made him shiver. Taking care, he slipped under the blankets, by his wife's side. One by one, they would all become shades. Better to pass into the other world with a strong spirit, in the fullness of a passion, rather than fade and wither gloomily with the years. He thought of the woman who lay at his side, who for so many years had kept closed in her heart the memory of the eyes of her loved one as he told her he did not wish to live.

The first thing that strikes us here is the simplicity and precision of the opening sentence in the English, 'The air of the room chilled his shoulders' (the man is leaning on his elbow, his shoulders are uncovered, hence the air of the room chills them) and the difficulty of rendering *exactly* that sense in Italian while retaining the spareness of the original: 'L'aria della stanza gli faceva venire freddo alle spalle' (*The air in the room made his shoulders cold*), while correct, would perhaps be longer than we want. The translator's decision to keep things as short and simple as possible is a sensible one. This leads us to a second observation: that if we consider the very first sentence of the whole passage, 'She was fast asleep', as forming an integral part of the first main paragraph, and not a paragraph in itself, then all the five paragraphs of this passage (as we shall see) start with a single terse, predominantly monosyllabic sentence. In each case these opening sentences both introduce and set off the rhythms that then develop later on. Such an observation validates the translator's decision to sacrifice exact semantic content for faithfulness to brevity and rhythm.

Likewise easily observable here is the substitution of the two English words 'stretch' and 'lay' with the single Italian 'si infilò' (*he slipped/slid himself in*), a move which forms part of the general and probably inevitable jettisoning of the verb 'lay' and the links it establishes throughout the passage. More serious and more revealing is the divergence between 'tutti sarebbero diventati ombre' (*they would all become shades*) which refers us to a future time, and the English 'they were all becoming shades', with its disturbing and crucial suggestion that the process has already begun, that Gabriel and his wife, like Aunt Julia, are *already* dying. One also notes a shift and loss of focus in the last sentence where the Italian makes the object of thought Gabriel's wife, rather than the way in which she has hidden the story of Michael Furey from her husband:

> He thought of how she who lay beside him had locked in her heart

> Pensò a quella donna che gli giaceva a fianco, che per tanti anni aveva tenuto chiuso nel suo cuore

> He thought of the woman who lay at his side, who for so many years had kept closed in her heart

But none of these differences seem to amount to much more than the inevitable difficulty of arriving at exact equivalences of the original in an elegant Italian. And if the changes in translating 'lay' and 'were becoming shades' both detract from a suggested equivalence between the couple in bed and the already dead Michael Furey, the comparison is anyway amply hinted at in the sentence beginning 'Better pass boldly into that other world ... than fade and wither dismally with age.'

So is all well? Let us backtrack for a moment and re-read all three paragraphs of the English through to this point. In doing so, we cannot help feeling that these last few sentences represent a dramatic shift of tone, which is muted in the translation. What is this shift and why is it partly lost? Once again one has to look for the kind of devices usually associated with poetry before the precise nature of the difference between original and translation becomes apparent, and with it Joyce's strategy for achieving an emotional climax to a story in which there is very little action.

When asked to find examples of poetic technique in this paragraph, students will invariably point to the strong alliteration of plosives in 'Better pass boldly into that other world, in the full glory of some passion', an acoustic effect only partly lost in the Italian 'Meglio passare nell'altro mondo con animo forte, nel pieno di una passione' (*Better to pass into the other world with a strong spirit, in the fullness of a passion*). But perhaps even more pertinently one notes in 'Better pass boldy' a use of ellipsis as a form of poetic licence (a more standard English would offer: 'How much better it would be to pass boldly ...') and, in general, an intensification of the poetic register in terms of diction and syntax. In the space of a few lines we have the archaic locution of 'passing into ... that other world' alongside such words as 'boldly, glory, passion, fade, wither, dismally'– all very much the vocabulary of late Victorian poetry. This is then followed by the now distinctly archaic 'He thought of *how she who lay beside him*', followed by the traditionally poetic 'locked in her heart', in a sentence where 33 of the 36 words are monosyllables and where there is no punctuation whatsoever. In short, Joyce is using an increasingly lyrical syntax and diction of an absolutely traditional kind (in this he is worlds away from Lawrence), a style that might become trite were it not for the spareness of the content, the subtle rhythms of the prose.

Does the Italian register this shift? Clearly it should be easier to render a style that is 'traditional' to a language (rather than idiosyncratic), if only because one feels one might reasonably resort to a style traditional to the translator's language. But the problem here is that Italian does not have such abundant and neatly defined sources of diction, and indeed what lyrical diction is available is less frequently recovered in modern prose and hence would be difficult to use with the sort of subtlety Joyce achieves. Certainly a limited change in diction is apparent in the Italian, with the appearance of words like 'malinconicamente' (*melancholically*) and 'animo forte' (*strong spirit*), but it is difficult for the translator to draw on something that the reader immediately recognizes as a peculiarly poetic diction, perhaps because this is simply not available for translating the particular words in question.

Even more difficult in Italian is the suggestion of a peculiarly poetic phrasing and focusing. 'Meglio passare' (*Better to pass*), with its elision of 'sarebbe' (*it would be*), does have something of the drama of the English in it, yet remains very ordinary, everyday Italian. (I do not mean here that Italian does not have resources in this area. On the contrary. Merely that it is difficult to draw on them when the content is established by the English.) The slight archaism of 'how she who lay beside him' is lost in the prosaic 'quella donna che gli giaceva a fianco', and finally, the splendid rhythm of the last sentence in the English becomes merely long and unconvincing in the Italian:

> 'Pensò a quella donna che gli giaceva a fianco, che per tanti anni aveva tenuto chiuso nel suo cuore il ricordo degli occhi del suo inna-morato mentre le diceva che non desiderava vivere.'

He thought of the woman who lay at his side, who for so many years
had kept closed in her heart the memory of the eyes of her loved one
as he told her he did not wish to live.

The truth is, perhaps, that to achieve a stronger lyric effect in the Italian would
require a radical rethinking of the sentence and the introduction of simile or
metaphor, which would hardly be acceptable in a passage whose spareness is
one of its main qualities. The question becomes the impossible one of 'how
would Joyce have written this if he were Italian?

The decisive shift in tone we have talked about is now amply confirmed
in the next, penultimate paragraph:

Generous tears filled Gabriel's eyes. He had never felt like that
himself towards any woman, but he knew that such a feeling must
be love. The tears gathered more thickly in his eyes and in the partial
darkness he imagined he saw the form of a young man standing under
a dripping tree. Other forms were near. His soul had approached that
region where dwell the vast hosts of the dead. He was conscious of,
but could not apprehend, their wayward and flickering existence. His
own identity was fading out into a grey impalpable world: the solid
world itself which these dead had one time reared and lived in was
dissolving and dwindling.

Lacrime generose riempirono gli occhi di Gabriel. Non aveva mai
provato sensazioni simili per nessuna donna, ma sapeva che quel
sentimento doveva essere amore. Lacrime più copiose gli velarono
gli occhi e nella penombra gli parve di vedere la figura di un giovane
in piedi, sotto un albero grondante di pioggia. Altre figure gli erano
vicine. La sua anima aveva avvicinato la regione in cui dimora la folla
sterminata dei morti. Ne era cosciente, ma non riusciva a coglierla,
quella loro effimera e tremolante esistenza. La sua stessa identità si
stava smarrendo in un mondo grigio e impalpabile, e lo stesso mondo
materiale, il mondo sul quale quei morti avevano vissuto e procreato,
si andava dissolvendo e rimpicciolendo.

Generous tears filled Gabriel's eyes. He had never had feelings like
that for any woman, but he knew that that sentiment must have been
love. Thicker tears veiled his eyes and in the penumbra it seemed he
saw the figure of a young man standing, under a tree dripping with
rain. Other figures were nearby. His soul had approached the region in
which the endless crowd of the dead dwell. He was aware of, but could

not grasp, their ephemeral and tremulous existence. His very identity was swooning into a grey and impalpable world, and the material world itself, the world on which those dead people had lived and procreated, was dissolving and shrinking.

Again the terse opening sentence, again the rhythmical, at first monosyllabic prose. But we should now be in a position to appreciate the general change of diction and the use of a more archaic word order in the sentence: 'His soul had approached that region where dwell the vast hosts of the dead'. The problem for the translator is once again to achieve this shift of register while maintaining a fair translation of the content. Hence the introduction of a word like 'dimora' (*dwell*). But the archaism of placing the verb before its subject (something fairly ordinary in Italian) is lost and likewise the strong rhythmical conclusion to the sentence with its two anapaests ending on the strongly stressed 'dead' (' ... where dwell the vast hosts of the dead').

In the following two sentences Joyce abandons the predominantly monosyllabic for a series of multi-syllable words, again taken from a recognizably lyrical diction: 'wayward, flickering, fading, impalpable, dissolving, dwindling'. Again, it is difficult in Italian to register this shift. Looking at the translation in detail, however, one does wonder why the repetition of the verb 'fade', so powerfully used in the previous paragraph and appropriately translated with 'svanire' (*fade*), cannot be retained in the Italian. For repetition here underlines the fact that Gabriel feels that *he himself is dying*, a sentiment central to the passage. Likewise we notice how the verb 'rimpicciolire' (shrink) translates only a limited sense of 'dwindling', losing the overtones of sickness and decline typical of the verb's use in poetry. Finally, the more alert will notice the tiny but intriguing detail that in the last sentence Joyce uses the unusual collocation 'one time' (to mean 'in the past') rather than 'once' and that this is eliminated in the Italian. A reading of the sentence soon makes it clear that 'one time' was preferred for the rhythm it gives to the sentence and perhaps its archaic sound; it thus seems fair enough to eliminate it, if its presence makes no such contribution in Italian.

The intensification of the poetic register throughout the text naturally reaches its climax in the final paragraph where it now becomes all too easy to see how impossible it would be to achieve the same effect in any translation:

A few light taps upon the pane made him turn to the window. It had begun to snow again. He watched sleepily the flakes, silver and dark, falling obliquely against the lamplight. The time had come for him to set out on his journey westward. Yes, the newspapers were right: snow

was general all over Ireland. It was falling on every part of the dark
central plain, on the treeless hills, falling softly upon the Bog of Allen
and, farther westward, softly falling into the dark mutinous Shannon
waves. It was falling, too, upon every part of the lonely churchyard
on the hill where Michael Furey lay buried. It lay thickly drifted on
the crooked crosses and headstones, on the spears of the little gate,
on the barren thorns. His soul swooned slowly as he heard the snow
falling faintly through the universe and faintly falling, like the descent
of their last end, upon all the living and the dead.

Un lieve battito sul vetro lo fece voltare verso la finestra. Aveva
ripreso a nevicare. Restò a osservare, assonnato, i fiocchi di neve,
argentei e scuri, che scendevano obliquamente davanti al lampione.
Era giunto il momento di mettersi in viaggio verso occidente. Sì, i
giornali avevano ragione: nevicava su tutta l'Irlanda. La neve cadeva
in ogni parte della bruna pianura centrale, sulle colline brulle, scendeva
piano sulla palude di Allen, e più a occidente, calava lieve sulle cupe
onde tumultuanti dello Shannon. E cadeva anche su tutto il solitario
cimitero di campagna, là in cima alla collina dov'era sepolto Michael
Furey. S'ammucchiava sulle croci contorte e sulle pietre tombali,
sulle punte del piccolo cancello, sui cespugli brulli. E l'anima gli si
velava a poco a poco mentre ascoltava la neve che calava lieve su
tutto l'universo, che calava lieve, come a segnare la loro ultima ora,
su tutti i vivi e i morti.

A light tap on the glass made him turn toward the window. It had
started snowing again. He lay watching, sleepy, the snowflakes, silver
and dark, that fell obliquely in front of the street lamp. The moment
had come to set off on a journey to the west. Yes, the newspapers were
right: it was snowing over all of Ireland. The snow fell in every part
of the dark central plain, on the bleak hills, it descended softly on the
bog of Allen. And further west, it fell light on the gloomy tumultu-
ous waves of the Shannon. And it fell too all over the lonely country
cemetery, there at the top of the hill where Michael Furey was buried.
It settled on the crooked crosses and the grave stones, on the spikes of
the little gate, on the bleak bushes. And his soul faded little by little as
he listened to the snow falling light on all the universe, falling light,
as if to mark their last hour, on all the living and the dead.

Any translation of such a text is bound to be a series of defeats and small con-
solatory victories. The differences are all too evident: the loss of alliteration

(except in the brilliant 'ascoltava la neve che calava lieve su tutto l'universo' – *he listened to the snow falling light on all the universe*), the impossibility of following the play of inversions with verb and adverb ('falling softly', 'softly falling' – 'falling faintly', 'faintly falling'), the inability to repeat the eloquent way the symbols of snow and death are tied up with the supremely passive verb 'lay' ('where Michael Furey lay buried. It lay…' translated with 'era' – *was* – and 's'ammucchiava' – *it settled/heaped up*), or again the way the assonance of 'His soul swooned slowly' disappears in 'E l'anima gli si velava' (*And his soul faded*), and so on.

In each of the cases mentioned the loss is one of lyricism and poetic effect, just as it was in the first paragraph, though what I want to stress is the way the translation also fails to register the gradual escalation of this effect through the passage as a whole. In this paragraph, for example, Joyce begins to insert the adverb between the verb and its object ('He watched sleepily the flakes'), repeats a number of words obsessively ('dark' three times, translated with a different word on each occasion) and very curiously introduces the name 'Shannon' as an adjective before 'waves': 'the dark mutinous Shannon waves' (rather than the more normal 'the dark and mutinous waves of the Shannon').

Traditionally poetic collocations like 'crooked crosses' and 'barren thorns' reinforce the effect. In Italian this heightened poetic sense has to be carried almost entirely through the content, since none of these techniques can easily be conveyed in Italian, though it should be said that the translator introduces some melancholy repetition with 'brullo' (*bleak*), which also calls to mind the word 'bruna' (*brown/dark*). To make matters worse, some of that content will not have the same connotations outside the English language. The idea of 'going west', for example, links the idea of travelling to the western Ireland of his wife's infancy (and the nation's purest un-English heartland) with the idea of death. But to 'go west' is not used as a euphemism for death in Italian.

Comparison with the Italian also draws our attention to the fact that there are two expressions that remain obscure in the English, but which are ironed out in the Italian into something rather more ordinary. In the fourth sentence, 'snow was general all over Ireland' has become 'nevicava su tutta l'Irlanda' (*it was snowing over all of Ireland*), while in the last sentence, 'like the descent of their last end' is translated as 'come a segnare la loro ultima ora' (*as if to mark their last hour*).

'Snow was general' is presumably some newspaper or weather forecaster's expression of the time. But the effect of the word 'general' is to suggest that the snow has some kind of power over the country, giving the sentence an ominous feel. Coming in the last line of the story, the expression 'the descent of their last end' is not immediately comprehensible and gives the sentence a very mysterious feel. It is a technique we observed in Lawrence: what is not easily comprehensible must mean more than what could easily be said. But the expression is not a complete enigma. Those with a good memory will recall that the same words were used earlier on in *The Dead* during a conversation about certain monks who slept in their coffins. When the Protestant Mr Browne expresses his surprise at this morbid habit, a certain Mary replies: 'The coffin ... is to remind them of their last end'.[3] On this occasion the expression is translated in the Italian as 'il passo fatale'[4] (*the fatal step*, a common euphemism for death).

The last line of the story thus recovers this ominous, colloquial and disturbingly tautological expression for death, rendered all the more peculiar by the notion of 'descent' – 'the descent of their last end' – as if somehow the snow were death itself falling from the sky, as if it were an accepted fact that death descends upon us.

Much has been said and theorized about the story *The Dead* in terms of Joyce's attitude towards Ireland, the importance of the notion of the journey westwards towards an older Ireland, of the statue of Patrick Morkan, the titles of the songs, Gabriel's response to the Irish nationalists, etc. Certainly the introduction to the standard Italian edition of *Dubliners* concentrates entirely on this aspect.[5] But it is interesting to note that, in terms of style, none of the effort Joyce puts into his writing seems to be directed at an elucidation or examination of the political or social situation and hence none of this aspect is actually lost in translation, since it all remains at the level of surface content. The references are all still there in the Italian, for those who can understand them. And this is something that could not be said of the passages we looked at from *Women in Love*. In this passage from *The Dead,* then, Joyce's stylistic efforts are directed not towards the expression of complex ideas, but to a convincing and poetic evocation of a state of mind, a chilling awareness of mortality as something inextricably related to the loss of passion and to one's place in the history of one's race. What is lost, even in this excellent translation, is not complexity of thought, but the slowly increasing intensity and melancholy grace with which that evocation is achieved.

There is nothing new in suggesting the importance of the evocative aspect in Joyce's work. The idea is there in the very title of *Dubliners,* obvious in

---

[3] *Dubliners,* cit., p. 230.

[4] *Gente di Dublino,*cit. p. 192.

[5] I refer again to the Garzanti edition, which appears to be the most widely read.

the struggle to recapture the flavour of childhood in *A Portrait of the Artist as a Young Man,* and overwhelming in the meticulous reconstruction of Dublin in *Ulysses.* Frank Budgen's remark in *The Making of Ulysses* that it was 'essential to Joyce that we shall not substitute our own home town for his',[6] has been widely quoted and seems to be a faithful reflection of the determination with which Joyce set out to recreate a particular time and place. *Ulysses* is certainly more specifically about Dublin, its people, its language than it is a story whose outcome might be a matter of urgency to the reader.

But if comments on the evocative nature of Joyce's work are commonplace, little appears to have been said about the kind of difficulties this function of literature can present in translation, the extent to which the supremacy of 're-creation in language' over story line will affect the success of the book in another language. At the most elementary level, for example, it will be clear that if I am writing in English and struggling to evoke an English scene I will select a diction, and perhaps a use of proper names, of people or places, or even songs, which I know will strike a chord in the minds of my English readers, particularly those of my own age, class and background. It is a technique used to great effect in *The Waste Land:*

> Trams and dusty trees.
> Highbury bore me. Richmond and Kew Undid me.

Or again:

> O City city, I can sometimes hear
> Beside a public bar in Lower Thames Street
> The pleasant whining of a mandoline.

There are times when you feel you need to know London like the back of your hand to appreciate the poignancy and wit of Eliot's poem. The same, I suspect, may be true of Joyce's Dublin, so lovingly and with such effort recalled. The problem for the translation is first that the names may mean very little to the foreign audience, may carry no connotations whatsoever, and second that they probably will not fit in with the rhythms of the translation's prose. Such difficulties were evident in the passage considered from *The Dead.* The implied passion behind the surname Furey was lost. The wistful archaism of the title, *Arrayed for the Bridal,* the song that the ailing Aunt Julia was singing, was

---

[6] *James Joyce and the Making of Ulysses,* Frank Budgen, Oxford University Press, 1972, p. 71.

lost. And at the end of the passage the strength and crudeness of 'the Bog of Allen' as the geographic feature through which to evoke central Ireland was lost in the rhythmically awkward 'palude di Allen'.

This kind of difficulty presents itself when working from any language into any other. Readers of foreign literature are used to accepting a loss of density in local cultural reference, in return for a corresponding exoticism arising from reading about distant places. Nevertheless, such loss and compensation do pose the problem of the translatability of certain strategies of evocation, in the sense that the original depends on a unity of language, place and people that cannot be carried over in translation.

In the case of Joyce, we can certainly say that the difficulties of reproducing the evocative nature of his work in translation are more evident in *A Portrait of the Artist* and *Ulysses,* as he becomes ever more determined to use all the resources of the English language to create the worlds, atmospheres, mental states and even literary styles he wishes to evoke. In this regard we can take as a starting-point the apparently simple language of the first page of *A Portrait,* and then compare it with the celebrated translation by Italian novelist Cesare Pavese.

Here, to refresh the memory, is the English:[7]

> Once upon a time and a very good time it was there was a moocow coming down along the road and this moocow that was down along the road met a nicens little boy named baby tuckoo ...
> His father told him that story: his father looked at him through a glass: he had a hairy face.
> He was baby tuckoo. The moocow came down the road where Betty Byrne lived; she sold lemon platt.
> *O, the wild rose blossoms On the little green place*
> He sang that song. That was his song.
> *O, the green wothe botheth.*
> When you wet the bed first it is warm then it gets cold. His mother put on the oilsheet. That had the queer smell.
> His mother had a nicer smell than his father. She played on the piano the sailor's hornpipe far him to dance. He danced:
> Tralala la la, Tralala tralaladdy, Tralala lala, Tralala lala.
> Uncle Charles and Dante dapped. They were older than his father and mother but Uncle Charles was older than Dante.

---

[7] James Joyce, *A Portrait of the Artist as a Young Man.* Definitive text corrected from the Dublin holograph by Charles G. Anderson, edited by Richard Ellmann. First published in Great Britain by Jonathan Cape, 1924, pp. 7-8.

Dante had two brushes in her press. The brush with the maroon velvet back was for Michael Davitt and the brush with the green velvet back was for Parnell. Dante gave him a cachou every time he brought her a piece of tissue paper.

The Vances lived in number seven. They had a different father and mother. They were Eileen's father and mother. When they were grown up he was going to marry Eileen. He hid under the table. His mother said:

– O, Stephen will apologize.

Dante said:

– O, if not, the eagles will come and pull out his eyes –

Pull out his eyes,

Apologise,

Apologise,

Pull out his eyes.

Apologise

Pull out his eyes,

Pull out his eyes,

Apologise.

*

The wide playgrounds were swarming with boys. All were shouting and the prefects urged them on with strong cries. The evening air was pale and chilly and after every charge and thud of the footballers the greasy leather orb flew like a heavy bird through the grey light. He kept on the fringe of his line, out of sight of his prefect, out of the reach of the rude feet, feigning to run now and then. He felt his body small and weak amid the throng of players and his eyes were weak and watery. Rody Kickham was not like that: he would be captain of the third line all the fellows said.

Since the first part of this text is apparently so simple, I have often invited students to translate the passage themselves and report on the difficulties they encounter. These can be listed as follows:

- the problem of finding an equivalent for the jolly raconteur's expansion of the traditional 'once upon a time';
- the problem of finding the Italian baby-language equivalents for 'moo-cow', 'nicens', and above all 'baby tuckoo', since there is some concern as to whether tuckoo means anything (does it come from 'tuck' as in 'to tuck in a piece of clothing', or as in 'to tuck into some food'?);

- the problem of adequately translating the verse, especially as students know from previous studies of *A Portrait* that colours and images take on an important symbolic role throughout, and then the difficulty of achieving the baby version of the same verse;
- the problem of translating the verse beginning 'Pull out his eyes', since it seems impossible to retain both rhyme and content.

Apart from these points, none of which were considered insuperable, students usually see no difficulties in translating the piece, aside, they will say, from the trivial problem of some vocabulary they are not familiar with: 'lemon platt', 'hornpipe', 'press', 'cachou'. Had they their dictionaries with them, it would not occur to them, they say, to mention this as a problem. They are thus surprised and concerned when I tell them that I myself have no idea what 'lemon platt' is, apart from the fact that it must be a sweet of some kind. Likewise with 'cachou'. 'Hornpipe' I am able to explain is a particular dance, traditionally danced by sailors, for which there is no translation in Italian. 'Press' like 'lemon platt' and 'cachou' is something of a mystery for me, but its involvement with brushes and tissue paper suggests that it is some kind of piece of equipment used for ironing (though I still cannot visualize it). The young Stephen presumably gets a sweet every time he brings his aunt (but Italians who did not know the book had imagined Dante was a man) a piece of tissue paper to put over the clothes being ironed.

These vocabulary problems then, rather than being simply words that need looking up ('platt' in any event does not appear in my *Chambers English Dictionary),* turn out to be one of the major problems in the translation. Because if they are not immediately familiar to a contemporary English reader, one must ask oneself whether they were familiar to readers when the book was written, and, in any event, whether they should be translated with easily comprehensible or similarly 'difficult' (perhaps dated, perhaps local) words.

But more importantly, the discovery of this translation problem points the students to one of the text's major stylistic techniques: the use of fragments of culture-specific material to establish the authenticity of these memories by suggesting a full, real, contingent world around them, and most of all to evoke the way that world is perceived by the child in bits and bobs which he does not feel the need to explain, not appreciating that the reader does not understand.

It may be important, then, that these words be a little obscure, that they suggest a group of initiates who would know them and a narrative driven by a consciousness so young as not to be aware that it is a member of such a group. In this way naivety is established. The problem for a foreigner approaching the text is that when he does not know a word he cannot be sure if this is because his vocabulary is inferior to the average native speaker's, or because the writer wished the word to remain obscure.

So much for the problems observed by students when making their own attempts. Not many conclusions could be drawn from them and, interestingly enough, it is only when closely comparing their own and above all Pavese's translation with the original, that other stylistic elements, equally difficult to translate, emerge.

Here is Pavese's translation:[8]

> Nel tempo dei tempi, ed erano bei tempi davvero, c'era una muuucca che veniva giù per la strada e questa muuucca che veniva giù per la strada incontrò un ragazzino carino detto grembialino ...
>
> Il babbo gli raccontava questa storia: il babbo lo guardava attraverso un monocolo: aveva una faccia pelosa.
>
> Grembialino era lui. La muuucca veniva per la strada dove abitava Betty Byrne, che vendeva filato di limone.
>
> *Oh, le belle rose di selva là nel verde giardinetto.*
>
> Cantava questa canzone. Era la sua canzone.
>
> *Oh, le belle lose veldi.*
>
> Quando bagnate il letto, prima è caldo, poi viene freddo. La mamma metteva la tela incerata. Era ciò dava l'odore strano.
>
> La mamma aveva un odore più buono del babbo. Gli suonava sul piano la tarantella per farlo ballare. Lui ballava:
>
> *Tralala lalla*
> *tralala lallara*
> *tralala lalla*
> *tralallà*
>
> Lo zio Charles e Dante battevano le mani. Erano più vecchi del babbo e della mamma, ma lo zio Charles era più vecchio di Dante.
>
> Dante aveva due spazzole nel suo armadietto. La spazzola col dorso di velluto marrone era per Michael Davitt e la spazzola col dorso di velluto verde era per Parnell. Dante gli dava una pasticca ogni volta che le portava un pezzo di carta velina.
>
> I Vances abitavano al numero sette. Avevano un altro babbo e un'altra mamma. Erano il babbo e la mamma di Eileen. Quando fosse cresciuto, avrebbe sposato Eileen. Si nascondeva sotto il tavolo. La mamma diceva: – Oh, Stephen, andrai in ginocchio.

---

[8] James Joyce, *Dedalus,* quoted from the Adelphi edition, Milan, 1976. Translation by Cesare Pavese, pp. 25-7.

Dante diceva:
– Altrimenti verrà l'aquila e gli porterà via un occhio.
Via un occhio,
in ginocchio,
in ginocchio,
via un occhio.
In ginocchio,
via un occhio,
via un occhio,
in ginocchio.

*

Il gran campo da gioco sciamava di ragazzi. Tutti urlavano e i prefetti li incitavano con gran voci. L'aria della sera era pallida e fredda e dopo la carica e il tonfo dei giocatori, la sfera di cuoio infangato volava come un uccello pesante nella luce grigia. Egli si teneva sull'orlo della sua fila, fuori degli sguardi del prefetto, fuori della portata dei piedi villani, ogni tanto fingendo di correre. Si sentiva il corpo piccolo e debole tra la folla dei giocatori e aveva gli occhi deboli e acquosi. Rody Kickham non era così: sarebbe stato capitano della terza fila, dicevano tutti i compagni.

Obviously back-translation is more difficult where the translator himself uses local idioms, plays with the language, introduces rhymes. This is a very literal rendering to help the English reader to see what has happened.

In the time of times [*idiom*], and they really were good times, there was a cooooow that came down the road and this cooooow that came down along the road met a cute boy called little blazer [*playing with the Italian word grembiule, a little child's school uniform, at the time of translating*].
Daddy used to tell him this story: Daddy looked at him through a monocle: he had a hairy face.
He was little blazer. The cooooow came along the road where Betty Byrne lived, who sold lemon floss.
Oh, the beautiful wild roses, there in the little green garden.
He used to sing that song. It was his song.
Oh the beautiful gween woses.
When you wet the bed, first it's warm, then it gets cold. Mummy would put the waxed sheet. It was that made the strange smell.
Mummy had a nicer smell than Daddy. He [*or she*] would play the tarantella on the piano to make him dance. He danced:

Tralala lalla
tralala lallara
tralala lalla
tralallà

Uncle Charles and Dante clapped their hands. They were older than
Daddy and Mummy, but Uncle Charles was older than Dante.

Dante had two brushes in her cabinet. The brush with the maroon
velvet back was for Michael Davitt and the brush with the green velvet
back was for Parnell. Dante gave him a sweet every time he took her
a piece of tissue paper.

The Vances lived at number seven. They had another daddy and another mummy. They were Eileen's daddy and mummy. When he had
grown up, he would marry Eileen. He used to hide under the table.
Mummy would say: Oh, Stephen, you will get on your knees.

Dante said:

Otherwise the eagle will come and pluck out an eye.

Pluck out an eye
On your knees
On your knees
Pluck out an eye
On your knees
Pluck out an eye
Pluck out an eye
On your knees

*

In the big playing field the boys would swarm. Everyone shouted
and the prefects urged them on with loud voices. The evening air was
pale and cold and after the charge and thud of the players, the muddy
leather sphere flew like a heavy bird in the grey light. He stayed on the
edge of line, away from the eyes of the prefect, away from the reach
of rude feet, every now and then pretending to run. He felt his body
was small and weak in the crowd of players and his eyes were weak
and watery. Rody Kickham was not like that: he would be captain of
the third line, all the boys said.

The first thing that has to be said is that one can only admire Pavese's re-
sourcefulness in solving precisely those problems indicated by the students: the
charming opening line, the clever handling of the verse, and so on. But one of
the challenges of choosing this passage, with its apparently simple technique
of a child's vision followed by a paragraph of sophisticated adult narrative,
blending back into child's vision, was to show that even here translation may

encounter all kinds of difficulties in following the style of the original. Here are the main divergences between the two texts:

- The introduction of 'veniva' (*it came,* or *used to come* or *would come*) in the third line of the Italian, where the English had the vernacular 'and this moocow that was down along the road ...'
- 'Grembialino' (*little apron/uniform*) is more specific and recognizable than 'tuckoo'. Students often translate with the equally acceptable 'merendino' (*little snack*).
- 'Monocolo' is more specific than 'glass'. Many of the students had imagined the father looked at the child through the distorting medium of a drinking glass; or indeed a mirror.
- The momentarily confusing play with 'he' ('he had a hairy face. He was baby tuckoo'), where the child does not take the trouble to qualify the pronoun, is lost in the Italian. Though some confusion is retained in 'Cantava questa canzone' (*he would sing this song*). For a moment we do not know who is singing it.
- 'Era ciò che dava l'odore strano' (*it was that that made the strange smell*) is again a little more adult and syntactically predictable than 'That had the queer smell' (as opposed to 'it was that that had ...').
- In the sentence beginning 'Erano più vecchi del babbo' (*they were older than Daddy*) Pavese introduces a comma absent in the original, just before that beautiful non-sequitur 'but Uncle Charles was older than Dante'.
- 'Armadietto' (*little cabinet/cupboard*) is more easily comprehensible and generic than 'press'. Likewise 'pasticca' (*sweet/pastille*) for 'cachou'.

But it is the paragraph that begins 'The Vances lived' which presents us with the most interesting divergence, one which, as it were, puts all the others in focus. Quite simply, in the fourth sentence of the paragraph, Pavese substitutes Joyce's plural, 'when they were grown up', with a singular, 'quando fosse cresciuto' (*when he was grown up*). But let us look at the paragraph as a whole to see how this comes about.

> The Vances lived in number seven. They had a different father and mother. They were Eileen's father and mother. When they were grown up he was going to marry Eileen. He hid under the table.

> I Vances abitavano al numero sette. Avevano un altro babbo e un'altra mamma. Erano il babbo e la mamma di Eileen. Quando fosse cresciuto, avrebbe sposato Eileen. Si nascondeva sotto il tavolo.

> The Vances lived at number seven. They had another daddy and another mummy. They were Eileen's daddy and mummy. When he had grown up, he would marry Eileen. He used to hide under the table.

The first thing to note is the curious preposition in the first sentence, 'The Vances lived *in* number seven', suggesting the child's vision of the people going in and out of the physical place, the house, and substituting for the more normal 'at number seven'. Pavese does not risk this, despite the fact that Italian prepositions function in a similar fashion. Then we have some very confused use of pronouns in the following three sentences. First, 'They had a different father and mother" Here we discover that the term 'The Vances' in the first sentence, rather than referring, as would be normal, to the family as a whole, referred only to the children in the family, who presumably represent Stephen's chief interest. This comes across well in the Italian.

Then, in another sentence beginning with 'they', we have: 'They were Eileen's father and mother'. Again the referent for the pronoun has changed, this time from the children to the parents, but with the further confusion that now only one child is referred to: Eileen. Presumably the other Vances at the beginning of the paragraph (who did not include the parents!) must have been her brother(s) and/or sister(s). Again the Italian, correctly employing only the inflected verb form without the pronoun, achieves the same effect.

But in the next sentence Pavese loses either his nerve or his concentration. In the English, 'When they were grown up he was going to marry Eileen', the referent for 'they' has shifted yet again, this time from Eileen's parents to Stephen and Eileen. But there is a moment of disorientation before we appreciate this. For a moment we ask ourselves, what does he mean, 'When they (Eileen's parents) were grown up'? Here Pavese translates 'Quando fosse cresciuto, avrebbe sposato Eileen' (*when he had grown up he would marry Eileen*). The use of the singular and the masculine ending for 'cresciuto' (*grown up*) make it clear who the subject of the verb is, and the little game Joyce is playing with this childish grammar breaks down at its wittiest moment.

This apparently tiny change in the translation will serve to make us aware of the technique Joyce is using (and indeed used earlier on in the repetition of 'he' with different referents). Pavese switches to the singular to *avoid confusion,* but Joyce is deliberately creating confusion to suggest that the childish centre of consciousness driving the narrative does not appreciate the problems his audience may be experiencing with his careless grammar. The strategy is obviously in harmony with the use of a diction at once highly local and specific – 'lemon platt, baby tuckoo' – and not entirely comprehensible.

The translator's problems in conveying Joyce's evocation of the child's mentality are not limited to the diction and the deixis. There are also some difficulties with tense. For example, the sentence that follows the play with the pronouns, 'He hid under the table', involves another difficult choice. Pavese has translated the word 'hid' as 'nascondeva' (*he hid/used to hide/would hide*), using the imperfect to suggest repeated action. He then goes on, logically enough, to translate 'mother said' and 'Dante said' as 'diceva' (*said/used to say/would say*).

And this is fair enough. But it is worth noting that once again the English is grammatically vague as the child's mind is vague, or rather, as he is unaware of what would be needed to explain things precisely to his reader/audience. Apart from the past progressive of the very first sentence of the passage, which are his father's words, only the simple past tense is used throughout, with no indication as to whether the actions are repeated or unique. Perhaps this business of Stephen's hiding under the table and being punished only happened once. Or perhaps it happened every day. We do not know. As we do not know exactly what 'glass' means, or 'baby tuckoo', or 'lemon platt'. Pavese, however, is forced to choose. In the Italian system of tenses it must be clear whether the action happened once or was repeated. It is impossible to evoke the same naivety through the grammar. Or at least, not in the same way. Creating the text directly in the Italian one would look for specifically Italian ways that a child's language can be naive. There are many.

Problems with tense are not limited to the past. For a divergence in the next lines shows that while sometimes confusing in its deixis and dramatic structure, Joyce's original is extremely precise in terms of remembered detail. The English gives: 'O, Stephen will apologise' and the Italian,' 'Oh, Stephen, andrai in ginocchio.' (*Oh, Stephen, you will go on your knees*).

Let us quickly admire and then forget Pavese's clever switch from 'apologize' to 'andare in ginocchio' (go on your knees) which is of course required to set up the rhyme 'occhio – ginocchio' (*eye – knee*), and concentrate instead on the change to the second person (rather than the third) and the different uses of the future tense in the two languages.

The implications of the English third person with the strong 'will' form ('Stephen will apologise') are complex. This structure is used not when we first give someone an order, but when they have already refused to obey our first order. The 'will' form here indicates 'I'm not taking "no" for an answer'. It is the most coercive form available and suggests an elided conversation that has gone as follows: 'Apologise, Stephen.' 'No!' 'Stephen, apologise.' 'No!' 'Oh, Stephen will apologize.' The equivalent of the third person with the 'will' form, in Italian, would be the more colloquial: 'O sì che Stephen andrà in ginocchio' (Oh yes Stephen will go on his knees), which again would suggest a preceding refusal. As things stand that refusal is not indicated in the Italian. The English version is thus not only more elliptic and more dramatic than Pavese's, but it also sets up the theme of Stephen's resistance, society's insistence. Throughout the book Stephen will refuse, in one way or another, to apologize (and hence conform), while others insist that he do so.

Looking at the last and very different paragraph of the passage, it is clear that the translator's task here is to register the shift in voice from that of the simplistic child to the sophisticated adult. Returning to what was previously said about the use of the past tense, it is worth noting that Joyce immediately suggests the change in voice by introducing the descriptive past progressive form, 'The wide playgrounds were swarming ...', a form and diction too sophisticated for the young Stephen; since the Italian has already had to make ample distinction between the past tenses in the earlier passage, it is unable to indicate this switch, though of course the register of the verb 'sciamare' (*swarm*) does the job well enough.

Other differences between original and translation in this paragraph have to do with tiny problems of tone. For it is clear that this is not only a more adult narrative voice, but also a lyrical one, not unlike the voice of those last pages of *The Dead.* That is, not only does the syntax become more sophisticated, but the diction changes too and there are some unusual collocations: 'strong cries', 'pale and chilly air', 'greasy leather orb', etc. For the most part Pavese, who is himself a master of lyric prose, has no difficulty following this. Nevertheless the one or two divergences are interesting. For example the change from 'after *every* charge and thud' to 'dopo la carica e il tonfo dei giocatori' (*after the charge and thud of the players*), seems to suggest some misunderstanding of the game, as if the flight of the ball somehow occurred after all the charging and thudding were over. It is difficult to see why the English could not have been followed here.

The other change that students will note is the translation of 'greasy leather orb' as 'sfera di cuoio infangato' (*sphere of muddy leather*). The ball is greasy, in the sense of difficult to catch, because it is muddy of course. But likewise one must remember that 'greasiness' is an image that is to be associated with the lumpen, sensual, anti-intellectual side of life throughout the book. Unfortunately there is no alternative for 'infangato' (*muddy*) in the Italian here, nothing that the translator can do to get the nuance which is there in the English and hook the word on to the developing image cluster. As for the use of 'sfera' (*sphere*), if nothing else· it draws our attention to Joyce's most curious use of the poetic 'orb', a word that, apart from meaning a circle or sphere, also has connotations of bereavement (of children!) and blindness. Did Joyce, doubtless aware of those connotations, choose the word to suggest some lesion in

Stephen's infancy, the parents' loss of the child at public school, or to conjure up the idea of blindness, the child's weak eyes as it were projected on to the ball? Or, since one is dealing with a rugby ball rather than a football, was it more a question of the word orb not so obviously making the reader think of something spherical when the object in question is not in fact round but oval? Or was it just the portentously glum and dead monosyllabic sound of the word that attracted the writer as for the first time he introduces the symbol of the bird, not here as an image of freedom, but as something heavy and trapped in the grey light? Inevitably translation draws us to that area where the writer's choices are both mysterious and mystery-making.

More generally speaking, the main purpose of this paragraph, apart from narrating very dramatically the fact that Stephen is now at school, is the way it slows the prose down, provides a traditional narrative voice against which Stephen's childish voice becomes more recognizable. And indeed towards the end of the paragraph we slip back into the child's voice and point of view: 'Rody Kickham was not like that: he would be captain of the third line all the fellows said'. The absence of a comma after 'line' marks the return to that ungrammatical voice. It seems unnecessary for Pavese or his editors to put it in.

Volumes have been written on the opening paragraphs of *A Portrait* and most of them concentrate on the way this page sets up the tensions that will dominate the rest of the book: the use of symbolism, the introduction of church, state and family, the references to the five senses, the dramatization of the boy's hearing and then reproducing language, etc. However, the difficulties encountered when translating the passage suggest that much of Joyce's linguistic effort has gone into discovering a style which will effectively, wittily and rapidly evoke a child's perception of his surroundings. The use of a deliberately confusing syntax in combination with highly specific cultural references serves to achieve this end, and it might be argued that this technique is more important to the success of the opening than its patterns of imagery. In any event, the imagery comes across perfectly well in translation, the diction and deixis slightly less so.

In this regard, just to underline the use of specific cultural reference, we could quote a sentence from the paragraph following the passage we have looked at:

> Rody Kickham had greaves in his number and a hamper in the refectory.[9]

---

[9] *Portrait*, p.8.

I had to turn to Pavese's translation to understand 'greaves' and 'number'.

> Rody Kickham aveva parastinchi nel suo armadio e un cestino nel refettorio.[10]

> Rody Kickham had shin-pads in his locker and a basket in the refectory.

But even if I did not understand Joyce's original, what I recognized in the sentence that an Italian reader could not is the jargon of the public school and the pun of the name Kickham (who is to become captain of the third line). Such is the way Joyce evokes Stephen's childhood. To a great extent it is an evocation of a particular idiom wielded by an initiate who does not appreciate that his audience may not be initiates. The fact that a translation is more comprehensible than the original does not mean that it is equally effective.

Let us now put some pressure on this idea of the evocation of a childish and idiomatic language. Inevitably that language will change as Stephen grows. At the beginning of *A Portrait* there is the frequent use of vocabulary specific to the public school – 'wax' (bad temper), 'pandybat' (a stick for punishing the pupils), 'feck' (to steal), etc.; the biblical language of the prayers – 'Visit, we beseech thee, O Lord this habitation'; and then Stephen's first curiosity with common words (the onomatopoeia, for example, of the word 'suck'). Later on there will be all kinds of reflections on language (the 'dead language' of 'The ivy whines upon the wall'), the beauty of the word 'ivory', the cadences of the terrible sermon at the centre of the book, the charm and power of poetry. In each case, the translator faces all kinds of problems. In particular, there is a danger of translating very local vocabulary with equally local vocabulary in the target language ('hornpipe' becomes 'tarantella' on the first page, a specifically southern European dance with various connotations not there in the English). But in general Pavese avoids this trap, for culture-specific language in the translation would make us start thinking of Naples or Rome, rather than Ireland, whereas the experience described is an Irish experience not an Italian one. Other problems are obvious: the lack of a recognizable biblical style in Italian, the problem of translating onomatopoeia, the difficulty of suggesting the captivating cadence of a poetic line. And all this without considering the difficulties not just of getting each thing right, but right in relation to each other. Using painting as a metaphor, one might say that just as each colour used on a canvas changes and is changed by all the other colours, so is each

---

[10] *Dedalus*, p.27

style conditioned by and conditioning of all the others.

One mentions this chequered and constantly shifting aspect of Joyce's work (a milder form of the same thing was observed in *The Dead*), not so much to despair of translation as to get a better appreciation of the original, and likewise to suggest how impossible it would be to choose anything like a representative passage. The difficulties, for example, encountered in those first pages of *A Portrait* are quite different from those of the epiphany described in this paragraph:

> He was alone. He was unheeded, happy, and near to the wild heart of life. He was alone and young and wilful and wildhearted, alone amid a waste of wild air and brackish waters and the seaharvest of shells and tangle and veiled grey sunlight and gayclad lightclad figures of children and girls and voices childish and girlish in the air.[11]

Pavese gives this as:

> Era solo. Nessuno gli badava e lui era felice, accanto al cuore selvaggio della vita. Era solo e giovane e risoluto e selvaggio, solo in un deserto di aria selvaggia e di acque salmastre, in mezzo alla messe marina di conchiglie e di ciuffi, alla luce grigia e velata del sole, alle figure, vestite gaiamente e leggermente, di ragazzi e bambine e alle voci infantili nell'aria.[12]

> He was alone. No one was watching him and he was happy, close to the wild heart of life. He was alone and young and resolute and wild, alone in a desert of wild air and salt waters, in the middle of the marine harvests of shells and tufts, of the grey and veiled light of the sun, of the figures, gaily and lightly dressed, of children and little girls and childish voices in the air.

It is interesting here how completely, even in this solid translation by a considerable writer, the Italian fails to convey the urgency and excitement of the original. There are no alternative strategies it seems to get over the effect of 'gayclad lightclad', nor the torrent of alliteration and assonance. Even the rushing, urgent syntax of the English (not unlike the sentence foreseeing Aunt Julia's death in *The Dead*) is broken up and made easier to understand. And here perhaps there is something of that loss of meaning through altered

---

[11] *Portrait,* p. 155.
[12] *Dedalus,* p. 210

diction and syntax that we saw with Lawrence, in the sense that *A Portrait* presents these epiphanies as moments when all phenomena and language, negative and positive, flow together, are lost in each other rather than opposing each other.

The word 'tangle' is important in this regard, as is the flagrant mix of words with negative connotations – waste, brackish, tangle – in the generally exhilarating, positive and entirely unpunctuated whole, and again the way all these disparate phenomena are linked together with nothing more helpful than eight egalitarian 'and's.

Particularly intriguing in a translation of this quality is Pavese's difficulty with the list that forms the second part of the long third sentence, beginning '…alone amid a waste of wild air and brackish waters and the seaharvest…'. Pavese breaks up the list by using first 'in' (*in*) for 'amid' and then 'in mezzo a' (*in the middle of*) where the English has nothing. He then recalls the 'a' of 'in mezzo a' four times, thus allowing the Italian to eliminate a number of 'and's. If this has the effect of re-creating the insistence of the English, it entirely sacrifices the sense of confusion, since the reader's attention is constantly taken back to 'in mezzo a' (*in the middle of*) and thereby to Stephen's position in the midst of these phenomena, rather than being allowed to lose himself in them, as Stephen is lost.

Confusion, and the generally vertiginous flow, is further eliminated by the introduction of five commas where there are none in the English, while at the end the word 'girlish' has to be cut out since it seems to pose insuperable problems in the Italian (as it did in *The Dead*). Unfortunately, the result of the omission of 'girlish' is that Pavese actually fails to describe the simple reality of what is going on on the beach. Joyce lists 'gayclad lightclad figures of children and girls and voices childish and girlish in the air'. The distinction between the neuterless children and then the girls surely suggests a situation of infants being watched over by adolescent girl babysitters, such as the one Stephen is about to see wading in the sea. The Italian, 'in mezzo ... alle figure ... di ragazzi e bambine e alle voci infantili nell'aria' (*in the middle... of the figures ... of children and little girls and of childish voices in the air*), suggests the opposite: some older, perhaps adolescent children of both sexes playing with some infant girls. On reading the Italian, grammatically precise and syntactically all too helpful, one cannot help wondering why all the little ones are girls. Where are the infant boys?

But my purpose in presenting this passage is to suggest that when we have prose like this we are posed with the problem of whether the translation must be more determinedly creative in its own language, as in the translation of poetry, where it is generally accepted that the translator will draw on the poetic resources of his own language at the expense of semantic content in the hope of producing *a similar effect* to the original. Inevitably, the question of how many liberties a translator can take is a vexed one (though I feel the word 'liberties' is always ill-chosen in this regard; it is more a problem of what one is being faithful to). In any event, it is a question that can no longer be baulked when we arrive at the unceasingly creative prose of *Ulysses.*

If *A Portrait* is varied and constantly changing in style, *Ulysses* is heroically protean. In his essay, 'Righting Ulysses', Fritz Senn concludes that *'Ulysses* refuses to stay put. Once we know what it *is* we are sure to be wrong.[13] For the translator, as we have seen with passages from Joyce's earlier work, the difficulty is one of registering these changes in a language whose range of styles and resources cannot be expected to correspond exactly to those being used in the original. For example, it is a difficult enterprise to translate pastiche, in which *Ulysses* abounds, if the original model for that pastiche does not exist in the translator's language. There is the danger of losing the irony and fun that are the main pleasure of the text. In a chapter like *The Oxen of the Sun* with its grand tour through the whole history of English prose, it is difficult to see how a translation can be achieved without altering the content to accommodate the history of an entirely different language. Even some of the shorter and simpler sentences in the book have an inner dynamism that pose huge problems for the translator. Fritz Senn remarks on the sentence 'He [Bloom] pulled the door to after him and slammed it tight till it shut tight',[14] where the use of three verbs for the same action and the repetition of 'tight' suggest both Bloom's uneasy state of mind as he climbs into a funeral carriage, and also his meticulousness and determination to solve little problems, get things right. Comparison of this with the Italian 'Si tirò dietro lo sportello e lo sbatté finché non fu ben chiuso',[15] (*he pulled the door behind and slammed it till it was well shut*) shows how much the uneasiness and irritation encountered in closing the door are lost when the sentence is ironed out into something more stylistically 'normal'. It is worth pointing out that the stylistic devices Joyce uses here are not unlike some of those seen in the passages from *Women in Love*.[16] But once again, the loss in translating Joyce is a loss above all of mood, not of polemic.

---

[13] Fritz Senn, 'Righting Ulysses', an article in *James Joyce: New Perspectives,* Harvester, 1982, p. 27.

[14] *Ulysses.* Oxford University Press, 1993 (World's Classics). Reprint of the original 1922 edition, p. 88. All further quotations are from this edition.

[15] *Ulisse,* Oscar Mondadori, Milan, 1978. Translation by Giulio de Angelis, p. 120. All further quotations are from this edition.

[16] *Women in Love,* cit., pp. 56-7.

Adventure is of the essence in this kind of endeavour and the admirable translation of *Ulysses* by Giulio de Angelis offers plenty of material for reflection. Take the short paragraph:

> Kidneys were in his mind as he moved about the kitchen softly, righting her breakfast things on the humpy tray. Gelid light and air were in the kitchen but out of doors gentle summer morning everywhere. Made him feel a bit peckish.[17]

> I rognoni erano nel suo pensiero mentre si muoveva quietamente per la cucina, sistemando le stoviglie per la colazione di lei sul vassoio ammaccato. Luce e aria gelida nella cucina ma fuori una dolce mattina d'estate dappertutto. Gli facevano venire un po' di prurito allo stomaco.[18]

> Kidneys were in his thoughts as he moved quietly around the kitchen, putting out the dishes for her breakfast on the battered tray. Light and freezing air in the kitchen but outside a sweet summer morning everywhere. Brought a little itch to his stomach.

As ever one cannot help but notice the translation's tendency to reduce the quirks of the original to a norm. So the wit of 'in his mind' rather than 'on his mind' (distortion of idiom, as in Lawrence) is lost (necessarily in this case), the potentially significant verb 'righting' is lost (Bloom's habit of getting things right), and likewise the elision of an article before 'gentle summer morning'. But if we expected this to be the trend throughout, then we are pulled up short by 'Gli facevano venire un po' di prurito allo stomaco' (*Brought a little itch to his stomach*), a far more bizarre expression than the very ordinary English that closes the paragraph: 'Made him feel a bit peckish.'

In the paragraphs that follow this passage, the translator offers other curiosities where the English is fairly simple: for example, 'la gatta interita girò attorno a una gamba del tavolo con la coda ritta' (the chilled cat went round a table leg with tail erect), for Joyce's 'The cat walked stiffly round the leg of the table with tail on high.' In terms of assonance and alliteration 'interita' forms an internal rhyme with 'ritta' (*erect*) and picks up the 't' of 'tavolo' (*table*). In this sense it fits well into the sentence. But few readers (native Italians) will ever have seen the word (it means stiff with cold). A few paragraphs further on we have two complete neologisms, 'ammusava' (mixing 'annusare', *to*

---

[17] *Ulysses*, p. 53.
[18] *Ulisse*, p. 75

sniff, and 'muso', *muzzle*) for the English 'tipped' and then 'leccottìo' (mixing 'leccare', *to lick*, with 'ottìo', a suffix indicating sound) for 'licking lap'.

In a more traditional text such invention would cause concern, but it is clear that in translating *Ulysses* de Angelis is trying to draw, where he can, on the resources of Italian to create linguistic games that will make up for his loss of those games in other parts of the text. Comparison of translation and original here offers an excellent opportunity to reflect on the process of evocation through invention that appears to drive the English and to ask whether reproduction of that process 'means the same thing' or at least 'has the same effect' in Italian as in English. Does English perhaps have a tradition of playing with vocabulary (made all the easier by the lack of inflection – nouns and adjectives that can become verbs, etc.) which Italian does not? Or might it be that Italian 'plays in a different way'? These are not questions I feel capable of dealing with here, but it is inescapable that texts of this creative intensity alert us to the notion that a certain kind of richness may reside only in a certain language.

Here, in any event, to conclude this chapter on Joyce, is a passage from *Ulysses* at the book's most playful. We are in the chapter known as *The Sirens*. While Bloom is in the back room of a pub eating, Blazes Boylan (about to become Bloom's wife's lover) and Lenehan are at the bar flirting with the barmaids. The dominant themes of the chapter are musical, and indeed in the background someone is singing a song at the piano. To help those coming cold to the passage, the barmaid Miss Douce is referred to as 'sparkling bronze' in honour of her red hair.

> Sparkling bronze azure eyed Blazure's skyblue bow and eyes. – Go on, pressed Lenehan. There's no-one. He never heard.
> – ... *to Flora's lips did hie.*
> High, a high note, pealed in the treble, clear.
> Bronzedouce, communing with her rose that sank and rose sought Blazes Boylan's flower and eyes.
> – Please, please.
> He pleaded over returning phrases of avowal.
> – *I could not leave thee ...*
> – Afterwits, Miss Douce promised coyly.
> – No, now, urged Lenehan. *Sonnezlacloche!* O do! There's no-one.
> She looked. Quick. Miss Kenn out of earshot. Sudden bent. Two kindling faces watched her bend. Quavering the chords strayed from the air, found it again, lost chord, and lost and found it faltering.
> – Go on! Do! *Sonnez!*

Bending, she nipped a peak of skirt above her knee. Delayed. Taunted them still, bending, suspending, with wilful eyes.

– *Sonnez!*

Smack. She let free sudden in rebound her nipped elastic garter smackwarm against her smackable woman's warmhosed thigh.

– *La cloche!* cried gleeful Lenehan. Trained by owner. No sawdust there.

She smilesmirked supercilious (wept! aren't men?), but lightward, gliding, mild she smiled on Boylan.

– You're the essence of vulgarity, she in gliding said.

Boylan, eyed, eyed. Tossed to fat lips his chalice, drank off his tiny, chalice, sucking the last fat violet syrupy drops. He spellbound eyes went after her gliding head as it went down the bar by mirrors, gilded arch for ginger ale, hock and claret glasses shimmering, a spiky shell, where it concerted, mirrored, bronze with sunnier bronze.[19]

It should be said that of all the passages looked at so far in this book, this is the first that presents even native readers with real problems of comprehension. Indeed, much of the fun here comes from the effort involved in understanding the playful manner in which the scene is being described, the habit, typical of classical epics, of referring to the characters through some quality (bronze), the general mixture of narrative ellipsis with mock heroic tone ('communing with her rose that sank and rose'), the amusing and Joycean collision of words – afterwits, smackwarm – not to mention a determined musicality that aims at tying in with the Homeric episode of the Sirens which is here being parodied. The danger, as far as a translation is concerned, is that it may become nothing more than a crib of the English for those who are bewildered.

Here is de Angelis's version:

Scintillante bronzo azzurrocchiava il fiocco e gli occhi azzurrocielo di Blazzurro.

– Andiamo, insisteva Lenehan. Non c'è nessuno. Non l'ha mai sentito.

– ... *alle labbra di Flora s'appressava.*

Alta, una nota alta, scampanò acuta, limpida.

Bronzodouce, congiunta alla sua rosa or saliente or ritrosa, cercava il fiore e gli occhi di Blazes Boylan.

– Per favore, per favore.

Invocava fra ricorrenti frasi di devozione.

---

[19] *Ulysses,* p. 255-6.

– *Mai ti potrei lasciar ...*

– Tra un pochinino, promise Miss Douce, pudicamente.

– Ma no, ora, insisteva Lenehan. *Sonnez la cloche!* Via! Non c'è nessuno.

Ella guardò. Presto. Miss Kenn fuori portata d'orecchio. Chinata a un tratto. Due volti infiammati la osservavano chinarsi.

Tremuli gli accordi si staccarono dal motivo, lo ritrovarono, accordo perduto, e lo perdettero e ritrovarono smorente.

– Andiamo! Via! *Sonnez!*

Chinandosi, s'afferrò un lembo di gonna sopra al ginocchio. Differiva.

Ancora li tormentava, chinandosi, in sospeso, con occhi malandrini.

– *Sonnez!*

Schiocco. Lasciò libera a un tratto di scatto la giarrettiera elastica estesa schioccalda contro la coscia schioccante caldicalzata di donna.

– *La cloche!* gridò Lenehan giubilante. Ammaestrata dal proprietario. Niente imbottitura lì.

Lei sorriseghignò sussiegosa (addolorata! non sono dei begli) ma, scorrendo verso la luce, mite sorrise a Boylan.

– Lei è la quintessenza della volgarità, disse scorrendo.

Boylan occhieggiava, occhieggiava. Riversò il calice accostato alle grosse labbra, scolò il suo picciol calice, sorbendo le ultime grosse gocce violette sciroppose. I suoi occhi ammaliati seguivano la testa scorrente per il bar lungo specchi, arco dorato per bicchieri da gazosa, vino del Reno e chiaretto baluginanti, una conchiglia spinosa, ove concertava, specchiava, bronzo con bronzo più solare.[20]

Sparkling bronze azureyed the bowtie and skyblue eyes of Blazure.

– Come on, insisted Lenehan. There's no one. He's never heard it.

– *... to Flora's lips he came...*

High, a high note, rang out sharp, clear.

Bronzedouce, together with her rose now rising now reluctant, looked for the flower and eyes of Blazes Boylan.

– Please, please.

He invoked amid repeated phrases of devotion.

– *Never could I leave you...*

– In an itsybitsy, promised Miss Douce, coyly.

– But no, now, insisted Lenehan. *Sonnezlacloche!* Go on! There's no one.

---

[20] *Ulisse,* pp. 363-4.

> She looked. Quick. Miss Kenn out of earshot. Bent suddenly. Two
> inflamed faces watched her bend.
>
> Tremulous the chords left the tune, found it again, chord lost, and
> lost it and found it dying away.
>
> – Come on! Now! *Sonnez!*
>
> Bending, she took hold of a hem of skirt above the knee. Delayed.
> Still she tormented them, bending, in suspension, with roguish eyes.
>
> – *Sonnez!*
>
> Smack. She let go with a sudden snap the extended elastic suspender,
> smackwarm against her smacking warm-stockinged woman's thigh.
>
> – *La cloche!* Shouted Lenehan jubilant. Trained by owner. No pad-
> ding there.
>
> She smilesniggered supercilious (sorrowful! Aren't men beasts) but,
> passing toward the light, mild she smiled at Boylan.
>
> – You are the quintessence of vulgarity, she said passing by.
>
> Boylan eyed, eyed. Poured his chalice pressed to fat lips, drained his
> little chalice, drinking up the last fat violet syrupy drops. His enchanted
> eyes followed the head passing down the bar along the mirrors, gilded
> arch for glimmering ginger ale Rhine wine and lighter red glasses, a
> spiky shell, now concerting, mirroring, bronze with sunnier bronze.

The first thing to be said about this translation is that it could not, like others we have looked at, give the reader the impression that the original was a
conventional piece of prose without particular stylistic effects. Faced with an
onslaught of wit and the determination to have the passage throb with musicality, the translator is left with no alternative but to imitate, as far as is possible,
Joyce's game. Otherwise little would remain. Without its special effects the
text would be in danger of disappearing altogether. Paraphrase would be pitiful.
Thus one can hardly pretend, as Lawrence's translator sometimes appeared to
do, that there is nothing special about the text.

As far as the foreign reader is concerned, one advantage of looking at a
translation of such a text is that it alerts him to the fact that his difficulty with
the English, if he has already tried to read it, is not merely a question of not
being familiar with the vocabulary or up to the syntax. He realizes that much
of the text is wilfully bizarre and thus appreciates that the focus of Joyce's attention has shifted away from the object of evocation, still central in *Dubliners*
and *A Portrait,* and towards the medium of evocation, the language.

Does this lead us then to the conclusion that this translation is closer to
its original than the translations examined from *Women in Love*, in the sense
that it reveals the intention of the original in a way that those translations

sometimes did not? As always a detailed look at divergences will help us to appreciate exactly what has happened.

> Sparkling bronze azure eyed Blazure's skyblue bow and eyes.

> Scintillante bronzo azzurrocchiava il fiocco e gli occhi azzurrocielo di Blazzurro.

> Sparkling bronze azureyed the bowtie and skyblue eyes of Blazure.

The deliberately trite, heavily accented rhythm of Joyce's first sentence is blurred but not entirely lost, while the linguistic invention and the use of al-literation and internal rhyme remains. The English evokes two things here: the exchange of glances in the pub and a certain way the British have of imagining epic verse. It struggles to be at once exact and information-packed on the narrative level, but funny too in the way this information is delivered in mock heroic overtones. If the Italian loses anything aside from the very strong rhythm, it is this gesture towards what is not so much Homeric epic as a British tradition in parodying it.

> – Go on, pressed Lenehan. There's no-one. He never heard.

> – Andiamo, insisteva Lenehan. Non c'è nessuno. Non l'ha mai sentito.

> – Come on, insisted Lenehan. There's no one. He's never heard it.

The dramatic ellipsis of the second line presents no problem at all, once the general situation has been understood. Clearly Lenehan wants the barmaid ('bronze') to do something, something audible, something intimate, for Blazes Boylan. Since she is already exchanging glances with him it seems likely she will comply.

> –   ...to Flora's lips did hie.

> –   ...alle labbra di Flora s'appressava.

> – ... to Flora's lips he came...

The problem with a snatch of song overheard from the piano is to indicate the archaic, pastoral diction ('hie' = to go) which forms one of the references to a more idyllic past against which the dubious taste of the present situation is set. This is nicely done in the Italian with some old fashioned phrasing and a conveniently literary diction, 'appressava' (*neared/approached*) in particular whose high register is not really conveyed in my back-translation 'came'.

> High, a high note, pealed in the treble, clear.

> Alta, una nota alta, scampanò acuta, limpida.

> High, a high note, rang out sharp, clear.

The next line presents impossible problems and the first easily identifiable loss. The English picks up the word 'hie' and repeats the sound in 'high', describing the musical note. In so far as *The Sirens* 'falls under the bodily sign of the ear',[21] it is clear that Joyce would not have written this line had the previous line not ended with 'hie', or alternatively he would not have written the previous line had it not given him the opportunity to lead into this line. Whatever the case, the two lines are linked in a way they cannot easily be in any translation.

Does this matter? Two reflections are possible here: one is that this kind of mental connection is Joyce's way of keeping us in touch with Bloom who is overhearing and watching this scene, and asking himself whether Boylan has perhaps forgotten the appointment with his (Bloom's) wife. That is, we feel it may be Bloom making these connections (hie, high). More pertinently perhaps there is the fact that much of *Ulysses* is concerned with displaying all the possible and often arbitrary ways things and above all words can be connected and arranged, the way 'meaning' generates itself endlessly. In this sense there is a loss. Joyce would not have put these two sentences together had he been originating the text in Italian.

But another aspect to consider is the syntax. Joyce has a way of wielding grammar that allows us to read it in two ways. Here we could read: 'High ... pealed in the treble', where 'treble' is the subject of 'pealed'. Or alternatively 'a high note pealed in the treble', where 'a high note' is the subject and 'the treble' an acoustic range. As we shall see later on in the passage, it often seems that the language has not settled into its final meaning but remains in a state of potential. This syntactical fluidity is difficult to achieve in the Italian.

> Bronzedouce, communing with her rose that sank and rose sought Blazes Boylan's flower and eyes.

---

[21] Frank Budgen, *The Making of Ulysses,* Oxford University Press, 1972, p. 135.

Bronzodouce, congiunta alla sua rosa or saliente or ritrosa, cercava il fiore e gli occhi di Blazes Boylan.

Bronzedouce, together with her rose now rising now reluctant, looked for the flower and eyes of Blazes Boylan.

These, like the opening lines, offer a mix of witty narrative compression with lofty diction: It seems here that the translation, in discovering the possibility of 'ritrosa' (reluctant, bashful, drawing back), while departing slightly from an exact semantic translation, perfectly conveys Joyce's method, his play with the relationship between meaning and sound ('ritrosa' rhymes with 'rosa'). Furthermore, since 'ritrosa' means 'withdrawing' in the sense of 'shy', the Italian offers an ironic vision of the barmaid as timid pastoral shepherdess, which is absent at this point in the English, but entirely appropriate (see Miss Douce's later coyness) and in harmony with the song played in the background. The only objection might be how deep the translator has had to quarry in the language to come up with his solution. 'Sank and rose' seems so obvious in the English, as if handed to Joyce on a plate (which is often his point one feels); 'saliente o ritrosa' makes us think how hard the translator had to work, so that you wonder whether anybody but a translator with this particular problem to solve would ever have written this in Italian.

– Please, please.
He pleaded over returning phrases of avowal.

– Per favore, per favore.
Invocava fra ricorrenti frasi di devozione.

– Please, please.
He invoked amid repeated phrases of devotion.

Aware of the assonance between 'please' and 'plead', the translator manages something similar with 'per favore' (*please*) and 'invocava' (*invoked*). Then fortunately 'frasi' (phrases) is an exact cognate of 'phrases' in both the linguistic and musical contexts. But is there a pun in the archaic 'avowal'? Could we read 'a vowel'?, i.e. the returning vowel in 'please, please'. One never knows with Joyce. In any event there is nothing the translation can do about it.

– Afterwits, Miss Douce promised coyly.

– Tra un pochinino, promise Miss Douce, pudicamente.

– In an itsybitsy, promised Miss Douce, coyly.

Here, in 'tra un pochinino' (*in an itsybitsy*) one has another resourceful attempt to discover in Italian something that might match an invention in the English. 'Afterwits' presumably mimics Douce's Irish accent and the little-girl coyness with which she says this. 'Pochinino' gets that over well enough. But Joyce knows that when we look at the letters of his new word 'afterwits', or listen to its pronunciation, we (or perhaps it is a question of Bloom listening from the other room) will also hear the word 'halfwits', which might be a fair enough description of Boylan and Lenehan, at least from Bloom's point of view.

If we were to hazard a guess now at the intention driving this text, we might reasonably settle on words like 'abundance', 'richness', or even 're-dundance'. Connections, ideas, are endless. That is the text's epic quality. Registering a minimal and inevitable loss here one does no more than remark the disappearance of one tiny snake from Gorgon's head. It is worth observing, though, how the translator tries to get the monster to grow another by discovering the heavy alliteration of the p's, absent in the English: 'Tra un *p*ochinino, *p*romise Miss Douce, *p*udicamente;' something that does not come over in the back-translation.

> – No, now, urged Lenehan. *Sonnezlacloche!* O do! There's no-one.

> – Ma no, ora, insisteva Lenehan. *Sonnezlacloche!* Via! Non c'è nessuno.

> – But no, now, insisted Lenehan. *Sonnezlacloche!* Go on! There's no one.

The dialogue presents no problems, since here the need for authenticity returns Joyce to standard spoken discourse. Indeed, he seems to use dialogue to help us keep in touch, just in case we are finding the going rather heavy. In touch up to a point... We now know that Lenehan wants her to *'Sonnez la cloche'*. But do we know what that means?

> She looked. Quick. Miss Kenn out of earshot. Sudden bent. Two kindling faces watched her bend.

> Ella guardò. Presto. Miss Kenn fuori portata d'orecchio. Chinata a un tratto. Due volti infiammati la osservavano chinarsi.

> She looked. Quick. Miss Kenn out of earshot. Bent suddenly. Two
> inflamed faces watched her bend.

The trick with these lines is the way the syntax becomes even more elliptic to
suggest the speed of the action as Miss Douce tries to establish whether the
coast is clear for their little game. Since Joyce is never afraid of a little dramatic
confusion, one wonders whether the initial 'Ella' (*she*) is really necessary in
the Italian (though one appreciates the decision to go for a high register. Use
of personal pronouns is not necessary here and this one is archaic).

Otherwise one notes the difficulty of getting the Italian to be as quick and
sharp as the original ('earshot' becoming 'portata d'orecchio' (here, the back-
translation 'earshot' is generous), 'sudden bent', 'chinata a un tratto' – *bent
all at once*). Would Joyce have looked for different images in Italian, images
which would have given him the acoustic effect desired? One suspects so.

In the last sentence the difference between 'kindling' and 'infiammati'
(*inflamed*) again draws attention to the way Joyce keeps his syntax at a level
of potential rather than definition. 'To kindle' is more usually transitive than
intransitive. We expect an object. Are the two men kindling themselves in
kindling her? Curiously, 'to kindle' also means 'bring forth young'. But one
has to stop somewhere.

> Quavering the chords strayed from the air, found it again, lost chord,
> and lost and found it faltering.

> Tremuli gli accordi si staccarono dal motivo, lo ritrovarono, accordo
> perduto, e lo perdettero e ritrovarono smorente.

> Tremulous the chords left the tune, found it again, chord lost, and lost
> it and found it dying away.

Of all the phrases in the text this is probably the densest and hence the least
translatable. 'Quavering' offers a description of the trembling chords and assonance with the word 'stray' and a joke with the musical term 'quaver' (half
a crotchet). 'Air' suggests either the way the music strays from the air in the
room, or the way it loses the tune. The language then dithers splendidly, groping for the chord (again there is that sense of endeavour to get things right),
at which point we realize that we may now be talking about Douce feeling
in her skirts for her garter (cord), since that, as we are about to see, is what
'*sonnez la cloche*' involves.

As earlier on, the Italian is quite heroic in its determination to keep up with the game, first with the suggested play with 'tremuli' (*tremulous*, referring to the chords) and 'tremoli' (*tremolos*, the musical term), then the decision to pun on 'accordo' (*chord*) but also 'accordo' (*agreement*, i.e. Lenehan's agreement with Miss Douce), and then the very literary 'smorente' (literally, *fading to the colour of death*). All this is admirable, particularly the play with 'accordo' (*chord/agreement*), absent in the English, and reminds us that a chord is an agreement of different notes. 'Smorente', however, does not offer the range of interpretation we get from 'faltering', which could refer to the singing voice, or to the movement of the hand under the skirt looking for the garter. And it is this joke – that the text may be talking about Miss Douce as much as about the music – which is central here.

> – Go on! Do! *Sonnez!*
> Bending, she nipped a peak of skirt above her knee. Delayed. Taunted them still, bending, suspending, with wilful eyes.

> – Andiamo! Via! *Sonnez!*
> Chinandosi, s'afferrò un lembo di gonna sopra al ginocchio. Differiva. Ancora li tormentava, chinandosi, in sospeso, con occhi malandrini.

> – Come on! Now! *Sonnez!*
> Bending, she took hold of a hem of skirt above the knee. Delayed. Still she tormented them, bending, in suspension, with roguish eyes.

First the simple dialogue, for breathing space, then the monosyllabic speed of the next line with the visual precision of 'nipped' (her teasingly dainty fingers) and the pun on 'peak' (the men are about to 'peek'). The Italian, in contrast to previous efforts, has nothing to offer here, returning the description to a more ordinary kind of prose. The same is true of the next sentence where the pun on 'suspend' (she pulls her suspenders and keeps the men in suspense) is lost in 'in sospeso' (*in suspension*), which seems merely desperate in the Italian. Also lost is the suspense arising from the assonance of the two participles, 'bending, suspending', the second a syllable longer and tenser than the first. This is perhaps the moment to reflect on the extraordinary energy involved in maintaining this level of density, not just over this one page we have chosen, but over hundreds of pages. And the extraordinary resources that would be required to match this wordplay line by line. Not bound by any need to stay true to an original, Joyce's prose is effusive, it never ceases to abound with meaning. For all its heroism, a translation cannot avoid a certain patchiness. Either it falls off, or we feel all the strain of its groping for games while staying within the semantic prison of the original. In any event, it should be clear by now that the principle of never-ending abundance lies at the heart of the text.

> – Sonnez!
> Smack. She let free sudden in rebound her nipped elastic garter smackwarm against her smackable woman's warmhosed thigh.
> – La cloche! cried gleeful Lenehan. Trained by owner. No sawdust there.

> – Sonnez!
> Schiocco. Lasciò libera a un tratto di scatto la giarrettiera elastica estesa schioccalda contro la coscia schioccante caldicalzata di donna.
> – La cloche! gridò Lenehan giubilante. Ammaestrata dal proprietario. Niente imbottitura lì.

> – Sonnez!
> Smack. She let go with a sudden snap the extended elastic suspender, smackwarm against her smacking warm-stockinged woman's thigh.
> – La cloche! Shouted Lenehan jubilant. Trained by owner. No padding there.

How clever the acoustics of 'a un tratto di scatto!' (*a sudden snap*) 'Rebound' and 'nipped' are gone, but to compensate we have the assonance of 'elastica estesa' (extended elastic) and again the hard clicking sounds of the neologism's 'schioccalda' (*smackwarm*) and 'caldicalzata' (*warmstockinged*). Though this works wonderfully from the onomatopoeic and clownish points of view, the translator finds nothing to get over the sense of 'smackable', which says much about the way the men's minds work (here I must point out that the 'smack' I have used to translate 'schiocco' in the back-translation refers only to the sound smack, but not to the idea of a blow, which is not there in 'schiocco'). Quite simply, 'smackable' would require too many words to explain, would spoil the rhythm of the description, to which, in a chapter obsessed with the musicality of words, the translator rightly decided to give precedence.

At this point Lenehan completes the expression *'Sonnez la cloche'*, which has been suspended over the previous paragraph, and at last all is explained. The fun of the following lines lies in the association (presumably Lenehan's, or Bloom's imagination of Lenehan's thought) of Miss Douce with a racehorse ('trained by owner'), horseracing being a theme that runs throughout *Ulysses.* And here since the richness lies in making the association, rather than in any linguistic trick, the Italian has no difficulty following. In passing

I shall admit that I have still to understand what 'No sawdust there' means. Is 'Niente imbottitura' (*no padding*) an exact translation? But how could a horse be padded? Perhaps I am ignorant. In general, in a text of this kind with its mixture of creativity and local mimicry one expects there to be moments of incomprehension. In general, as with the opening pages of *A Portrait,* things tend to be a little clearer in the translation.

> She smilesmirked supercilious (wept! aren't men?), but lightward, gliding, mild she smiled on Boylan.

> Lei sorriseghignò sussiegosa (addolorata! non sono dei begli) ma, scorrendo verso la luce, mite sorrise a Boylan.

> She smilesniggered supercilious (sorrowful! Aren't men beasts) but, passing toward the light, mild she smiled at Boylan.

Again it is not the neologisms that mark the difference between the texts, but the problem the translation has with the compression of the original. 'Wept!' is presumably an elision of the expression, taken from the Bible, 'Jesus wept!', here a vulgar exclamation of dismay. 'Addolorata' is a brilliant solution. On the one hand it can just mean regretful, sorrowful. But on the other, the Addolorata is of course Our Lady of Sorrows. 'Aren't men?', however, simply forces the Italian to add something explanatory, in this case 'aren't men beasts'.

These exclamations are then followed by the lyric, rhythmic and beguilingly jolly 'but lightward, gliding, mild she smiled on Boylan'. This time the translator can find nothing in his own language that will allow him to play similar games, whether of rhythm, diction or assonance, with the same content. The distance between 'lightward gliding' and 'scorrendo verso la luce' (*passing toward the light*) is great indeed.

> – You're the essence of vulgarity, she in gliding said.

> – Lei è la quintessenza della volgarità, disse scorrendo.

> – You are the quintessence of vulgarity, she said passing by.

The fun here is the superb and superbly hypocritical way Miss Douce dismisses the men in a comment that gains strength from being so immediately comprehensible in a generally difficult text, the distorted syntax of 'she in gliding said' then returning us to the poetic, or mock heroic, register. The only problem here is the difficulty in Italian of setting off the simplicity of the speech locution with the literary word order of the narrative.

> Boylan, eyed, eyed. Tossed to fat lips his chalice, drank off his tiny, chalice, sucking the last fat violet syrupy drops. He spellbound eyes went after her gliding head as it went down the bar by mirrors, gilded arch for ginger ale, hock and claret glasses shimmering, a spiky shell, where it concerted, mirrored, bronze with sunnier bronze.

> Boylan occhieggiava, occhieggiava. Riversò il calice accostato alle grosse labbra, scolò il suo picciol calice, sorbendo le ultime grosse gocce violette sciroppose. I suoi occhi ammaliati seguivano la testa scorrente per il bar lungo specchi, arco dorato per bicchieri da gazosa, vino del Reno e chiaretto baluginanti, una conchiglia spinosa, ove concertava, specchiava, bronzo con bronzo più solare.

> Boylan eyed, eyed. Poured his chalice pressed to fat lips, drained his little chalice, drinking up the last fat violet syrupy drops. His enchanted eyes followed the head passing down the bar along the mirrors, gilded arch for glimmering ginger ale Rhine wine and lighter red glasses, a spiky shell, now concerting, mirroring, bronze with sunnier bronze.

The back-translation is over-generous here: the game of putting together past participle and identical preterite ('eyed eyed') is something Joyce does frequently in *Ulysses* (a few pages further on we have 'Lydia, admired, admired'[22]). Clearly this is part of the general mining of words that share the same sound but have a different meaning ('hie', 'high', for example). It also suggests a mischievous complicity between man and woman which lies at the heart of the *sonnez la cloche* episode. So it is surprising that the Italian decides to interpret this with a simple repetition of the imperfect tense: 'Boylan occhieggiava occhieggiava' simply repeats the same past tense, as it were, Boylan looked, looked). 'Lydia admired, admired' is more understandably translated as 'Lydia ammirata, ammirava'[23] (*Lydia being admired admired in turn*). But in any event, the same effect is impossible in a language that does not offer the coincidence of identical past participle and preterite.

'Tossed to fat lips his chalice' involves the same mock heroic literary echoes found all over *Ulysses*; such extravagant diction is a staple of a certain kind of British bar talk (something Stephen and his friends constantly indulge in). The

---

[22] *Ulysses,* p. 275.
[23] *Ulisse,* p. 378.

Italian not only has difficulty in conveying this kind of diction, but given the absence of this sort of pub culture the effect is not perhaps the same. As for the rest of this paragraph, one can only marvel at the almost exasperated evocation involved in striving to create through language the spellbound effect that drink and Douce are having on Boylan. Deploying a combination of bizarre syntax and lush vocabulary that we will find in another great stylist, Henry Green, the sentence bewilders us as the mirrors and bottles and beautiful woman bewilder Boylan. Once again this is partly achieved by keeping the syntax in a state of potential rather than achieved definition. 'He spellbound eyes went' could mean 'He went with spellbound eyes', or 'He was spellbound and his eyes went'. The Italian, 'I suoi occhi ammaliati seguivano', *His enchanted eyes followed*), is perfectly defined and comprehensible.

The grammar of the English is again unclear in the last part of the sentence. '... gilded arch for ginger ale, hock and claret glasses shimmering, a spiky shell ...' suggests, at least to this English reader, that the gilded arch behind the bar contains ginger ale bottles (perhaps providing one of the two bronzes of 'bronze with sunnier bronze'), and hock and claret glasses which are shimmering. The Italian however suggests another reading, equally legitimate: '... arco dorato per bicchieri da gazosa, vino del Reno e chiaretto baluginanti...' (gilded arch for glimmering ginger ale Rhine wine and lighter red glasses, a spiky shell). One is suspicious of this reading, partly because it involves supposing a very unusual position for the participle 'shimmering', which we would expect to precede 'ginger ale' (though Joyce is capable of this and more), and partly because while one might speak of hock glasses or claret glasses, in the sense of something specifically used for those drinks, one does not speak of 'ginger ale glasses'.

But such distinctions are trivial and make little difference. The important thing to bear in mind is the effect of the English, the way it will not sit still but wriggles about in its mobile syntax. The verb 'concerted' caps this virtuosity, bringing together ideas of musical arrangement, framing and agreement (of Miss Douce with her reflected image). The Italian offers a reasonably effective cognate here, though the notion of framing is missing.

Finally, in the very last segment of the sentence, 'bronze with sunnier bronze', the Italian does achieve the same level of ambiguity as the English. What can it mean, 'concerted, mirrored, bronze with sunnier bronze' ('concertava, specchiava, bronzo con bronzo più solare' – *concerting, mirroring, bronze with sunnier bronze*)? Are we talking merely about the reflection of Miss Douce's red hair? Or are we talking about the way the bar mirror brings together, perhaps harmonizes, reflected ginger ale bottles (not in the Italian), which are bronze in colour, and the reflection of Miss Douce? In which case which is sunnier? Etc. Perhaps all we are really talking about is Joyce's attempt, as already suggested, to give a sense of Boylan's wonder, and to generate that wonder in ourselves. Certainly the clarity of the Italian (in general) takes off some of the dazzle that we feel when trying to look hard at the English.

So much for our comparison of translation and original. It might well be argued that it was unnecessary to analyse such a long passage to appreciate what is happening here. But in a book where abundance almost becomes the subject-matter, where the relentlessness of Joyce's strategy is of the essence, it seemed important to suggest the Herculean nature of the translator's task and, above all, the way the constant slippage between original and translation becomes a problem not just of quantity, but of quality.

What conclusions can be drawn? Slight differences in semantics occur either when the translator is inventing in order to stay close to the spirit of the original ('la sua rosa or saliente or ritrosa' – *her rose now rising now reluctant*), or when the English is generating a multiplicity of meanings that cannot be achieved in the same space in the Italian. It would be hard to say, however, that any of these changes in semantic content or losses of double meaning were important in terms of understanding what is going on, and in any event the translator manages some appropriate inventions not there in the English. Nor could we genuinely say that the translation loses a lyrical power aimed at intensifying our involvement in the narrative (as was the case with *The Dead* and *A Portrait)*. No, what is lost here, to a point but by no means entirely, is the reading experience itself, the fun being had with language, the suggestion of the arbitrary way words rub together to create meaning, the extent to which the text mixes an evocation of a dramatic scene with an evocation of ways of evoking that scene, of evoking bawdiness, evoking music, rhythm and so on.

Again it might be objected that although the Italian loses much it does manage to suggest this fun. Certainly we could hardly accuse Giulio de Angelis of not trying. All the same, you have to ask yourself: is this the way Italian plays? This invention of compound words, the deployment of bizarre and loose syntax, have a long tradition in English. Many other writers before and after have played the same games. This is not the case in Italian. There are no texts in Italian towards which *Ulysses* looks backwards or forwards (as might be the case with Lewis Carroll and Dylan Thomas, to name but two writers in English).

Joyce writes a text whose multi-layered quality becomes its own subject. On the grand scale there is the parallel with the *Odyssey*, on a small scale there are the many puns and ambiguities. In the case of the latter, the many layers of complexity are generated through all those occasions where the language suggests more than one meaning, or begs questions as to tone, register, attitude and so on. To this extent the text becomes radically dependent on the language in which it was written, the translation a heroic half measure, an exploration of the difference between the two languages. In a novel where the traditional narrative line is very much in the background while the language sparkles blindingly in the fore, a medium too bright to see through, reading the translation has the effect of putting on dark glasses. All is slightly clearer, slightly less exhilarating.

4. Translating the Smoke Words of *Mrs Dalloway*

The 1993 Feltrinelli edition of Virginia Woolf's *Mrs Dalloway* opens with an introduction by the translator.[1] Like Joyce, Virginia Woolf is seen as an important and difficult author, so it's understandable and appropriate that Feltrinelli should have chosen a well-known university professor to translate and introduce the book. What is less understandable is that the translator dedicates so little of her twenty-three-page introduction to a consideration of the language of the book, and none at all to the problems it poses for translation and the consequent status of the Italian text.

True, there are one or two quotes from Woolf's diary vis-à-vis her intentions language-wise. Then in a discussion of the book's handling of time the translator remarks that '...the whole system of tenses is rather inconsistent and confused. The present tense of the characters is given in the past, and as a result their past ought to be expressed with the past perfect, though this isn't the case; the tense remains the same, so that, from a formal point of view, the two tenses (the present and the past) are indistinguishable. What dominates is an imperfect tense, that above all conveys the non-closure of the energy of the novel's action' (p. xvii).

Such a remark, however intriguing, is hardly exhaustive and may generate legitimate uneasiness. For apart from the fact that any advanced student of English will be aware that the past perfect is not automatically applied to a time previous to the immediate narrative time (and indeed rarely used at all in the sort of spoken English on which Woolf's internal monologues so effectively draw), one wonders what the translator means here by the English 'imperfect' (any verb structure indicating repeated action? Or the use of continuous verb forms?). Interestingly, there is no comment on the fact that the extreme flexibility of the English past tense (the preterite) is supremely adapted to the generation of temporal confusion, a confusion that Italian, with its more precise distinctions between imperfect and past historic, will be obliged to resolve (ie. to interpret). Nor does the translator remark that this vocation for confusion, or apparent confusion, is by no means limited to the verb tenses.

---

[1] Virginia Woolf, *La Signora Dalloway*, Feltrinelli Editore, Milan, 1993. Translation and introduction by Nadia Fusini. All quotations in Italian taken from this edition. Page numbers of text and introduction are indicated in brackets at the end of each quotation.

Aside from this brief comment on the language, most of the introduction is dedicated to an analysis of the content of the novel and its two centres of emotion: Clarissa, all acceptance and openness; Septimus, all rejection and closure. These positive and negative poles are echoed, comments the translator, in an up and down rhythm throughout the text (the observation is well established), and, introducing a quotation from the first page of the book ('What a lark, what a plunge!'), she goes on to remark:

> 'up and down, repeatedly something climbs, rises, lifts itself up, (What a lark – *che spasso, che allegria, che euforia, che gioia!* [*fun, jollity, euphoria joy*]) and something falls, plunges (What a plunge – *che tuffo, che caduta, che tristezza, che terrore!* [*dive, fall, sadness, terror*]).' (p. xviii)

Turning to the translation itself, we find that the translator has translated that expression from the first page – 'What a lark! What a plunge!' – as 'Che gioia! Che terrore!' (*What joy! What terror!*)

I hope at this point that the purpose of this brief comment on the translator's introduction will become clear. In the translation we considered of *Women in Love* it was evident that many of the problems in the translation were the result of a lack of critical awareness of Lawrence's philosophies, his literary strategies. And this will be true of other translations we will consider, though it was decidedly not the case with the Italian version of *Ulysses.* Here, with Woolf, we have a translator who has engaged at a critical level with the text, and has formed a strong sense of the book's strategies. If there is a problem, then, it is not a lack of critical awareness, but a tendency to distort the text to fit the translator's interpretation. For only an act of radical interpretation backed up by an overall critical vision of the book could lead a translator to transform the innocent 'What a lark! What a plunge!' (and surely here the plunge is the lark and vice versa) into 'Che gioia! Che terrore!' What is more, such a translation actually eliminates the evocation of an up and down movement that the translator, in her introduction, had set out to comment upon. The metaphor is eliminated in favour of its presumed referent. But here is the famous first page.

> Mrs Dalloway said she would buy the flowers herself.
> For Lucy had her work cut out for her. The doors would be taken off their hinges; Rumpelmayer's men were coming. And then, thought Clarissa Dalloway, what a morning – fresh as if issued to children on a beach.

What a lark! What a plunge! For so it had always seemed to her when, with a little squeak of the hinges, which she could hear now, she had burst open the French windows and plunged at Bourton into the open air. How fresh, how calm, stiller than this of course, the air was in the early morning; like the flap of a wave; the kiss of a wave; chill and sharp and yet (for a girl of eighteen as she then was) solemn, feeling as she did, standing there at the open window, that something awful was about to happen; looking at the flowers, at the trees with the smoke winding off them and the rooks rising, falling; standing and looking until Peter Walsh said, 'Musing among the vegetables?' – was that it? – 'I prefer men to cauliflowers' – was that it? He must have said it at breakfast one morning when she had gone out on to the terrace – Peter Walsh. He would be back from India one of these days, June or July, she forgot which, for his letters were awfully dull; it was his sayings one remembered; his eyes, his pocket-knife, his smile, his grumpiness and, when millions of things had utterly vanished – how strange it was! – a few sayings like this about cabbages. (pp. 1-2) [2]

One of the advantages and pleasures of teaching young students is that they often remind you of how you first felt on reading a passage yourself. Here, the response of most foreign, and many English, students is one of bewilderment. The hinges have been taken off with a vengeance. 'What a plunge!'. In classrooms in Milan a reading of the Italian will often be required merely to establish more or less what has happened.

La signora Dalloway disse che i fiori li avrebbe comperati lei.
Quanto a Lucy aveva già il suo daffare. Si dovevano togliere le porte dai cardini; gli uomini di Rumpelmayer sarebbero arrivati tra poco. E poi, pensò Clarissa Dalloway, che mattina – fresca come se fosse stata appena creata per dei bambini su una spiaggia.
Che gioia! Che terrore! Sempre aveva avuto questa impressione, quando con un leggero cigolio dei cardini, lo stesso che sentì proprio ora, a Bourton spalancava le persiane e si tuffava nell'aria aperta. Com'era fresca, calma, più ferma di qui, naturalmente, l'aria la mattina presto, pareva il tocco di un'onda, il bacio di un'onda; fredda e pungente, e (per una diciottenne com'era lei allora) solenne, perché in piedi di fronte alla finestra aperta, lei aveva allora la sensazione che

---

[2] Virginia Woolf, *Mrs Dalloway,* Harcourt Brace Jovanovich, New York, 1953. All quotations from the English original are taken from this edition. Page numbers are indicated in brackets at the end of each quotation.

sarebbe successo qualcosa di tremendo, mentre continuava a fissare i fiori, e gli alberi che emergevano dalla nebbia che a cerchi si sollevava fra le cornacchie in volo. E stava lì e guardava, quando Peter Walsh disse: 'In meditazione tra le verze?' Disse così? O disse: 'Io preferisco gli uomini ai cavoli?' Doveva averlo detto a colazione una mattina che lei era uscita sul terrazzo – Peter Walsh. Stava per tornare dall'India, sì, uno di questi giorni, in giugno o a luglio forse, non ricordava bene, perché le sue lettere erano così noiose; ma certe sue espressioni rimanevano impresse, gli occhi, il temperino, il sorriso, quel suo modo di fare scontroso, e tra milioni di cose ormai del tutto svanite – com'era strano! – alcune espressioni, come questa dei cavoli. (p. 1)

Mrs Dalloway said she would buy the flowers herself.

As for Lucy she already had her work to do. The doors would have to be taken off their hinges; Rumpelmayer's men would arrive soon. And then, thought Clarissa Dalloway, what a morning – fresh as if it had just been created for children on a beach.

What joy! What terror! She had always had that impression, when with a light squeak of the hinges, the same that she heard right now, at Bourton she threw open the shutters and plunged into the open air. How fresh and calm it was, stiller than here, of course, the air in the early morning, it seemed the touch of a wave, the kiss of a wave; cold and sharp, and (for an eighteen-year-old as she then was) solemn, because standing in front of the open window, she had the sensation then that something awful would happen, as she went on gazing at the flowers, and the trees that emerged from the fog which lifted in circles among the rooks in flight. And she stood there and watched, when Peter Walsh said: "Meditating among the vegetables? Did he say that? Or he said: "I prefer men to cabbages?" He must have said it at breakfast one morning when she had gone out on the terrace – Peter Walsh. He was about to return from India, yes, one of these days, in June or July maybe, she couldn't rightly remember, because his letters were so boring; but some of his expressions had stayed with her, his eyes, his penknife, his smile, that argumentative manner of his, and among millions of things now entirely vanished – how strange it was! – some expressions, like this about the cabbages.

Woolf plunges us *in medias res*. She wants to remove doors and hinges, from standard narrative, from the syntax, and ultimately, as we shall see, from between people. But before jumping to too many conclusions, let us see what can be learnt from a comparison of translation and original.

The first thing to notice is that the book sets off very confidently in a simple past tense and there, frankly, it remains. To this extent it is entirely traditional and it is difficult to understand what the translator means in her introduction when she talks about the character's present being rendered in the past. In this opening section there are also four uses of the past perfect to signal switches back to previous time. Once signalled, the text then returns to the simple past. This is standard practice in English and presents no difficulty for the Italian, though two of those past perfects are translated, appropriately, with Italian imperfects since they refer to repeated action. But it is not in the verb tenses that the idiosyncrasies of Woolf's style lies, however complex the handling of time may be.

The first difference that one notices comes at the beginning of the second paragraph:

> Mrs Dalloway said she would buy the flowers herself.
> For Lucy had her work cut out for her.

> La Signora Dalloway disse che i fiori li avrebbe comperati lei.
> Quanto a Lucy aveva già il suo daffare.

> Mrs Dalloway said she would buy the flowers herself.
> As for Lucy she already had her work to do.

The English begins the second paragraph with the explanatory 'For'. Following a standard style, this would not require a new paragraph, and perhaps not even a new sentence. There is thus a strong sense of fragmentation. 'Quanto a' (*As for*) is not so obviously explanatory, thus not so obviously sheared away from its normal position in the same paragraph (imagine the paragraph beginning 'Dato che' – *given that*). This is not a criticism. 'Quanto a' (*as for*) seems an excellent solution. Yet one notes its difference from the more radical 'For'.

More generally, the second paragraph displays a slight tendency on the translator's part to introduce explanatory material: 'Si dovevano togliere le porte dai cardini' (*The doors would have to be taken off their hinges*) instead of the balder 'The doors would be taken off their hinges.' And then: 'gli uomini di Rumpelmayer sarebbero arrivati tra poco' (*Rumpelmayer's men would arrive soon*), for 'Rumpelmayer's men were coming'. There is nothing to object to here. It is normal practice in translation to look for the way something 'would be said' in one's own language. The process often involves the introduction or omission of small pieces of information of the 'tra poco' (*soon/in a short while*) variety, perhaps in order to establish a desired rhythm. However, we may note that the balder English more strongly foregrounds the symbolic gesture of the removal of the doors, while the lack of precise information helps to give the impression of a mind (Mrs Dalloway's) at work on its own, rather than a narrator attentive to the reader's need for information.

Now comes the first real problem: 'And then, thought Clarissa Dalloway, what a morning – fresh as if issued to children on a beach.'

Italian students invited to translate this paragraph invariably feel they need help, they need to be told *what it means*. What is it that is issued (given out, distributed?) to children on beaches that establishes such a high standard of freshness? Or is everything issued to children on beaches necessarily impeccably fresh? Or does the sentence mean: only children on a beach could have inspired the 'issuing' of a morning of such freshness? In which case, who can be spoken of as doing the issuing (especially given that both Woolf and Mrs Dalloway are declared agnostics, if not atheists)?

The Feltrinelli translation clears the mystery up a little:

> E poi, pensò Clarissa Dalloway, che mattina – fresca come se fosse stata appena creata per dei bambini su una spiaggia.

> And then, thought Clarissa Dalloway, what a morning – fresh as if it had just been created for children on a beach.

As with 'tra poco' (*soon*) in the previous sentence, the translator has now introduced 'appena' (*just*) pinning down the time she referred to in her introduction as deliberately vague, but more crucially she has decided to translate 'issued to' as 'created for' thus making the sentence at once more easily comprehensible while at the same time conferring upon it fairly orthodox religious implications ('rilasciata a' – *issued/distributed/given out to* – would have been the semantically exact, though hardly felicitous, translation of 'issued to'). Here, in the Italian, it seems that a generous deity makes the freshest mornings for children on a beach. This, like the question of opening the second paragraph with 'For', is something we shall have to return to.

The most glaring difference between the two texts comes in the already discussed opening line of the third paragraph. But seeing it in context now, one is bound to appreciate that with the fresh morning and the attractive image of children on a beach, the expression 'What a lark! What a plunge!' necessarily comes over as *wholly positive* in the English. It is the exhilarating plunge of those children into the sea, of the younger Clarissa leaving the French windows for the garden at Bourton, of the older Clarissa setting out into the bustle of Westminster, of Woolf herself embarking on her new narrative, her new style. Only later will it become clear that the loss of self involved in plunging into the outside world may also be awesome, awful, dangerous, so that the word 'plunge' will be used again when Septimus Warren Smith leaps from a window to his death. By going directly for the possible emotions underlying the English words and translating with 'Che gioia! Che terrore!' (What joy! What terror!) the translation rather jumps the gun here and does not allow the reader to savour the slow accumulation of positive and negative connotations around 'plunge'. A less interpretative translation, a translation less aware of the later suicide, or, better still, more aware of how delicately Woolf will be setting up the pattern of images that links that suicide to Clarissa, might have been satisfied with a translation such as 'Che spasso! Che tuffo!' (What fun! What a dive!), which would be more in line both with Clarissa's mood and those children on their beach.

Before comparing the English and Italian of the third paragraph, it is worth making the general comment that it is here that the text suddenly becomes complex and, at first glance, confusing. Following the apparently unnecessary paragraph break after the first sentence (itself of exemplary brevity and simplicity), then the short second paragraph explaining the decision of the first, we now have something long, intricate, meandering, fifteen lines that take us back and forth across thirty and more years, mixing dialogue, description, exclamations, questions. And the confusion, as we shall see, is not generated by any vagueness with the tenses, which do all the work they can, but by the stretched and convoluted syntax which strains to keep up with, or rather, is there to represent, the rapid series of associations (some occurring within others) which are Clarissa's thoughts as she physically walks out of her front door and mentally goes back to her adolescence when she went out of a different door and spoke with a man who may or may not be about to return.

Beginning as it does with 'What a lark! What a plunge!' the rest of the paragraph is presented as an *explanation* of that exclamation. For we have a 'For' again. One might have imagined that the exclamation was inspired by the idea of children leaping into the sea, and perhaps it was, but now Clarissa decides to explain it in terms of the excitement, at different moments in her life, of going out through a door on a fresh morning. Looking at the Italian translation of the second sentence, one notices that the 'For' is again omitted, that once again time has been foregrounded ('proprio ora' – *right now*), as it is not in the English, that the adverbial expression of place ('at Bourton') has been moved, that 'French windows' has been translated as 'persiane' (*shutters*) and that the verb 'tuffare' (*dive*) now appears for the first time:

For so it had always seemed to her when, with a little squeak of the hinges, which she could hear now, she had burst open the French windows and plunged at Bourton into the open air.

Sempre aveva avuto questa impressione, quando con un leggero cigolio dei cardini, lo stesso che sentì proprio ora, a Bourton spalancava le persiane e si tuffava nell'aria aperta.

She had always had that impression, when with a light squeak of the hinges, the same that she heard right now, at Bourton she threw open the shutters and plunged into the open air.

Clearly the translator decides to introduce the 'proprio ora' (*right now*) to draw the reader's attention more determinedly to Clarissa's exit from her Westminster home (which is indeed almost lost in the English). Likewise the moving forward of 'at Bourton' may help the reader to orientate himself more quickly, to appreciate that the French windows were not opened here, where Clarissa lives now, but somewhere else. Certainly in the English the position of 'at Bourton' between verb and indirect object – 'and plunged at Bourton into the open air') – is unusual. One might normally have expected: 'she had burst open the French windows at Bourton and plunged into the open air'. Writing it in this more standard fashion, however, makes us aware of how much more dramatic and teasing Woolf's version is in having us wait that moment longer to find what exactly was plunged into and where. Perhaps because the word 'plunge' originally appeared immediately after 'beach', its repetition here half leads us to expect that it might be the sea Clarissa leapt into. Or perhaps a pool, or a street. It is the nothingness of 'open air' that surprises us ('plunged at Bourton into the open air'). Since the Italian did not use 'plunge' (*tufo*) in close association with the children and the sea, so that its use here is not a repetition, the game of association is lost. In any event, we must also remember that since the reader does not know where Bourton is, or was, or what it has to do with Clarissa, the sentence is anyway disorientating. It lacks the explanation 'her childhood home', 'her country home' which would put us at our ease. The passage is intended to be disorientating. It is a lark, a plunge. The attempts, on the translator's part, to make the text more accessible are not in line with its general drift.

What is truly curious, though, is the decision to translate 'French windows' as 'persiane' (*shutters*). The 'French window' is a 'portafinestra' (literally, *doorwindow*), whereas 'persiane' refers to a kind of shutter that has slats to let the light through, something extremely unusual in England. Using 'persiane'

seems to break the link between the doors Rumpelmayer's men will be taking away, the French windows and the door Clarissa is opening to go out into
Westminster to buy the flowers. What possible reason could there be for using
the word 'persiane' then, especially when 'portafinestra' seems so admirably
suited to linking the idea of doors and windows? Does the translator feel that
the 'foreignness' of 'French' in 'French windows' is important (in the sense
that Clarissa is plunging into otherness) and can somehow be evoked through
the etymology of 'persiane'? The explanation is far-fetched, I am afraid. More
likely what we have here is a banal mistake. In which case the interesting
thing to observe is the difference between elements which are deliberately
disorientating (Woolf's associations and syntax), but which ultimately, as we
proceed with the book, will make sense, and an element such as this which is
accidentally disorientating and can never make any sense.

The next sentence is the longest and most meandering and above all contains a couple of images which, like 'fresh as if issued to children on a beach',
are difficult to pin down. The work of the translator is admirable here, and
yet... one notices the absence of an 'and yet'. As follows:

> How fresh, how calm, stiller than this of course, the air was in the
> early morning; like the flap of a wave; the kiss of a wave; chill and
> sharp and yet (for a girl of eighteen as she then was) solemn, feeling
> as she did, standing there at the open window, that something awful
> was about to happen; looking at the flowers, at the trees with the smoke
> winding off them and the rooks rising, falling; standing and looking
> until Peter Walsh said, 'Musing among the vegetables?' – was that it?
> – 'I prefer men to cauliflowers' – was that it?

> Com'era fresca, calma, più ferma di qui, naturalmente, l'aria la
> mattina presto, pareva il tocco di un'onda, il bacio di un'onda; fredda
> e pungente, e (per una diciottenne com'era lei allora) solenne, perché
> in piedi di fronte alla finestra aperta, lei aveva allora la sensazione che
> sarebbe successo qualcosa di tremendo, mentre continuava a fissare i
> fiori, e gli alberi che emergevano dalla nebbia che a cerchi si sollevava
> fra le cornacchie in volo. E stava lì e guardava, quando Peter Walsh
> disse: 'In meditazione tra le verze?' Disse così? O disse: 'Io preferisco
> gli uomini ai cavoli?'

> How fresh and calm it was, stiller than here, of course, the air in the
> early morning, it seemed the touch of a wave, the kiss of a wave; cold
> and sharp, and (for an eighteen-year-old as she then was) solemn,

because standing in front of the open window, she had the sensation
then that something awful would happen, as she went on gazing at the
flowers, and the trees that emerged from the fog which lifted in circles
among the rooks in flight. And she stood there and watched, when Peter
Walsh said: "Meditating among the vegetables? Did he say that? Or
he said: "I prefer men to cabbages?"

The translator efficiently resolves the problem of 'stiller than this' with the
slightly more explanatory 'più ferma di qui' (*stiller than here*), then cleverly
introduces 'pareva' (*it seemed*) where another 'come' (*like*) might appear to
be introducing a further exclamation ('Com'era fresca' – *how fresh it was* –;
'come' can mean both the exclamatory 'how' and the comparative 'like'). But
now one runs up against the problem of the onomatopoeia in 'the flap of a
wave; the kiss of a wave', reminding us again of those children on the beach
and thus increasing the text's inner unity. What the exact sense of 'flap' might
be here it is difficult to decide. Does it refer to sound or movement, or both,
or is it there to contrast with the hiss and caress of 'kiss', the wave quietly
breaking – flap – and then retreating – kiss (but kisses are not a retreat)?

   In any event one can only feel that the translator does well in her choice of
'tocco' (*touch*) and 'bacio' (*kiss*), though perhaps 'schiocco' (smack) would
have provided a harder sound against which to set off the anyway frequently
collocated 'bacio' (*kiss*). The translation is likewise to be admired in the earlier
part of the sentence for managing to follow fairly closely the syntax of the
original which is so important for suggesting the chain of association. But
every student will notice that the translator eliminates that 'yet'.

   chill and sharp and yet (   ) solemn

   fredda e pungente, e (   ) solenne

   cold and sharp, and (   ) solemn

The two interesting aspects of Woolf's original are, first: how the 'yet' followed by the parenthesis creates expectation (and yet what? in what way
contrasting to 'chill and sharp'?) and second, that when we arrive at 'solemn'
we are not quite sure that it does indeed offer any contrast. 'Bright and merry,
and yet solemn' would not surprise us. The contrast is clear. Likewise 'chill
and sharp and yet merry' would be perfectly understandable. But in what
way can 'solemn' be said to stand in contrast to 'chill and sharp'? Is this why
the translator eliminates the 'yet', as she previously tried to make one or two

questions of time and place clearer? This is something which, again, we shall have to return to.

The next part of the sentence demands some syntactical rearrangement in the Italian. The explanatory element in 'feeling as she did' is simply resolved with the introduction of 'perché' (*because... she had the sensation*), but this then creates complications when the English follows with three verbs in apposition to 'feeling': 'looking' and 'standing and looking' with the result that here, at last, the Italian syntax diverges significantly ('mentre continuava a fissare' – as *she went on gazing*) and ultimately breaks the sentence in two, just before the 'until Peter Walsh' that, in the English, interrupts the long tension of the repeated present participles ('feeling ... looking ... standing and looking until Peter Walsh...'), a tension increased by the fact that what Clarissa looks at (the smoke, the rooks) likewise generates three participles ('winding', 'rising' and 'falling'). The problem here is that, in losing the list of verbs followed by 'until', the Italian also loses the sense of Peter Walsh's breaking the intensifying spell of those participles, the sense of Peter Walsh perhaps being the 'something awful' that was 'about to happen'. Let us read it again:

> feeling as she did, standing there at the open window, that something awful was about to happen; looking at the flowers, at the trees with the smoke winding off them and the rooks rising, falling; standing and looking until Peter Walsh said...

Such an interpretation may seem far-fetched, but its latency will be confirmed as again and again the book presents one person's interruption into another's chain of thought as something disquieting and destructive, and most destructive of all is Peter Walsh, who, with his sarcasm and his pocket-knife, has a tendency of barging into other people's bedrooms, and relationships, and interrupting them. Watch, in the back-translation from the Italian, how the effect of growing suspense broken by Peter Walsh's intervention disappears:

> because standing in front of the open window, she had the sensation then that something awful would happen, as she went on gazing at the flowers, and the trees that emerged from the fog which lifted in circles among the rooks in flight. And she stood there and watched, when Peter Walsh said

Such subtleties, however, one becomes aware of only with a thorough knowledge of the book. What is more obvious on making a first comparison between the English and Italian is the difficulty of dealing with these images of smoke and rooks:

> looking at the flowers, at the trees with the smoke winding off them
> and the rooks rising, falling

The Italian version draws our attention to the fact that it is not easy to understand exactly what Woolf means here.

> mentre continuava a fissare i fiori, e gli alberi che emergevano dalla
> nebbia che a cerchi si sollevava fra le cornacchie in volo

> as she went on gazing at the flowers, and the trees that emerged from
> the fog which lifted in circles among the rooks in flight

The focusing is shifted by the introduction of the strong 'fissare' (*gaze*) and the sentence is italianized, as it were, by the decision to use the relative pronoun 'che' (*that*) after 'alberi' (*trees*) rather than 'con' (*with* – as in, 'trees with the smoke winding off them'), thus necessitating the introduction of a superfluous verb 'emergevano' (*emerged*). Basically, rather than a series of substantives tenuously linked with a 'with' and an 'and', we have a more elaborately articulated sentence where the relationship between the substantives is clarified (indeed, as far as the rooks and the smoke are concerned, invented).

The Italian version thus generates a greater sense of control, departing from the fragmentation of the English. But most noticeably of all, 'smoke' has been explained as 'nebbia' (fog) while that strange image 'winding off' has been made a little easier to understand with 'a cerchi si sollevava' (lifted in circles) even though this eliminates the fog's exact relationship with the trees (that of slowly revealing them).

But does fog in fact rise 'a cerchi' (*in circles*)? One has to say no, it does not. It melts. Smoke, on the other hand, is famous for 'wreathing' or 'spiralling', and yet one cannot help feeling it unlikely that there would be fires beneath the trees. The image remains impenetrable in the English (an impenetrability that goes hand in hand with the groping, meandering syntax), rather less so in the Italian.

Then at the tail end of the phrase, the rising and falling motion, so frequently referred to by the book's commentators (including the translator in her introduction), is eliminated in the translation as the rooks proceed steadily 'in volo' (*in flight*) through what is now an entirely standard (but certainly attractive) Italian sentence structure.

The last part of the paragraph presents perhaps only one major problem: 'Musing among the vegetables?'. The difficulty here lies in the range of connotation presented by 'musing'. The busy, invasive, if inconclusive, Peter

Walsh no doubt means to accuse Clarissa of being 'absent-minded' among the vegetables. He is being sarcastic. He likes to attack women for the frivolousness of their activities. In short, he is interrupting her, as he will later interrupt her in her house, walking straight up to her bedroom, not respecting her space. But one cannot help sensing the possibility, through the etymology of 'muse', of some hint of creativity, of Clarissa's, and Woolf's, *poeticizing* among the vegetables (as indeed Woolf does so often and so well). In which case Peter Walsh becomes a kind of 'man from Porlock' interrupting Clarissa's creativity (certainly much of *Mrs Dalloway* revolves around the question of how much value is to be attached to Clarissa's musings). In any event, there is little a translation can do to maintain this ambiguity here since there is no Italian word that carries the connotations of 'muse' in its verb form. More interesting is the translator's decision to clear up the anomaly 'cauliflowers', 'cabbages'. In the English we have first, 'I prefer men to cauliflowers', but then later, 'a few sayings like this about cabbages'. The Italian chooses a cabbage diet for both.

So much for a fairly close analysis (though all kinds of other things might have been noticed, for example, the change in focusing from 'it was his sayings one remembered' to 'ma certe sue espressioni rimanevano impresse' (*but some of his expressions had remained impressed*); or indeed the difficulty of translating 'sayings', or 'grumpiness', etc.). The question is, can we now use the divergences between the Italian and English texts to get some sense of what Woolf is up to? Can we put things together?

Summarizing the differences in the Italian, we have:

- the elimination of conjunctions perhaps felt to be unnecessary or misleading or merely out of place in Italian (the explanatory 'for' twice, the contrasting 'yet' once);
- a tendency to make difficult images a little clearer;
- a tendency to shift the syntax, or introduce elements, again in aid of clarity (the placing of 'a Bourton', the introduction of adverbs of time);
- a tendency to interpret what is vague ('Che gioia! Che terrore!' – *What joy! What terror!*);
- a difficulty (inevitably) with Woolf's frequent use of present participles and the tension they generate.

In general, then, we can say that Woolf's text presents problems for the translator when it seems deliberately 'muddled'. Even the question of 'cauliflowers' and 'cabbages' may be taken as an example. How much should the translator clear up? Let us return to the question of those two 'for's.

In the opening pages of *Mrs Dalloway* four of ten paragraphs will begin with the same explanatory 'For'?[3] As suggested earlier, one might choose to call this fragmentary, in the sense that it splits off something that could have remained in the previous paragraph. But one might equally say that this use of an explanatory conjunction to open a paragraph creates a very strong connection with the previous paragraph. This is particularly and perplexingly the case in places where it is not clear that an explanatory 'for' is justified, in the sense that what follows in the new paragraph cannot easily be understood as an explanation of what preceded. This was true to a certain extent of the 'For so it had always seemed to her ...' in the second sentence of the third paragraph, but even more in the passage from the third to the fourth paragraph, thus:

> She stiffened a little on the kerb, waiting for Durtnall's van to pass. A charming woman, Scrope Purvis thought her ... There she perched, never seeing him, waiting to cross, very upright.
> For having lived in Westminster – how many years now? over twenty – one feels ... a particular hush ... before Big Ben strikes.

Here Clarissa stopped by the kerb, it seemed, to let a van pass, not because she felt any particular hush (an unlikely feeling as a van passes). What then is her feeling of that hush supposed to be explaining? Why this gesture of logical connection with the previous passage, this 'For', if there is no connection? Is it that, while generating a sense of fragmentation by breaking a paragraph around an explanatory 'For', Woolf, precisely in then making the 'For' inexplicable from a logical point of view, also generates a second impression of the interconnection of *everything* (or at least in Clarissa's mind)? Certainly this would put Woolf in line with so much of the modernist adventure for which the process of dismantling in order to reassemble was always a favourite strategy, most emblematically in cubism.

In any event, of these four paragraphs beginning with 'For' in the opening pages, the Italian translates only one with an explanatory conjunction (not the one quoted above, which is simply ignored.[4] Again, this is not meant as a

---

[3] *Mrs Dalloway*, cit., pp. 3, 4, 5 and 9.

[4] 'Si irrigidì appena sul marciapiede, aspettando che passasse il furgone di Durtnall. Una donna affascinante, pensò di lei Scrope Purvis ... Se ne stava posata lì, senza neppure vederlo, in attesa di attraversare la strada, ben diritta.

Quando si vive a Westminster – da quanti anni ormai? più di venti ... prima dei rintocchi del Big Ben si sentiva un silenzio particolare.' (2)

Back-translation:

She stiffened a little on the pavement, waiting for Durtnall's van to pass. A charming woman,

criticism. It may be that the translator feels that there are genuine problems with starting certain paragraphs with 'perché' (*because*) though she does occasionally do so. But the important thing is that this divergence between the texts alerts us to a strategy Woolf has. Further attention to paragraph openings throughout the book shows many of them beginning with an explanatory 'So' or a conjunction 'And'. Again a number of these are not obviously explanatory of what has come before, or do not clearly follow on from it. So we are bound to conclude that while there seems to be unnecessary fragmentation at the syntactical level (i.e. there is no need for the new paragraph) there is a wilful rejection of fragmentation and even normal distinction at the semantic level (things are presented as explanations when they are not), and above all a sense of disjunction between the two levels (of syntax and semantics). It is as if Rumpelmayer's men (what a wonderfully invasive name Rumpelmayer is, a huge German crowbar jammed between the hinges of English prosody) had not just taken the doors away, but lifted semantics off their syntactical hinges too. In many of these places the translation follows the English without any effort at all. In others, it ignores the possibly anomalous conjunction or explanatory word.

In so far, then, as the use of 'for' and 'yet' can generate senses both of confusion and interconnection (indeed con-fusion *is* interconnection), one can now begin to see some similarity between this and the translator's other major problem in the opening page: those elusive (confusing?) images that Woolf uses to describe the morning, starting with 'fresh as if issued to children on a beach'.

Like the kind of clauses that traditionally follow an explanatory 'for' or an 'and yet', we expect the image that follows an 'as if' to have clarificatory powers. We will be told something more about this fresh morning. But here instead the image offers a combination of evocation and mystification, not clarification at all. Semantically, the expression is mystifying, particularly the use of the verb 'issued' (can anybody think of some extraordinarily fresh thing which is regularly issued/given out to children on beaches?); in terms of evocation the expression brings in the picture of 'children on a beach' and so establishes the way the fresh morning encourages Clarissa to look back to her childhood and adolescence. These are the hinges, not of traditional novels, or traditional houses, but of the mind or, more specifically, of the stream of

---

Scrope Purvis thought of her … She stood still there, without even seeing him, waiting to cross the road, very upright.

When one lives in Westminster – for how many years now? more than twenty … before the chimes of Big Ben you heard a particular silence.

consciousness as perceived by the modernists.

Later, when we arrive at the image of 'the trees with the smoke winding off them' we are bound to appreciate that, for all its fanfare of breaking down barriers, there is something hermetic about this approach. We shall never know exactly what Woolf meant by those words. And hermeticism is notoriously difficult to translate, offering as it does, to reader and translator, only a shell of someone else's jealously guarded meaning (in that sense hermeticism confers upon the stream of consciousness a certain authenticity, if only by giving us the feeling that having penetrated another's thoughts does not guarantee that we will understand them).

But let us return to 'issued' or 'issue'. The dictionary gives the most basic sense as 'a going or flowing out' or, as a verb, 'to come out, to proceed, as from a source'.[5] The word occurs a number of times in *Mrs Dalloway* and is used to refer to life gushing forth in its most basic and, above all, undefined form. Leaving Clarissa's house later in the day, Peter Walsh's train of thought will be interrupted by a sound:

> a frail quivering sound, a voice bubbling up without direction, vigour, beginning or end, running weakly and shrilly and with an absence of all human meaning into
> ee um fah um so
> foo swee too eem oo
> the voice of no age or sex, the voice of an ancient spring spouting from the earth; which issued, just opposite Regent's Park Tube Station, from a tall quivering shape, like a funnel, like a rusty pump, like a wind-beaten tree. (p. 122)

Just as *Mrs Dalloway* frequently gives us images of up and down movements, so it swings from greater to lesser coherence, or definition, and back. At the most incoherent ('ee um fah um so'), the most undefined (notice the series of different, surely incompatible, images to describe the old woman), lies the most vital, that which issues or is issued (translated 'veniva' – *came* – in the Italian here), and it is this vitality that the novel seeks to unleash, or draw on, when it blurs definition. This prompts the consideration that incoherence or loss of definition in Woolf has a coherent and definite purpose, is of a certain kind, forms part of a strategy, and that it usually occurs when the language is at its most vital and poetic. This is what happens in an image like 'looking ... at the trees with the smoke winding off them'. We sense the evocative power

---

[5] *Chambers English Dictionary,* Cambridge University Press, 1988.

of this image perhaps above all in its elusiveness, its evasion of exact definition, the mind struggling to grasp the world, to come to terms (in the literal
sense of the expression) with what it sees and feels.

Like the verb 'issue' the word 'smoke' returns frequently in *Mrs Dalloway*.
Smoke is something that blurs, and in doing so unites. When it retreats, definition emerges. Woolf clinches the relationship between smoke and the vitality
of that which issues without definition in the last sentence of her description
of the old woman's timeless, incomprehensible song.

> Cheerfully, almost gaily, the invincible thread of sound wound up
> into the air like the smoke from a cottage chimney, winding up clean
> beech trees and issuing in a tuft of blue smoke among the topmost
> leaves. (p. 125)

The appearance, indeed repetition, of the verb 'wind' should come as no surprise. Not only is it traditionally collocated with smoke, but frequently used
in *Mrs Dalloway* to refer to the process of losing or regaining definition. Here
are a few lines from earlier on in the book:

> And everywhere, though it was still so early, there was a beating, a
> stirring of galloping ponies, tapping of cricket bats; Lords, Ascot,
> Ranelagh and all the rest of it; wrapped in the soft mesh of the grey-
> blue morning air, which, as the day wore on, would unwind them,
> and set down on their lawns and pitches the bouncing ponies, whose
> forefeet just struck the ground and up they sprung, the whirling young
> men, and ... (p. 6)

The translation of the first of these two pieces is as follows:

> Allegro, quasi gioioso, il filo invincibile del suono si avvolgeva nel-
> l'aria come il fumo che esce dal comignolo, e s'avvolge intorno ai
> faggi sottili e s'arriccia in un ciuffo di fumo azzurrognolo tra le foglie
> più alte. (p. 73)

> Cheerful, almost joyous, the invincible thread of sound wound itself
> in the air like smoke that comes out of the chimney, and winds itself
> round the slender beeches and curls in a tuft of bluish smoke among
> the higher leaves.

The translator introduces the word 'gioioso' (*joyous*) picking up the word
'gioia' (*joy*) which she has frequently used and indeed used to translate 'lark' on

the first page. This helps to give a cohesion similar to that of Woolf's text, even if the meaning shifts slightly. She also faithfully keeps 'avvolgeva' (*wound*) though she has been obliged to lose this before in places where it was used in the negative form 'unwind' or 'wind off'. The continuity of 'issued', however, is quite lost, this sense of what is most vital emerging in an indefinite form to then drift away and reveal a more defined territory as it does so. Instead of looking for some alternative, the Italian prettifies with 's'arriccia in un ciuffo di fumo bluastro' (*curls in a tuft of bluish smoke*).

But perhaps the most intriguing loss comes with the translation of the word 'clean,' to describe the beech trees, as 'sottili' (*thin/slender*). Once one has appreciated the book's fascination with definition and blurring, its use of smoke as an image of that which blurs and is vital, or at least part of a vital process, then its picture of the 'clean' trees begins to make sense. 'Clean' partly refers to the smoothness of beech bark and partly to the tree's definition, its starkness before, and after, being wrapped, blurred, in smoke. It also offers an attractive monosyllabic assonance ('clean beech trees'). The Italian 'faggi sottili' (*slender beeches*) loses all this. As it likewise loses, in the second passage quoted here, both the use of 'unwind' and the introduction of an upward movement ('and up they sprung'):

> E dovunque, anche se era ancora presto, si sentiva nell'aria il fremito, lo slancio dei puledri al galoppo, il battere delle mazze da cricket; Lords, Ascot, Ranelagh e tutti gli altri campi, avvolti nella soffice garza dell'aria del mattino grigio azzurra, che, col procedere del giorno, si sarebbe diradata, scatenando per prati e declivi i puledri vigorosi che, sfiorando appena il terreno con gli zoccoli, facevano grandi balzi, giovani uomini volteggianti ... (p. 3)

> And everywhere, even though it was still early, one heard in the air the frenzy, the lunge of galloping foals, the bang of cricket bats; Lords, Ascot, Ranelagh and all the other fields, wrapped in the soft gauze of the grey blue morning air, that, as the day went on, would thin, unleashing across fields and slopes the vigorous foals that, hardly touching the ground with their hooves, made great leaps, young men whirling

The English gives: 'wrapped in the soft mesh of the grey-blue morning air, which, as the day wore on, would unwind them'. Here it is the indefinite, that which was issued, whether to children on a beach or from the mouth of the old woman, that 'unwinds' the world of definition and multiplicity, gives birth to it (as the smoke 'winds off' the trees of the first page). This relationship is lost in 'sarebbe diradata' (*would thin*). Then this move towards definition is always accompanied by an upward motion (here 'up they sprung', elsewhere, Clarissa returning upstairs to her bedroom and herself, or standing 'very upright' by the kerb), while the opposite move, away from definition, is downward, a plunge, into the open air at Burton, into the street in London.

Definition, indefinition. *Mrs Dalloway* tells the story of a woman who moves back and forth with great assurance, if not always without pain, between the retreat into self and the giving of self, its dispersion in the other (her walk through the streets, her party, which is 'an offering'). Life is understood, relationships are presented, in terms of the negotiation, happy or otherwise, of self and other, the limitation of self ('the narrow bed') and the euphoria of extension of self in some transcendental flux ('somehow in the streets of London, on the ebb and flow of things, here, there, she survived' – p. 12).

The great drama of Clarissa's youth was the need to reject a suitor who, forever toying with the pocket-knife of dissection, would have required too much of her, demanded the total plunge, the total surrender of self to his projects. Blander, the husband she chose understands better the back and forth of identity, the need for space. All the other characters in the book establish their qualities (the variety is infinitely nuanced) in relation to defence of self, surrender of self, respect of self in others. Notably, creativity is the key to a successful merging of self and other ('making it up, building it round one, tumbling it, creating it every moment afresh' – p. 5). One does things, whether manually or mentally, with the world and the people one finds around one and this involves a negotiation of self and other. Thus Clarissa's party. Thus the hat making of Septimus's wife Lucrezia ('She built it up; first one thing, then another, she built it up, sewing' – p. 221). At the opposite extreme to Clarissa, Septimus has lost the ability to negotiate the two extremes of self and other. He is either entirely imposing or completely overwhelmed, in a state of beatitude (everything is as he imagines) or of horror (everything is against him).

Stepping back for a moment from the specific problems of syntax and semantics, we can say that the translator's overall task in *Mrs Dalloway* is first to signal that pattern of images which Woolf offers, quite consciously it seems, as a key to reading the book, then second, and this is far more challenging, to shadow the exact level of definition, if we can call it that, of the English, to reproduce coherence or creative incoherence in the translation, since the back and forth of Woolf's English between extreme simplicity and bewildering, lyrical complexity offers a stylistic presentation of the characters' swinging back and forth between the limitations of self and the dangerous exhilaration of merging with the other.

Looked at in this light, the paragraphing of the first page, for example, becomes entirely understandable: first the declaration of Clarissa's selfhood in a single line paragraph (one way or another this occurs on a number of occasions throughout the book), next a brief explanatory turn of the hinge in the second, then the plunge into otherness in a long paragraph of rapidly increasing complication and difficulty, until, with the interruption of both Peter Walsh and Durtnall's van, Clarissa 'stiffens a little' in the shorter fourth paragraph, to then stand 'very upright' by the kerb. Following this hypothesis, one appreciates the difficulties of the translation as it loses one or two images that will be important throughout the book ('issue', 'smoke', 'rising and falling'), and struggles most of all with the challenge of achieving the creative blurring of such things as 'the trees with the smoke winding off them'.

In the previous chapters on Lawrence and Joyce, we noted the didactic strain behind the stylistic strategies of the first, the mania for evocation, for language as a vehicle of evocation, in those of the second. Loss in translation was a loss of philosophical complexity in Lawrence. Loss with Joyce was much more to do with a loss of reading experience, a loss of intimate apprehension (though I am aware that these two aspects might, at a certain level, be made to meet).

One is struck, however, reading Woolf in English and Italian by her greater integration of these two aspects. In so many ways *Mrs Dalloway* seems a meticulously planned and deliberate book, which, as it seeks to establish the nature of self and other, also delineates, in a very traditional moral sense, its heroes and villains (most notably the invasive Dr Holmes), and thus comes close to *prescribing* something like proper behaviour. At this self-conscious, planned and, ironically, very logical and coherent level, it is a book that is constantly generating images of itself (the aeroplane that produces smoke letters that appear only to disappear,[6] the thread that runs through London connecting everybody with everybody else,[7] etc.).

Yet in its attempt to present the mind in creative operation, and above all a community of minds, a sense of individuals blurring into groups, indeed into the natural world, it is also a book that is intensely engaged in evocation, both of mental processes and the phenomena they elaborate, and again a book which must appear to be open to the random, to incident, to the inexplicable, since successful engagement with every form of contingency (the other) requires such openness. If it failed to achieve this, it would come across as too calculating, too similar to those villains, the doctors Holmes and Bradshaw. In short, even in the structure of the book as a whole, we return to the question of

---

[6] On pp. 29-42.
[7] Thread image is repeated throughout *Mrs Dalloway.* See, for example, p. 170.

definition, non-definition. Almost every time the Italian translation diverges from the original in some significant regard, it does so at the expense of this theme.

Consider the following four examples, which, in another text, might be considered mere mistakes. Here we have Lucrezia trying to penetrate her husband Septimus's hermeticism:

> 'Look,' she repeated.
> Look, the unseen bade him, the voice which now communicated with him who was the greatest of mankind, Septimus, lately taken from life to death, the Lord who had come to renew society, who lay like a coverlet, a snow blanket smitten only by the sun, for ever unwasted, suffering for ever, the scapegoat, the eternal sufferer, but he did not want it, he moaned, putting from him with a wave of his hand that eternal suffering, that eternal loneliness. (p. 37)

We have commented on the creative non-sequiturs of the novel's narrative voice, but these reach their extreme in Septimus, who is not so much making up reality, building it up from the phenomena round about, like Clarissa or Lucrezia, but entirely out of touch with it, generating a vision (here virgin snow) that the slightest incursion from the outside world must destroy. Hence he is the most susceptible of all characters to interruptions. The Italian is as follows:

> 'Guarda,' ripeté.
> Guarda l'invisibile gli ordinò la voce che comunicava con lui, che era il più grande degli uomini, Septimus, appena tornato in vita dalla morte, il Signore che avrebbe cambiato il mondo, e ora giaceva come una coperta a fiori, una coperta di neve battuta dal sole, per sempre integro, per sempre sofferente, il capro espiatorio, l'eterno sofferente; ma no, non voleva, si lamentò, scostando da sé con un cenno della mano quella sofferenza eterna, quella eterna solitudine. (p. 22)

> 'Look,' she repeated.
> Look at the invisible ordered the voice that communicated with him, who was the greatest of men, Septimus, just returned to life from death, the Lord who would change the world, and now lay like a floral blanket, a blanket of snow beaten by the sun, for ever whole, for ever suffering, the scapegoat, the eternal sufferer; but no, he didn't want that, he complained, pushing away from himself with a wave of the hand that eternal suffering, that eternal solitude.

Of course one might object that when one approaches the area of total incomprehensibility, one incomprehensibility is no better or worse than another. All the same the latitude, the laxity, the freedom of interpretation is surprising here. If nothing else, Woolf is surely interested in the irony of 'Look, the unseen bade him'. The person telling him to look, his wife, is herself unseen. What hope then that Septimus will look at other things? Indeed, when he thinks of that voice (and he does not give a name to it), the only thing that grabs his attention is the object of its address, himself, so that the bulk of the sentence is a long relative clause attached to that self, a clause that entirely forgets the voice that had been speaking ('the voice which now communicated with him *who was*'). The decision to translate 'Look, the unseen bade him, that voice which…' as 'Guarda l'invisibile gli ordinò la voce' (*Look at the invisible ordered the voice*), while it does offer us mystery, nevertheless by missing the relationship of apposition between 'the unseen' and 'the voice' it also misses the relationship the text establishes between Septimus and his wife (also it is ludicrous that a practical person like Lucrezia would tell him to look at the invisible).

Then what are we to make of the translation of 'lately taken from life to death' as the exact opposite 'appena tornato in vita dalla morte' (*just returned to life from death*)? Here Septimus perceives the truth. His unseeing hermeticism is a form of death. *Mrs Dalloway* frequently makes it clear that Septimus sees his inability to feel anything for others as a form of death. He is an intelligent, perceptive man. That is what makes his drama moving. The only explanation for the Italian must be that the translator somehow feels the text makes more sense this way.

Then 'to renew society' is so much more specific than the rather banal 'cambiare il mondo' (change the world). Crucially, Septimus's problems have to do with society, society's treatment of him and his inability to be 'in society' with others. More, much more, might be added about the problem of interpreting 'unwasted' (any giving of himself to others would be 'waste') as 'integro' (*whole*), about the introduction in the Italian of 'a fiori' (*floral*), about the removal of 'only' in 'smitten only by the sun' (the last phenomenon to whose incursion Septimus seems susceptible here), but the important thing to note is how, at the end of the sentence, when Septimus tries to escape from his isolation and madness, the English returns to something far more coherent, upon which the Italian promptly falls into line. There are no problems after 'but he did not want it'.

Perhaps the only sensible comment we can make here is that when the English reaches its maximum unhingedness (and 'unhinged', we remember, means mad in the vernacular) even an excellent translator such as we have here loses her bearings. And with them goes the method in Septimus's madness, or rather the key to our reading of that madness in terms of the matrix of the book as a whole. Compare this long passage with a simple omission occurring just a few pages earlier when Septimus is enjoying a moment of complete beatitude:

> Sounds made harmonies with premeditation ... A child cried. Rightly far away a horn sounded. (p. 33)

> I suoni componevano melodie volute ... Un bambino piangeva. A distanza suonò un clacson. (p. 19)

> Sounds composed desired melodies ... A child cried. Far away a horn blared.

Septimus is able to be receptive to the world only when he can imagine it in perfect harmony. The 'Rightly' confirms his craziness here. In his mind the child's cry and the distant horn are a premeditated harmony, part of a pattern. To miss out 'rightly' (and devalue 'with premeditation' in 'volute' – *desired*) is to miss out the whole sense of the text (out of embarrassment perhaps?). But more importantly, we recognize in that 'Rightly' the same element of non-sequitur, of sham connection, if we like, that is already there in a milder form in Woolf's, or Clarissa's, use of 'for' and 'so' where such explanatory conjunctions do not seem justified, as this 'rightly' is only a product of Septimus's madness. The text as a whole strains towards an underlying pattern. It is in that direction that creativity pushes. But he who perceives the pattern totally, or believes he perceives it, without nuance or qualification, is mad. Here one cannot help remembering Woolf's claim, in a letter to Jacques Raverat, that 'Madness has saved me'.[8] *Mrs Dalloway* is an infinitely complex book and the translator makes alterations at his or her peril.

Part of the complexity of Woolf's novel, its desire to generate a sense of the interpenetration of people in social situations, comes from a constant play with the pronouns, which occasionally leave us wondering who is being spoken of. This is sometimes too much for the translator. Here, then, is the third of my four short examples:

> 'Dear!' said Clarissa, and Lucy shared as she meant her to her disappointment. (p. 43)

---

[8] Quoted by the translator in her introduction (p. vi) and taken from Virginia Woolf, *Letters, 1923-1928*.

'Caro!' disse Clarissa, e Lucy condivise, e glielo fece intendere, il disappunto. (p. 25)

'Dear!' said Clarissa, and Lucy shared, and had her understand that she did, her disappointment.

The 'disappointment' surely makes it plain that that 'Dear' was very much an 'Oh dear'. Not a 'caro' (*dear* as a form of address to a dear person). It is the kind of ambiguity that understandably poses problems, while the failure to appreciate that it is Clarissa who meant Lucy to appreciate her disappointment, not Lucy who, appreciating it, wished to communicate her appreciation, is less understandable. But rather than judging the translation here (which one always does with a shiver of concern that others will pay the same attention to one's own translations), the interesting thing is to see how again it is the complexity arising from Woolf's search for a transcendental blurring that causes the problems.

Where it is not a personal pronoun, a relative pronoun can have the same effects, simply because in the stream of consciousness one does not stop to explain oneself. Here is one of the book's very few hints of lesbianism. Clarissa is worried about the loneliness of her narrow bed. (cf. p. 45)

> She could see what she lacked. It was not beauty; it was not mind. It was something central which permeated; something warm which broke up surfaces and rippled the cold contact of man and woman, or of women together. For *that* she could dimly perceive. She resented it, had a scruple picked up Heaven knows where, or, as she felt, sent by Nature ... yet she could not resist sometimes yielding to the charm of a woman. (p. 46)

Here the *'that'* (italicized because taboo perhaps?) surely refers, not to the 'something central', but to the question of 'women together', otherwise both the foregrounding of 'that' and the whole following sentence become inexplicable. Again the Italian chooses to drop the sham explanatory 'For'. But that is the least of its problems.

> Lei sapeva che cosa lei mancava. Non era la bellezza, non era l'intelligenza. Era qualcosa dentro, che si irradia dal centro; un calore che intacca le superfici e increspa gli orli del freddo contatto tra un uomo e una donna, o tra due donne. Oscuramente lei lo sentiva. Ne soffriva, era uno scrupolo che sa il cielo da dove le veniva, o forse le veniva,

pensava, dalla natura ... eppure a volte non riusciva a resistere, e cedeva
al fascino di una donna. (p. 27)

> She knew what she lacked. It wasn't beauty, it wasn't intelligence.
> It was something inside, that radiated out from the centre; a warmth
> that broke the surfaces and ruffled the borders of cold contact between
> a man and a woman, or between two women. Darkly she sensed it.
> She suffered from it, it was a scruple that came to her from heaven
> knows where, or perhaps came to her, she thought, from nature...
> and yet sometimes she couldn't resist, and gave way to the charm of
> a woman.

In the English everything turns around the sudden change of direction after
'women together'. Clarissa drops her reflection on what she is lacking and
begins to reflect on her attraction to other women. Missing the transition, the
Italian translates, 'Oscuramente lei lo sentiva' (*Darkly she sensed it*) where
here the 'lo' (*it*) now refers to, what? Her awareness of what she lacks? Or the
'calore che intacca' (*heat that breaks*)? Presumably the former, since this is
the only thing that would explain the decision in the next sentence to translate
'She resented it' as 'Ne soffriva' (*she suffered from it*). Here, having failed to
grasp the crucial transition, and thus failed to understand what the 'it' refers
to in 'resented it' (her attraction to women), the translator is interpreting
freely. But still the paragraph makes no sense (in Italian), because now 'era
uno scrupolo' (*it was a scruple*) becomes meaningless. How can a lack be a
scruple? The English, once one has appreciated the italicized and strongly
foregrounded *'that'*, is clear enough. Lacking something, Clarissa nevertheless
does feel attracted to women (*'that* she could dimly perceive'). She resents
this attraction. Her resentment is the result of a scruple against love between
women. ' ... yet she could not resist sometimes yielding ...'. The intriguing
thing to notice here is that while Woolf courts incoherence (and the stream
of consciousness necessarily does this, if only to establish a certain mimetic
authenticity), she never actually becomes incoherent, though is sometimes
hermetic. The translation tends both to explain *and* to get lost. In doing so it
does us the favour, as might a paraphrase, of revealing Woolf's art.

Aside from straightforward mistakes, the translation more frequently runs
up against the difficulty of giving the full meaning and implications of the
text. Consider:

> and she, too, loving it as she did with an absurd and faithful passion,
> being part of it, since her people were courtiers once in the time of the

Georges, she, too, was going that very night to kindle and illuminate;
to give her party. (p. 6)

e anche lei, che l'amava, come l'amava, di una passione assurda e
fedele, e ne era parte, poiché i suoi erano stati a Corte al tempo di re
Giorgio, anche lei quella sera si sarebbe accesa, illuminata – per la
sua festa. (p. 3)

and she too, who loved it, how she loved it, with an absurd and faithful
passion, and was part of it, since her ancestors had been in Court at
the time of King George, she too that evening was going to set herself
alight, to shine – for her party.

The small difficulty with the culture-specific 'Georges' (there were more than
one!) need hardly be worried over. It is the verbs 'kindle' and 'illuminate' one
has to watch. For both of these verbs can be transitive or intransitive, and in
a book which is very much about self and other it is natural that such a state
of affairs should give rise to ambiguities that Woolf would wish to play with.
Here the two verbs are given no object and thus might, formally, be considered
intransitive. Yet when immediately followed by 'to give her party' one cannot help feeling it far more likely that they have a transitive sense. Clarissa
is going to generate energy for those who come to her party. She is going to
kindle and illuminate others (as in the last lines of the book her mere presence so excites Peter Walsh). Indeed the party, as we have said, is frequently
presented as 'an offering'.

Italian of course has the problem that these verbs must either be declaredly
transitive or intransitive. Since there is no object, the translator is free to
imagine them intransitive, or (as in the Italian here) reflexive, though in fact
this decision runs contrary to the underlying sense of the sentence, suggests
vanity rather than generosity on Clarissa's part and, what is more, invites the
more serious omission of 'to give her party' (what the whole book is about)
in favour of 'per la sua festa' (*for her party*), this in order to make more sense
of the preceding reflexives. One need only look at the back-translation to see
how much has changed: 'she too was going that very night to set herself alight,
to shine – for her party'. The notion of giving is completely lost.

Compare this with another, more significant moment, when the translator has trouble with the verb 'to give'. Unable to face the interruption, the
intrusion of Doctor Holmes, Septimus climbs on the window-sill to commit
suicide, then stops.

He did not want to die. Life was good. The sun hot. Only human beings what did *they* want? Coming down the staircase opposite an old man stopped and stared at him. Holmes was at the door. 'I'll give it you!' he cried, and flung himself vigorously, violently down on to Mrs Filmer's area railings. (p. 226)

Non aveva voglia di morire. La vita era bella. Il sole caldo. E gli esseri umani? Un uomo che scendeva dalla scala di fronte si fermò, e lo fissò sbalordito. Holmes era ormai alla porta. 'Lo volete voi!' gridò, e si buttò di sotto con tutte le sue forze, con violenza, giù sulla cancellata del giardinetto della signora Filmer. (pp. 134-5)

He did not want to die. Life was fine. The sun hot. And human beings? A man going down the step opposite stopped, and stared at him amazed. Holmes was already at the door. 'It's you who want it!' he shouted and threw himself down with all his strength, violently, down on Mrs Filmer's garden railings.

In passing one might notice that yet again the translator cannot stop herself making the time frame more specific with the introduction of the redundant 'ormai' (*by now/already*). But such observations are mere details in a passage which offers crucial divergences.

Septimus's 'what did *they* want?' is the most eloquent statement of his isolation, his inability to achieve a relationship with others or to understand why doctors visit him or what they would like him to do. Certainly they don't want him to kill himself. Woolf never accuses Holmes or Bradshaw of wanting Septimus dead. Why, then, does the translator omit the phrase, 'What did *they* want'?[9] Presumably because she has already decided to translate 'I'll give it to you!' as 'Lo volete voi!' (*It's you who want it/it's what you want*). Omitting the first use of 'want' thus avoids repetition later on. More importantly there is the consideration that 'Lo volete voi!' would look rather odd if it were to come immediately after 'Cosa volevano loro?' (*What do they want?*) since 'Lo volete voi' (*It's what they want*) suggests that Septimus knows only too well what people want.

---

[9] Since writing this passage I have discovered that, in this particular. instance, the English Penguin edition differs from the Harcourt Brace edition in omitting this clause, as follows: ' ... The sun hot. Only human beings? Coming down the stairs ...' (Penguin Modern Classics, p. 165). The translation of 'Only' as 'E' (*And*) remains problematic, while since the cry 'I'll give it you' is standard to all versions, the decision to translate this as 'Lo volete voi' (*It's you who want it*) now becomes all the more inexplicable.

The omission of 'what did *they* want?' would thus seem to have to do with the translator's difficulty with the later 'I'll give it you!'. For some reason she finds a straightforward translation a problem, perhaps even embarrassing, in so far as Septimus's cry cannot, she perhaps feels, easily be made sense of. Yet within the book's intellectual framework it makes perfect sense. Unable to negotiate, as Clarissa does, with the other, with others, unable to give something but not too much (a marriage, a party), Septimus surrenders himself *entirely* to the other, accepts dissolution of identity in death, as Clarissa expects to be dissolved in the future, after a natural death. It is in this sense that Clarissa can later choose to see his death positively, and above all, in relation to her party, as another offering. To write 'Lo volete voi!' (*It's you who want it!*) reduces Septimus's strange, thought-provoking death cry to a mere accusation, making the ambiguous 'you' of Woolf's text (which might be Bradshaw and Holmes, or everybody, or, more positively, nature itself?) all too plain.

All in all, what is fascinating in the translation of this passage is the way the respect for Woolf's work suggested by the enthusiastic, academic and feminist introduction is not borne out in the most elementary questions of textual faithfulness. We can only assume that the translator feels she is improving the text by making it clearer. The result is that our attention is drawn to the social issue of how doctors should behave, not the deeper theme of an underlying transcendental reality uniting self and other.

For two final examples, let us risk moving from the sublime to the ridiculous and back again, for that after all is what so much of *Mrs Dalloway*, so much of modernism, is about. The differences between translation and original tell their story at every level, since to a great extent the book is about finding a way of considering all things on the same plane (surely the ultimate goal of transcendentalism). In the following passage, Mrs Dempster is making up the world in classic Woolf tradition as she fantasizes about the life of a passing girl, Maisie Johnson.

> You'll get married, for you're pretty enough, thought Mrs Dempster. Get married, she thought, and then you'll know. Oh, the cooks, and so on. Every man has his ways. But whether I'd have chosen quite like that if I could have known, thought Mrs Dempster, and could not help wishing to whisper a word to Maisie Johnson; to feel on the creased pouch of her worn old face the kiss of pity. For it's been a hard life, thought Mrs Dempster. What hadn't she given to it? Roses; figure; her feet too. (pp. 39-40)

I quote the last few lines of this passage to include the question 'What hadn't she given to it?' and demonstrate how pervasive this concept of 'giving to life' is throughout the book. But the part that is most perplexing here is the two sentences, 'Oh, the cooks, and so on. Every man has his ways'. What on earth can this mean? The Italian clarifies.

> Ti sposerai, perché sei abbastanza carina, pensò la signora Dempster. Sposati, pensò, e poi vedrai. Farai la cuoca, chissà. A ognuno la sua strada. Ma chissà se avrei fatto le stesse cose, avessi saputo qualcosa in più, pensò la signora Dempster, e avrebbe tanto voluto sussurrare una parolina all'orecchio di Maisie Johnson, e sentì sulla sacca rugosa della sua faccia di vecchia il bacio della pietà. Perché è stata dura la vita, pensò la signora Dempster. Che cosa non le aveva sacrificato? Le rose, il corpo, i piedi perfino. (p. 23)

> You'll get married, because you're pretty enough, thought Mrs Dempster. Marry, she thought, and then you'll see. You'll be a cook, maybe. To each his path. But heaven knows if I would have done the same, had I known a bit more, thought Mrs Dempster, and she would very much liked to whisper a word in Maisie Johnson's ear, and she felt on the wrinkled pouch of her old woman's face the kiss of pity. Because life had been hard, thought Mrs Dempster. What hadn't she sacrificed to it? Roses, her body, even her feet.

Mrs Dempster is just a tiny fragment of London life, one of those millions of creative minds making up the city. Woolf gives us no more than a glimpse of her, but is determined to suggest that there is a whole world behind that wrinkled face. Hence the importance of allusions we cannot understand, flotsam and jetsam from a world we do not know. 'Oh, the cooks, and so on.' What can it mean? That Maisie will have cooks in her household? Surely she cannot herself be a cook in the plural? Or is there, since Mrs Dempster is clearly a disillusioned soul who feels it might have been better not to marry, some suggestion that the turnover of cooks has to do with the tastes (or attentions?) of the husband? 'Every man has his ways.' 'Man' here must surely refer to the male of the species. Had Woolf wanted to write 'A ognuno la sua strada' (*To each his path*), the English offers the idiom 'To each his own.'

What becomes evident here is the density of Woolf's text, the generosity of her novel, a novel that makes plain, in its constant generation of 'non-essential' detail, in its vocation for the list, the heterogeneous list, that abundance is part of its aesthetic, part of its vision of a life into which we will ultimately all return: 'Somehow', Clarissa thinks, 'in the streets of London, on the ebb and flow of things, here, there, she survived, Peter survived, lived in each other, she being part, she was positive, of the trees at home; of the house there, ugly, rambling all to bits and pieces as it was; part of people she had never met' (p. 12). One of whom is Mrs Dempster, whose 'Oh, the cooks, and so on' is merely made banal in the Italian 'Farai la cuoca, chissà' (*You'll be a cook, maybe*). 'Chissà' (*who knows/maybe*), in fact, turns out to be doubly useful to the translator in this passage. The sentence in the English beginning: 'But whether I'd have chosen quite like that if I could have known ...' remains grammatically incomplete in that the second half of the 'if' clause never appears. The Italian clears this up with 'Ma chissà se avrei fatto le stesse cose' (*But who knows if I would have done the same things*). Again the openness of the English is lost.

Now, for a last comparison, back to the sublime. Here is Peter Walsh on his way to Clarissa's party with the intuition that he is about to have an experience. Of what? he asks himself.

> Beauty anyhow. Not the crude beauty of the eye. It was not beauty pure and simple – Bedford Place leading into Russell Square. It was straightness and emptiness of course; the symmetry of a corridor; but it was also windows lit up, a piano, a gramophone sounding; a sense of pleasure-making hidden, but now and again emerging when, through the uncurtained window, the window left open, one saw parties sitting over tables, young people slowly circling, conversations between men and women, maids idly looking out (a strange comment theirs, when work was done), stockings drying on top ledges, a parrot, a few plants. Absorbing, mysterious, of infinite richness, this life. (p. 248)

One is struck again here by Woolf's combination of a Joycean spirit of evocation with some very deft essay writing, as she combines her description of the London twilight with a subtle presentation of her novel's complex aesthetic. Towards the end of the piece, as so often, she includes one incomprehensible, or at least difficult, fragment, one element, that like something Peter Walsh only half glimpses through a drawing room window, eludes us – 'maids idly looking out (a strange comment theirs, when work was done)'. How are we to take this? Could 'comment' be a collective noun referring in general to what maids say when they have finished their work? That seems unlikely, if not impossible, given the indefinite article ('a strange comment'). And anyway why would this be so strange? Clearly this is the point in the passage where the translator will be under the greatest strain. The Italian is as follows:

Della bellezza, intanto. Non la cruda bellezza dell'occhio. Non era pura e semplice bellezza – Bedford Place che porta a Russell Square. Intanto colpiva l'asse diritto, l'ampiezza e la simmetria; e poi le finestre illuminate, il pianoforte, la melodia che veniva da un grammofono, il senso di un piacere ben nascosto, ma che di tanto in tanto veniva a galla, quando, attraverso una finestra senza tende, lasciata aperta, si intravedeva un gruppo di persone intorno un tavolo, dei giovani che si muovevano lenti nella stanza, uomini e donne che conversavano, cameriere oziose che guardavano fuori (che strani commenti, i loro, a lavoro finito), le calze stese ad asciugare sui davanzali, un pappagallo, delle piante. Avvincente, misteriosa, infinitamente ricca, la vita. (pp. 147-8)

Of beauty, for sure. Not the crude beauty of the eye. It wasn't beauty pure and simple – Bedford Place leading to Russel Square. Meantime one was struck by the straight line, the broadness and the symmetry; and then the lighted windows, the piano, the tune coming from a gramophone, the sense of a pleasure well hidden, but that surfaced every now and then, when, through a curtainless window left open, you glimpsed a group of people round a table, youngsters moving slow in the room, men and women talking, leisurely maids looking out (what strange comments, theirs, their work done), stockings stretched to dry on the sills, a parrot, plants. Engaging, mysterious, infinitely rich, life.

One notices first of all the loss of the contrast that the English establishes as it sets out to express Woolf's complex vision of beauty: 'It was straightness and emptiness of course ... but it was also windows lit up, a piano ...'. Woolf acknowledges ('of course') the importance of classical structure, of clarity, coherence (as her novel is, in large terms, very rigidly and clearly structured), but sees the need for it to be set off with great density and abundance of detail. The window becomes a crucial image here. It is the means by which one penetrates the cold structures of definition, gaining access into the abundant, seething world of others. It is through the French window that Clarissa goes into the garden at Bourton, through her window in Westminster that she is given the epiphany (p. 283) of the old lady opposite behind her window, through a window that Septimus gives his life away, and here, through a window that Peter Walsh receives the gift of a sense of life's abundance, the glimpse of things revealed, as the smoke lifts to reveal what is beneath it.

Given these premises, it is significant that Woolf twice uses the definite article before window here: 'but now and again emerging when, through *the* uncurtained window, *the* window left open, one saw parties'. The sense of repeated experience in 'now and again' and then the plural 'parties' make it clear that those definite articles are not there to refer to a particular window, but to make the word generic, 'the uncurtained window, the window left open'. This use of syntax to hint at symbolism (typical, as we saw in an earlier chapter, of Lawrence) is lost in the Italian which chooses to eliminate one window and to use an indefinite rather than definite article before the other ('una finestra senza tende, lasciata aperta' – *a curtainless window, left open*).

Then what is it exactly that is going on behind those windows: 'pleasure-making'. By using this participle structure Woolf links her description with the book's credo in people's creativity, the fertility of minds constantly generating the world around them. They are making pleasure. We think of the 'What a lark!' of the first page, of Peter Walsh's 'fun' as he 'invents' (p. 79) the girl he briefly follows through London streets, of the 'fun' Clarissa is made to feel by Septimus's decision to throw life away. It is this that is hidden behind the clean lines of austere, well-defined beauty, but which constantly emerges, issues, from behind open windows. Again the book's willingness to offer a deeper vision, its constant suggestion of an underlying network of ideas, is lost in the translation's retreat into 'il senso di un piacere ben nascosto' (*the sense of a pleasure well hidden*), where it is the hiddenness rather than the pleasure-making which gets the focus.

And 'a strange comment theirs, when work was done', this odd incomprehensible parenthesis that refers us perhaps to what remains hidden in Peter Walsh's mind, is rendered as 'che strani commenti, i loro, a lavoro finito' (*what strange comments, theirs, their work done*). So, in the Italian, everything is explained. There remains merely the niggling doubt that this was not in fact what Peter Walsh wanted to say. For in what way are maids' comments strange upon finishing their work? And anyway does not the text suggest that what we have here are not maids talking to each other, or indeed to anyone else, but solitary maids leaning on different window-sills? So is there any other way we could understand the text? Because to translate it the way the translator has translated it is to suggest that Woolf's original was careless.

On a number of occasions in *Mrs Dalloway* we find that a gesture or action or phenomenon is referred to as a speech act, a phenomenon of language, and vice versa. Consider this extreme example, as Septimus sits in Regent's Park:

> But they beckoned; leaves were alive; trees were alive. And the leaves being connected by millions of fibres with his own body, there on the seat, fanned it up and down; when the branch stretched he, too, made that statement. (p. 32)

Here we move from the stock poetic metaphor of the trees 'beckoning' (perhaps a speech act, perhaps a gesture) to the radically odd use of the word 'statement' to describe a branch stretching (the Italian rendered this as 'quando il ramo stendeva anche lui stendeva' – *when the branch stretched he too stretched* – p. 19).

Alternatively, we might consider those moments in the book when the old woman's song is likened first to running water, then to smoke, or when the smoke produced by the aeroplane becomes 'smoke words'. Or there are the frequent references to the 'thread' of thought and conversation. It seems that just as *Mrs Dalloway* sets out to convince us of the interpenetration between ourselves and the world, ourselves and others, so there are hints at an interpenetration between language and phenomena, a sort of smoky and rather poetic border where words may become things or gestures, and vice versa.

With this in mind, we might consider that Peter Walsh is thinking of this typical maids' habit, this gesture of leaning out of the window once work is over, as a comment, a statement. Their work finished, instead of rushing off on their own, they idly look out of the window. Peter, with his desire for bustle and precision, his incomprehension of idleness, finds this strange. In terms of the book's psychology, its sense of the back and forth of intensities of identity, the maids' evident desire for contact, generosity, openness (leaning out of an open window over the busy street), after a period trapped in work, is not strange at all. Hence Woolf is revealing Peter's limitation in not understanding how others behave. Strangest of all, however, would be the notion that Peter reflects on what strange conversations maids have when they finish work.

Perhaps one problem of the approach I am proposing in these pages, this idea of arriving at a deeper understanding of a text through an examination of the divergence between original and translation, is that there is, as it were, too much to say. One can become fascinated, as here, with the criteria that governed the translator's approach. Why, for example, when Clarissa refers to herself as 'a radiancy no doubt in some dull lives' (p. 55) does the Italian choose to eliminate the world 'dull' and offer 'un centro di luce, non c'è dubbio, per alcune vite' – *a centre of light, no doubt, for some lives* (p. 32)? Is there a sense of embarrassment for what might be seen as Clarissa's and perhaps Woolf's elitism? Is it a sneaking political correctness which does not allow us to write others off as dull? If so, could we relate such a decision to the following, clearly politically-engaged remark in the translator's introduction?

> Virginia Woolf loves to present women in the act of sewing, or knitting.
> But it would be quite wrong to see this as an indication of domesticity.
> On the contrary, they are awesome, disquieting images; indirect ways

of evoking symbolic meanings behind familiar gestures. This novel in
particular is full of female figures, minor reincarnations of female dei-
ties from times past, echoes, memories of a female world of maternal
powers not yet entirely extinct... (p. xxi)

The curiosity here is the translator's assumption, which is also perhaps the assumption of contemporary feminism, that power and domesticity are somehow
mutually exclusive. Surely, it was precisely their *domesticity* that made the
'Fates' so frightening. For the myth of the three goddesses reminds us that it
is in the domestic world that destiny lies, it is women who are men's destiny,
who spin and cut the thread. And no one could be more eager to offer a positive and vibrant picture of domesticity than Virginia Woolf, to see, what is
more, the domestic world as a predominantly feminine world, in contrast to
the male world.

Clarissa, with her clothes, her flowers, her party, is supremely domestic
and proud of being so, ready to defend the value of her sphere against that of
her politician husband and Peter Walsh and others. The only women in this
book who are decidedly not domestic, Miss Killman and Lady Bexborough,
are ridiculed for their religious and political ambitions. To speak then of 'a
female world of maternal powers' reminds us that there is nothing unusual in
finding 'disquieting images' which are also domestic. Quite the contrary. What
is it men are so frequently trying to escape, after all, if not the domestic?

Finally, to use the expression 'not yet entirely extinct' is to fail to appreciate
Mrs Dalloway's radical claim that this world of female divinities is *not at all
extinct;* it is as alive and well as ever. Many modern commentators are happy
to have the old mythology live on, so long as it accepts its moribund state of
near extinction in literary symbol. Virginia Woolf is not among them.

Such are the digressions into which one might be drawn. Yet even here
one cannot deny that comparison of the translator's vision with the author's
helps us to appreciate what Woolf is really about, helps us to see that her text
is not altogether in tune with those modern orthodoxies that do not wish us
to refer to people as 'dull' or think of female protagonists as 'domestic'. And
despite the fact that this translation simply is not faithful enough for us to
decide whether divergences in the text are the result of genuinely linguistic
difficulties, or more simply the consequence of the translator's imposing her
own vision on Woolf's work, nevertheless, close comparison does reveal
certain of Woolf's strategies, and most of all the text's constant back and forth
between the sharply defined and the creatively blurred. Where the language is
sharply defined there is simply no question of a translator's departing radically
from the semantic sense. In such places the Italian text is excellent. Where the

English is less clear (in the sense of superficial semantics) all kinds of liberties are taken, often at the expense of the poetic thrust of the text.

5. Translating the Matter of Samuel Beckett's Manner

In 1990 the city of Milan played host to an international conference on the most important comic writers of the 20th century. Conducting an interview with the organizer of the event, a journalist from the public radio news showed surprise at the inclusion of Samuel Beckett amongst those discussed, Beckett being well known, the journalist remarked, for his overwhelmingly depressing plays and novels. A few lines from Arsene's speech as it appears in the Italian translation of Beckett's novel *Watt* might explain how the journalist came by this opinion.

> Personalmente, com'è ovvio, rimpiango tutto. Non una parola, non un'azione, non un pensiero, non un bisogno, non un dolore, non una gioia, non una ragazza, non un ragazzo, non un dubbio, non una certezza, non uno scherno, non una voglia, non una speranza, non un timore, non un sorriso, non una lacrima, non un nome, non un volto, nessun momento, nessun luogo, che io non rimpianga, esageratamente. Uno schifo, dal principio alla fine. (p. 44)[1]

Translated back into English, this would read:

> Personally, as is obvious, I regret everything. Not a word, not an action, not a thought, not a need, not a pain, not a joy, not a girl, not a boy, not a doubt, not a certainty, not a sneer, not a desire, not a hope, not a fear, not a smile, not a tear, not a name, not a face, no moment, no place, that I do not regret, excessively. Filth, from first to last.

This is indeed black material, a list of virulent regrets presented without any attempt to make it palatable, nor any easily discernible organization (bar the occasional arrangement in opposites) that might make it intellectually satisfying. If there is any humour here, it is the grim humour of negative excess intensified by the provocative assumption that any other position would be

---

[1] All quotations from the Italian translation of *Watt* are taken from Samuel Beckett, *Watt,* Sugarco Edizioni, Milan, 1967. Translation by Cesare Cristofolini.

unimaginable: Personalmente, com'è ovvio, rimpiango tutto (*Personally, as is obvious, I regret everything*).

Here is Beckett's English original:

> Personally of course I regret everything. Not a word, not a deed, not a thought, not a need, not a grief, not a joy, not a girl, not a boy, not a doubt, not a trust, not a scorn, not a lust, not a hope, not a fear, not a smile, not a tear, not a name, not a face, no time, no place, that I do not regret, exceedingly. An ordure from beginning to end. (p. 44)[2]

What a difference rhyme and rhythm can make! The whole passage is transformed into a monosyllabic chant with a sniff almost, and absurdly, of the nursery about it. Curiously, the fast and rigidly formal rhythm allows for both lyricism and comedy as, after the insistent repetition of the rhyming anapaests ('not a word, not a deed, not a thought, not a need ...'), we get a sudden sad slowing down with two spondees ('no time, no place'), which then set us up for the unexpectedly pompous 'exceedingly' ('not a hope, not a fear, not a smile, not a tear, not a name, not a face, no time, no place, that I do not regret, exceedingly.'). The register shift is then confirmed by the very plummy 'ordure', creating the most comic moment just as the piece makes its most depressing statement: 'An ordure from beginning to end.'

But apart from our now feeling that Beckett might, after all, be a funny and certainly a very clever person, it is also clear that the meaning and focus of the passage shift considerably with the introduction of these formal structures and register shifts. Rather than a statement of terminal pessimism, it is one that draws our attention as much to its language as to its message. Indeed, we might say that what it makes us most aware of is the collision between its formal linguistic arrangement (at once trite and anodyne) and its utterly unpalatable content. It is precisely in that enigma, the collision of form and content, that the humour and the subject-matter lie.

The thrust of this book so far has been to suggest that when an artistic vision is embedded in a particular use of language, problems of translation will reveal the nature of that vision. Here, in this Italian version of *Watt,* we have lost some very traditional writing techniques – rhyme and rhythm – things we are quite accustomed to losing in literary translation. Indeed, it is more surprising when they are not lost. But because these elements were not even hinted at in the Italian, and because they stand in such a peculiar and unexpected

---

[2] All quotations from the original *Watt* are taken from the Jupiter Books edition, Calder & Boyars, London, 1972. Page numbers are indicated in brackets at the end of each quotation.

relation to the content, the overall loss is not just one of aesthetic pleasure, but of the text's meaning in the fullest possible sense. Even if we may not immediately be able to articulate it, a reading of passages from *Watt* first in Italian, then in English, allows us to savour Beckett's strategy, and to feel, if nothing else, that we know what he is inviting us to meditate on. In Chapter III, after a frightening description of a world divided by fences into separate segments, none of which even has a fence in common – a sort of geometric vision of isolation and the impossibility of communication – we have this in the Italian:

> Nessun recinto era comune a due proprietà, né alcuna parte di alcun recinto. Ma la loro vicinanza era tale, in certi punti, che un uomo largo di spalle o di bacino, attraversando questi passaggi così angusti l'avrebbe fatto con maggior facilità, e con minor rischio per la propria giacca, e forse per i propri calzoni, di lato che di fronte. Per un uomo con un gran sedere, invece, o con una gran pancia, il moto in senso frontale sarebbe stato una necessità assoluta, se non voleva perforarsi lo stomaco, o il culo, o magari tutt'e due, con una punta arrugginita, o con punte arrugginite. Una donna con gran sedere e gran seno, una balia obesa, per esempio, si sarebbe trovata in una necessità analoga, mentre persone dotate al tempo stesso di spalle larghe e pancia grossa, o bacino largo e gran sedere, o bacino largo e pancia grossa, o spalle larghe e gran sedere, o gran seno e spalle larghe, o gran seno e bacino largo, per nessuna ragione, a meno che avessero perso il lume della ragione, si sarebbero affidate a questo insidioso canale' (p. 161)

No fence was common to two properties, nor any part of any fence. But their proximity was such, at certain points, that a man with broad shoulders or hips, crossing these extremely narrow passages would have done so more easily, and with less risk to his jacket, and perhaps to his trousers, sideways rather than frontways. For a man with a big bottom, on the other hand, or with a big belly, frontal motion would be an absolute necessity, if he did not want to perforate his stomach, or his arse, or perhaps both, with a rusty barb, or rusty barbs. A woman with a big bottom and big breasts, an obese wet nurse, for example, would have found herself in an analogous position, while persons endowed at once with broad shoulders and big bellies, or broad hips and big bottoms, or broad hips and big bellies, or broad shoulders and big bottoms, or big breasts and broad shoulders, or big breasts and broads hips, for no reason at all, unless they had lost the light of reason, would entrust themselves to this insidious channel.

Here the possibilities of humour seem evident enough in the manic following through of every possible permutation and the rigidly formal organization
of grotesque physical detail. But when Italian students are invited to translate
this back into English the gap between their back-translations and the original
suggests that the hilarity Beckett had in mind has hardly been suggested by
the Italian.

> No fence was party, nor any part of any fence. But their adjacence
> was such, at certain places, that a broad-shouldered or broad-basined
> man, threading these narrow straits, would have done so with greater
> ease, and with less jeopardy to his coat, and perhaps to his trousers,
> sideways than frontways. For a big-bottomed man, on the contrary,
> or a big-bellied man, frontal motion would be an absolute necessity,
> if he did not wish his stomach to be perforated, or his arse, or perhaps
> both, by a rusty barb, or by rusty barbs. A big-bottomed big-bosomed
> woman, an obese wet nurse, for example, would be under a similar
> necessity. While persons at once broad-shouldered and big-bellied,
> or broad-basined and big-bottomed, or broad-basined and big-bellied,
> or broad-shouldered and big-bottomed, or big-bosomed and broad-
> shouldered, or big-bosomed and broad-basined, would on no account,
> if they were in their right senses, commit themselves to this treacherous
> channel. (p. 155)

What was generated with rhyme and rhythm in the first passage we considered is here achieved by obsessive and flaunted alliteration (the peculiarity
of 'broad-basined' tells us how hard the author is trying). Again this formal
element both underlines the passage's rigid structure while at the same time
making it delightfully absurd, especially since, within that structure, the diction
oscillates alarmingly between high and low registers. The resulting distance
between the amusing reading experience and the desolate world the passage
describes could not be more comically disturbing.

The working out of long series of permutations, typical of Beckett's second
novel *Watt,* is often compared by critics to passages in the later chapters of
Ulysses, so much so that *Watt* is sometimes considered as the final flowering
of Beckett's so-called Joycean period. But did the two writers really have
the same thing in mind when they embarked on these *tours de force?* Before
going any further it is worth quoting two remarks Beckett made about the
older writer.

In 1929, in an essay defending the early chapters of *Finnegan's Wake,*
Beckett first attacks traditional narrative styles for displaying a distressing

distance between their form and content, this partly because, he claims, the English language in general is 'abstracted to death'. Then he goes on to remark that in contrast 'His (Joyce's) work is not *about* something, *it is that something itself*'.[3] Joyce, in short, is praised for having invented a style and indeed a language that is radically close to what it speaks of, thus overcoming the limitations and above all the distancing effect of the language as normally used.

Our own examination of passages from various moments in Joyce's career has shown how the writer moves from a conventional form of evocation where the narrative gestures towards a traditionally recognizable 'real world' *(Dubliners)*, to a more complex aesthetic where the very energy and obstinacy with which the text sets out to evoke the world actually begin to focus our attention on the efforts and felicities of the language itself, rather than its apparent and declared subject. Translation of Joyce thus grows progressively more difficult as his work becomes more self-referential, self-contained, more and more a question of *a thing made of language,* with a density of interconnecting devices that can be bewildering. This is what Beckett appears to be endorsing when he states that Joyce's work 'is not *about* something, *it is that something itself*'. And he adds: 'When the sense is sleep, the words go to sleep. When the sense is dancing, the words dance'.[4] As if Joyce had somehow gone beyond mimesis, had recreated the world in a text.

But later Beckett became more sceptical, to the point that after Joyce's death he is quoted as saying to his friend Lawrence Harvey, 'Joyce believed in words. All you had to do was rearrange them and they would express what you wanted ...'.[5] The implication here is that Beckett now felt Joyce had been naive to 'believe in words', and that he himself did not 'believe' in them, nor in the effects that might be achieved by rearranging them. So, at first glance, observing Beckett's retreat from the highly elaborate syntax and diction of the early works, *More Pricks than Kicks* and *Murphy* (his so-called Joycean period), to the progressively leaner writing of *Watt* and *The Trilogy,* followed by the desperately spare prose of the later works, one might suppose that Beckett gets progressively easier for reader and translator in the same way that Joyce becomes richer and more difficult.

Nothing could be further from the truth. Beckett's rejection of Joyce's confidence in language, the exuberant virtuosity of *Ulysses* and *Finnegan's*

---

[3] Samuel Beckett, *Dante ... Bruno. Vico ... Joyce.* In *I can't go on, I'll go on,* Grove Weidenfeld, New York, 1976, p. 117.

[4] Ibid., p. 118.

[5] Lawrence Harvey, *Samuel Beckett: Poet and Critic,* Princeton University Press, 1970, p. 249.

Wake, does not mark a return to traditional forms of representation. Rather it seems that having now accepted as inevitable that there would always be an unbridgeable distance between words and their referents, he decided to draw attention to that distance, and not, like Joyce, attempt to overcome it. What does this mean in practical terms? Here is the opening passage of *Murphy,* written in 1935:

> The sun shone, having no alternative, on the nothing new. Murphy sat out of it, as though he were free, in a mew in West Brompton. Here, for what might have been six months he had eaten, drunk, slept, and put his clothes on and off, in a medium-sized cage of north-western aspect commanding an unbroken view of medium-sized cages of south-eastern aspect. Soon he would have to make other arrangements, for the mew had been condemned. Soon he would have to buckle to and start eating, drinking, sleeping, and putting his clothes on and off, in quite alien surroundings. (p. 5)[6]

Confronting the passage, a translator is at once aware that it lacks the alliteration, onomatopoeia and meticulous description one might find in Joyce. The sound of the words does not appear to present a problem here, nor does the text have a rhythm intended to match any particular movement described either in the physical world or indeed in the mind, though that is not to say that it is without its rhythm, as we shall see. What it does have in common with much of Joyce's writing is a certain mockery, but of what? Of Murphy, of London? And how exactly is that mocking tone achieved?

Students invited to translate the piece are usually (though not always) aware of the biblical reference of the first line ('The sun shone having no alternative on the nothing new') and the difficulty of presenting that allusion succinctly in a country which has little biblical tradition. They are also alive to the curiosity of 'putting his clothes on and off' and the glibly frightening use of the word 'cage'. They usually have to check in their dictionaries to find out that 'buckle to' is an idiomatic expression meaning 'to apply oneself zealously to a task', upon which they appreciate the strangeness of placing it before verbs like 'eating', 'drinking' and 'sleeping', none of which could properly be conceived of as tasks. Nevertheless, at first glance nothing seems insuperable in this passage. So the only published Italian translation comes as a surprise.

---

[6] All quotations from the original *Murphy* are taken from *Murphy,* Picador, London, 1973. Page numbers are indicated in brackets at the end of each quotation.

Il sole splendeva, senza possibilità di alternative, sul niente di nuovo. Quasi fosse libero, Murphy se ne stava all'ombra, seduto, nel vicolo cieco del Bambino Gesù, West Brompton, Londra. Là, da mesi, forse da anni, mangiava, beveva, dormiva, si vestiva e si svestiva, in un vano di media dimensione, esposto a nord-ovest, con una vista ininterrotta su altri vani di media dimensione, esposti a sud-est. Presto gli sarebbe toccato trovarsi un'altra sistemazione: del vicolo del Bambino Gesù era stata decisa la condanna. Presto gli sarebbe toccato imparare di nuovo a mangiare, a bere, a dormire, a vestirsi e svestirsi in un ambiente assolutamente sconosciuto. (p.9)[7]

The sun shone, without any possibility of alternatives, on the nothing new. As if he were free, Murphy stayed in the shade, sitting down, in the blind alley of Baby Jesus, West Brompton, London. There, for months, perhaps for years, he had eaten, drunk, slept, dressed and undressed, in a medium-sized room, exposed to the north-west, with an uninterrupted view of other medium-sized rooms, exposed to the south-east. Soon he would have to find another arrangement: the blind alley of Baby Jesus had been condemned. Soon he would have to learn again to eat, drink, sleep, dress and undress in absolutely unknown surroundings.

Our first thought is that the translator is taking unforgivable liberties. What is this business of the 'vicolo cieco del Bambino Gesù' (*the blind alley of Baby Jesus*)? And why has 'what might have been six months' been transformed into 'da mesi, forse da anni' (*for months, perhaps for years*)? These are major changes and they will remain inexplicable until we realize that the Italian version has been translated, not from the original English, but from the French. And the French translation was done by Beckett himself. This alerts us to one of the curiosities of Beckett's work: that much of it is available, as it were, in 'two originals'. Beckett frequently translated himself, from French into English and from English into French (this man who 'did not believe in words' was an exceptional linguist). And when he thus translated himself he frequently made changes, not to the overall shape and structure of the text, but to all kinds of details.

Leaving aside any discussion as to the wisdom of choosing to translate from Beckett's French rather than his (in this case) original English, what I

---

[7] All quotations from the Italian translation of *Murphy* are taken from *Murphy,* Einaudi, Turin, 1962. Translation by Franco Quadri. Page numbers are indicated in brackets at the end of each quotation.

want to suggest is that if we examine the changes Beckett himself made when he translated, we will get a better sense of what he considered important in his original text, what he is being faithful to, what he feared might be lost. The question as to whether this has been or could be achieved in Italian is another matter. Here is the French:

> Le soleil brillait, n'ayant pas d'alternative, sur le rien de neuf. Murphy, come s'il était libre, s'en tenait à l'écart, assis, dans l'impasse de l'EnfantJésus, West Brompton, Londres. Là, depuis des mois, peut-être des années, il mangeait, buvait, dormait, s'habillait et se déshabillait, dans une cage de dimensions moyennes, exposée au nord-ouest, ayant sur d'autres cages de dimensions moyennes exposées au sud-est une vue ininterrompue. Bientôt il lui faudrait s'arranger autrement, car l'impasse de l'Enfant-Jésus venait d'être condamnée. Bientôt il lui faudrait rapprendre, dans un cadre tout à fait étranger, à manger, à boire, à dormir, à s'habiller et à se déshabiller. (p.7)[8]

And once again, a back-translation:

> The sun shone, having no alternative, on the nothing new. Murphy, as if he were free, stayed to one side, sitting down, in the dead end of Baby Jesus, West Brompton, London. There, for months, perhaps for years, he had eaten, drunk, slept, dressed and undressed, in a medium-sized cage, exposed to the north-west, enjoying an uninterrupted view of other medium-size cages exposed to the south-east. Soon he would have to make other arrangements, because the dead end of Baby Jesus had been condemned. Soon he would have to start again, in a completely alien situation, to eat, drink, sleep, dress and undress.

The switch to 'il vicolo cieco del Bambino Gesù' (*the blind alley of Baby Jesus*) is now explained and the fact that Beckett himself chose to introduce the idea in the French makes it clear to us that he is not interested in maintaining the documentary authenticity (or anonymity) of 'a mew in West Brompton' (just as the switch to 'depuis des mois, peut-être des années' – *for months, perhaps for years* – suggests a relaxed approach to chronology). In short, we cannot imagine Beckett like Joyce sending postcards back home to have friends check the names of streets and shops, or the dates when things

---

[8] All quotations from Beckett's French translation of *Murphy* are taken from *Murphy,* Les Editions de Minuit, Paris, 1965. Page numbers are indicated in brackets at the end of each quotation.

happened. No, he appears to be more interested here in the notion that Baby Jesus and all he stands for is a dead-end which has to be abandoned because condemned, and interested again in expressing this notion in such a facetious manner as not to make it quite dear whether we should take it seriously or not. In any event, the decision to introduce this name in the French foregrounds one aspect of the text which is left more subtle in the English: the extent to which Murphy's being obliged to change his abode and habits is resonant with philosophical issues.

Why did Beckett feel this major change, which so alters the tone of what is after all the opening paragraph of his first novel, was appropriate? Comparing the original line by line with first the French and then the Italian gives us a sense of what has happened and why.

> The sun shone, having no alternative, on the nothing new.

> Le soleil brillait, n'ayant pas d'alternative, sur le rien de neuf.
> The sun shone, having no alternative, on the nothing new.

> Il sole splendeva, senza possibilità di alternative, sul niente di nuovo.
> The sun shone, without any possibility of alternatives, on the nothing new..

Becket may be concerned that the opening biblical reference, though perfectly translatable, is less effective in a language without the Anglo-Saxon biblical tradition. Thus, although he makes no changes here, he may already be wishing to underline the extent to which the book engages the largest possible issues.

> Murphy sat out of it, as though he were free

> Murphy, come s'il était libre, s'en tenait à l'écart, assis,
> Murphy, as if he were free, stayed to one side, sitting down,

> Quasi fosse libero, Murphy se ne stava all'ombra, seduto
> As if he were free, Murphy stayed in the shade, sitting down,

Neither French nor Italian offer the possibility of a straight translation of 'out of it' here, where 'out' is both colloquially acceptable as the opposite of being 'in' the sun, but at the same time suggests Murphy's desire, in sitting out of the sunshine, to put himself outside the whole deterministic (solar) system that it represents. This joke is mostly lost in the French, and totally so in the Italian, with the result that the phrase, 'Quasi fosse libero, Murphy se ne stava all'ombra' (*As if he were free, Murphy stayed in the shade, sitting down*) is merely enigmatic, rather than witty. Neither the French nor the Italian make clear the absurdity of Murphy's attempt to escape the world of 'having no alternative' by merely sitting out of the sun. In this sense adding 'l'impasse de l'Enfant-Jésus' (*the dead end of Baby Jesus*) will give a compensatory irony to Murphy's vain imaginings of freedom.

    in a mew in West Brompton.

    dans l'impasse de l'Enfant-Jésus, West Brompton, Londres.
    in the dead end of Baby Jesus, West Brompton, London.

    nel vicolo cieco del Bambino Gesù, West Brompton, Londra.
    in the blind alley of Baby Jesus, West Brompton, London.

The word 'mew' has no equivalent in French or Italian. A 'mews' may be a dead-end, but it is not necessarily so. In particular, when used to describe a street the word has a final 's' and a plural 'mewses'. So why doesn't Beckett put the 's' here? *Chambers*' entry for the word 'mew' is as follows: *'as verb,* to shed, to moult, or cast: to change, as the covering or dress: to confine, as in a cage; *as noun,* the process of moulting: a cage for hawks, esp. while mewing: a coop, a place of confinement: a retreat, a hiding place.'

    A hiding place where one is obliged to change! What could be more appropriate in this context, quite apart from the chance to remind us that words do not have a fixed meaning, but slip and slither with time? Clearly no word in French or Italian or indeed any other language is going to offer us a similar range of connotation. Hence Beckett searches in his translation for something else that will give density and finds it in this reference to Baby Jesus (an improbable name for a London street).

    Here, for what might have been six months

    Là, depuis des mois, peut-être des années
    There, for months, perhaps for years

    Là, da mesi, forse da anni
    There, for months, perhaps for years

Structures of the variety 'pour ce qui aurait pu être six mois' (*for what could have been six months*) lack the light wistfulness of the oft-used English 'might have been', whereas 'peut-etre pour six mois' (*perhaps for six months*) would lose the studied uncertainty here. Beckett thus decides again to foreground the comedy (and the uneasiness as to the status of both narrator and text) with 'depuis des mois, peut-être des années' (*for months, perhaps for years*) conveying a much greater uncertainty than the original English. Obviously, it would be hard for an ordinary translator to take such a liberty.

> he had eaten, drunk, slept, and put his clothes on and off, in a medium-sized cage of north-western aspect commanding an unbroken view of medium-sized cages of south-eastern aspect.

> il mangeait, buvait, dormait, s'habillait et se déshabillait, dans une cage de dimensions moyennes, exposée au nord-ouest, ayant sur d'autres cages de dimensions moyennes exposées au sud-est une vue ininterrompue.

> he had eaten, drunk, slept, dressed and undressed, in a medium-sized cage, exposed to the north-west, enjoying an uninterrupted view of other medium-size cages exposed to the south-east.

> mangiava, beveva, dormiva, si vestiva e si svestiva, in un vano di media dimensione, esposto a nord-ovest, con una vista ininterrotta su altri vani di media dimensione, esposti a sud-est.

> he had eaten, drunk, slept, dressed and undressed, in a medium-sized room, exposed to the north-west, with an uninterrupted view of other medium-sized rooms, exposed to the south-east.

The second part of this second sentence is full of parallels, opposites and apparent opposites, all balanced off against each other, as in a system such as the one Murphy vainly hopes he is sitting out of. The word 'cage' both picks up on the etymology of 'mew' and confirms the loss of freedom inside this system and the vanity of Murphy's wishes. It should be noted that Beckett is not interested in commenting on the squalor of down-market housing, nor, as Lawrence might, on the lack of spirituality of suburban sprawl. No, he is interested in establishing the formal and deterministic nature of the trap Murphy is in. The sun goes round the earth, as it must, the north-western houses rigidly and inevitably face the south-eastern, having put on one's clothes, why should one not be obliged to 'put them off' again?

Thus, if we accept that the switch of the name of the street indicates a lack of concern for documentary realism in favour of a teasing textual density, one now appreciates that the precise directions north-west and south-east were preferred to merely north or south (as medium-sized was preferred to merely small or big), not because Beckett is referring to any particular place of any particular size, but because the use of these longer hyphenated forms highlights the parallels; that is, the language itself, like the street (or like the deterministic geometry Beckett is using the street to refer to), begins to form an inward turning grid. And this is the text's rhythm.

How do the French and Italian translations fare here? Rather well. They mirror the same effects as the English, except in the following instances. 'Cage', kept in the French, has been watered down to 'vano' (*room*) in the Italian (though 'vano', which as a noun means 'room' and as an adjective means 'vain' is rather cleverly appropriate – 'vanity, all is vanity,' wrote the same man who told us that there was nothing new under the sun). In both languages the irony of 'commanding an unbroken view' is lost. There is some allusion to the jargon of the estate agent in the French and Italian (another 'system' into which we might slip) but the ridiculous notion that one in any way 'commands' from one's cage what is only a mirror image of that cage is lost.

> Soon he would have to make other arrangements, for the mew had been condemned.

> Bientòt il lui faudrait s'arranger autrement, car l'impasse de l'Enfant-Jésus venait d'ètre condamnée.

> Soon he would have to make other arrangements, because the dead end of Baby Jesus had been condemned.

> Presto gli sarebbe toccato trovarsi un'altra sistemazione: del vicolo del Bambino Gesù era stata decisa la condanna

> Soon he would have to find another arrangement: the blind alley of Baby Jesus had been condemned.

The French chooses 's'arranger' (make arrangements/organize oneself) very appropriately, but in Italian 'arrangiarsi' (*get by*) has all kinds of unwanted connotations and the translator rightly rejects it for the felicitous 'sistemazione' (arrangement), a choice which fits in very neatly with the passage's geometric vocation. In both French and Italian, however, the subtler philosophical overtones are drowned out by the louder humour of 'del vicolo del Bambino Gesù era stata decisa la condanna' – *the blind alley of Baby Jesus had been condemned* – (how much more melancholy the irony is in the English here, where it is Murphy's deceptively commanding and beloved cage that has been condemned).

> Soon he would have to buckle to and start eating, drinking, sleeping, and putting his clothes on and off, in quite alien surroundings.

> Bientòt il lui faudrait rapprendre, dans un cadre tout à fait étranger, à manger, à boire, à dormir, à s'habiller et à se déshabiller.

> Soon he would have to start again, in a completely alien situation, to eat, drink, sleep, dress and undress.

> Presto gli sarebbe toccato imparare di nuovo a mangiare, a bere, a dormire, a vestirsi e svestirsi in un ambiente assolutamente sconosciuto.

> Soon he would have to learn again to eat, drink, sleep, dress and undress in absolutely unknown surroundings.

Here the rather Irish change of register in 'buckle to' is lost in the French and Italian with the drier choices of 'rapprendre' (*start again*) and 'imparare' (*learn*). True, it is as strange to say that one must 'learn' to start eating, etc., as it is to say one must 'buckle to and start eating ...', but it is not so vividly comic and, crucially, it does not introduce a word whose meaning is so patently mutable. That is, the French and Italian do draw our attention to language as semantics, but not as register, nor to a more general feeling for what is appropriate. The English text has now moved from the abstractions of 'the nothing new' to the language of idiomatic exhortation (in an area where exhortation is pointless).

Likewise lost in translation here is the curiosity of 'putting his clothes on and off'. 'S'habiller' (*dress*) and 'se déshabiller' (*undress*) exactly like 'vestirsi' and 'svestirsi' keep the sense of mutually determining opposites, and this could have been achieved in English with 'dressing' and 'undressing'. But the unusual use of 'off' as the reflex opposite of 'on' generates more comedy and suggests that the geometry of the language is not without its hiccups.

Finally there are two words to keep an eye on in the last part of the sentence: 'quite' and 'alien'. Taking the second first, there is no word in French or Italian that will convey the entire semantic range of the English word (unknown, hostile, contrary to one's principles, from beyond our planet, etc.). Both 'étranger' (*foreign/strange*) and 'sconosciuto' (*unknown*) lose some of the portentousness and fun here. Then 'alien' is qualified by 'quite', a word with wittily antithetical energies.[9] It might mean 'totally alien' ('quite' as a maximizer) and it might mean no more than 'somewhat alien' ('quite' as a diminisher). On first reading we take the maximizer as the obvious meaning; later we may reasonably ask ourselves: how 'alien' can the kind of lodging (or 'arrangement') Murphy is likely to find really be? Well, 'quite alien' (after all, 'there is nothing new under the sun'). Again the begged question and attendant joke are lost in the translation.

Summing up, we may conclude that Beckett is operating a system of compensation as he translates himself into the French, making up for the loss of some of the word play generated in the original with the rather cruder humour of 'the blind alley of Baby Jesus'. The Italian translator likewise shows an ability for compensation in his use of 'vano' (*room/vain*) and 'sistemazione' (*arrangement*).

But does this conclusion really tell us anything about Beckett's relationship with Joyce or his scepticism about language? Does it establish the principles a translator should be applying as he translates Beckett?

The opening paragraph of *Murphy* describes a man forced to change his habits. In his earlier essay on Proust, Beckett had commented at length on just such circumstances, which he sees as constituting the key moments in *À la recherche du temps perdu.* He wrote:

> The periods of transition that separate consecutive adaptations ... represent the perilous zones in the life of the individual, dangerous, precarious, painful, mysterious and fertile, when for a moment the boredom of living is replaced by the suffering of being.[10]

Habit ('consecutive adaptations', 'cages') anaesthetizes for us the horrors and ecstasies of existence ('Habit is a great deadener', says Didi in *Waiting far Godot*[11]). Conversely, the loss of habit lays us open to them. The suggestion is that it is only when habit is lost that we really experience 'existence'; also, by implication, it is only then that we really appreciate the nature (and value) of habit, as both deceiver and comforter. But what is important from the linguistic point of view, from the translator's point of view, is that Beckett appears to see language as an element similar to habit, or rather, as the expression

[9] I am indebted here to Christopher Ricks's discussion of Beckett's use of 'quite' in the opening phrase of *Malone Dies:* 'I shall soon be quite dead at last ...'. Ricks, *Beckett's Dying Words,* Oxford University Press, Oxford, 1993, p. 129 and following.
[10] Samuel Beckett, *Proust and Three Dialogues with Georges Duthuit,* Calder, London, 1987, pp. 8-9.
[11] Samuel Beckett, *Waiting for Godot,* Faber & Faber, London, 1971, p. 95.

of habit *par excellence*, a 'deadener' that helps us to get through, but which at the same time keeps us away from a more immediate experience of reality (his complaint in the essay on Joyce that language was 'abstracted to death' gradually becomes a conviction that such abstraction is part of the very nature of language). In a letter to a friend written in 1937, two years after the completion of *Murphy* but before its publication, Beckett remarks:

> It is indeed becoming more and more difficult, even senseless, for me to write an official English. And more and more my own language appears to me like a veil that must be torn apart in order to get at the things (or the Nothingness) behind it. Grammar and Style. To me they seem to have become as irrelevant as a Victorian bathing suit or the imperturbability of a true gentleman. A mask. Let us hope the time will come, thank God that in certain circles it has already come, when language is most efficiently used where it is being most efficiently mis-used. As we cannot eliminate language all at once, we should at least leave nothing undone that might contribute to its falling into disrepute. To bore one hole after another in it, until what lurks behind it – be it something or nothing – begins to seep through; I cannot imagine a higher goal for a writer today.[12]

In the light of these comments our opening paragraph from *Murphy* makes a little more sense. It begins with a very traditional phrase 'The sun shone', arousing entirely conventional expectations that are then quickly and comically dashed. From being a traditionally positive thing, the sun is related to a negative and tedious determinism, but one underwritten by the religion (a dead-end?) to which the majority still subscribe. 'Murphy sat out of it, as though he were free' hints at grand metaphysical and existential questions, then deflated by the decidedly prosaic 'West Brompton'. In the next sentence, language is shown as rapidly falling into rigid patterns (north-western/south-eastern – drawing attention to what it has in common with a solar determinism), but also into traps of its own making: 'commanding' is the appropriate jargon word for speaking of a view from a window, but ridiculous once we have introduced the word 'cage'; 'to put on' seems to invite 'to put off', but this is, for purely arbitrary reasons, not standard discourse when referred to dressing. The exhortatory 'buckle to' (the kind' of imperative people tend to direct at Murphy) is immediately made crazy by being referred to what is, in any event, unavoidable (in this sense the sentence offers an early formulation of the thinking behind

---

[12] Samuel Beckett, *Disjecta*, Calder, London, 1983, pp. 171-3.

the Unnameable's famously contradictory but entirely understandable motto, 'I can't go on, I'll go on').

In short, here is an early example of Beckett making efficient use of the language by efficiently misusing it, 'boring holes in it'. He both illustrates language's habit-forming processes and then breaks them down or has them fall into absurdity. What is mocked, then, is not London, or Murphy, but language and the way we take its meanings for granted, as Murphy has taken his mew for granted, his cage. Here we see the greater appropriateness in the English that it is the 'mew' (cage) that has been condemned (Christianity, one feels, or at least 'il vicolo cieco del Bambino Gesù', being a habit Murphy must have abandoned long ago).

There is a similarity with Joyce, in the sense that the text draws our attention to itself as text and to words as words. And of course there is the same intellectual playfulness. But it differs from Joyce in the intention behind that focus and that play: rather than 'the thing itself', a triumph made of words, this opening paragraph to *Murphy* foregrounds an anyway unavoidable distance between words and their apparent content. In the same letter of 1937 Beckett concludes:

> '...for the time being we must be satisfied with little. At first it can only be a matter of somehow finding a method by which we can represent this mocking attitude towards the word, through words. In this dissonance between the means and their use it will perhaps become possible to feel a whisper of that final music or that silence that underlies all. With such a program, in my opinion, the latest work of Joyce has nothing whatever to do. There it seems rather to be a matter of an apotheosis of the word.[13]

With this in mind, one does not need to read much of *Murphy* to appreciate how un-Joycean this period of Beckett's work actually was. Joyce might well have been able to describe a character as 'a well-to-do ne'er do well' *(Murphy,* p. 14, omitted in the French and Italian), but he would not have done so as part of a process of having words cancel each other out, Beckett's project of, as it were, catching language out in its habit-forming process. 'She felt', we learn of Celia, Murphy's girlfriend, 'as she felt so often with Murphy, spattered with words that went dead as soon as they sounded; each word obliterated before it had time to make sense, by the word that came next; so that in the end she did not know what had been said. It was like difficult music heard for the first time.'

---

[13] Ibid.

(p. 27) The remark indicates that Beckett's intentions were already well formed when he wrote *Murphy* ('it will perhaps become possible to feel a whisper of that final music'), and also suggests the principle to which a translator could, or could try to remain faithful when translating this book: he must have the words of his own language cancel each other out, bump into each other, trip over each other, he must bring his own language into disrepute.

In his remarkable book *Beckett's Dying Words* (to which this essay owes a great deal) Christopher Ricks has shown Beckett trying to operate this principle as he translates *Murphy* into French. Here is Murphy, himself an expert with words and their allusions, trying one of his many ruses to beg himself some free tea in a cheap café. He has asked for the waitress to have his half drunk cup 'filled with hot':

> 'I know I am a great nuisance, but they have been too generous with the cowjuice.'
> Generous and cowjuice were the keywords here. No waitress could hold out against their mingled overtones of gratitude and mammary organs. (p. 51)

Ricks comments: 'Clearly Beckett despaired of rendering into French the fluid fostering sequence "generous", "cowjuice", "mingled overtones of gratitude and mammary organs".[14] So the French tries an entirely different trick:

> 'Je vous emmerde, je le sais bien, mais que voulez-vous, ils m'ont foutu tout plein de jus de vache.'
> 'Emmerde' et 'vache' furent ici les mots actifs, nulle serveuse ne pouvait résister à leurs harmoniques mélangées d'amour et de maternité. (p. 65)

> 'I'm pissing you off, I know, but what do you want, they have fucked me full up with cowjuice.'
> 'Pissing' and 'cow' were the keywords here, no waitress could resist their mingled harmonics of love and maternity.

The humour here, as with the opening paragraph of the book, is cruder and louder than the English and depends on the outrageous, but typically Beckettian and, within the context of the plot of *Murphy* (a series of star-crossed love affairs), entirely appropriate suggestion that 'emmerde' (*pissing off*, literally *shitting*) establishes a 'harmonique' with 'amour' (*love*). The Italian

---

[14] Ricks, *Beckett's Dying Words,* cit., p. 59.

translation gives:

> 'La smerdo, lo so, ma che cosa vuole, mi hanno fatto il pieno di broda di vacca.'
> 'Smerdo' e 'vacca' furono le parole attive; nessuna cameriera poteva resistere ai loro armonici miscugli di maternità e d'amore. (p. 70)

> 'I'm shitting you, I know, but what do you want, they've filled me up with cowsoup.'
> 'Shitting' and 'cow' were the keywords; no waitress could resist their mingled harmonics of maternity and love.

The English was 'I am a great nuisance'. Beckett gratefully accepted the French curiosity of 'emmerde' (scatology which has become acceptable), seeing the game he could then play with the assonant 'amour'. But 'smerdo' (*cover with shit*) is a rather different matter. Not only is it *not* acceptable in the social context of the café, it has not become domesticated and is not a common expression, but furthermore it lacks any phonetic harmonic with 'amore' (*love*). Is this why the translator inverts 'amore' and 'maternità', perhaps feeling there is more harmony between 'smerdo' (*I shit on*) and 'maternità' (or at least that maternity might involve some kind of 'smerdare'?) If so it uncouples the semantic connection between 'vacca' (*cow*) and 'maternità' (further reduced by translating 'jus' – *juice* – with 'broda' – *bad soup* – rather than, perhaps, 'spremuta' – *squeezed juice*) and leaves 'amore' very much out in the cold. That is, rather than having the impression of someone efficiently misusing language, having it trip over itself to reveal its absurdities, we read in vain for any sense at all. The whole thing has become merely bizarre.

Of course translating word play is always an arduous task and frequently unrewarding. One could point to failures on this score with any number of translations. But the special problem here is that word play has a particular role in Beckett's work, it reveals and breaks linguistic habits and, in drawing attention to the precariousness of language, cuts the ground from under the speculations of the author's famously eloquent characters and narrators. Here is Beckett, towards the end of *Murphy,* merrily giving the game away as the coroner who is examining Murphy's corpse is obliged to reflect that while a burnt body makes it easy to guess the cause of death, identification becomes correspondingly more difficult.

> 'Then perhaps I may venture to proceed,' said the coroner, 'to the other matter, the identity of the ... deceased. Here I need hardly say we

find ourselves embarrassed by that very feature of the – the –'

'Tragic occurrence,' said Dr Killiecrankie.

'Very feature of the tragic occurrence that stood us in such good stead in the matter of the manner of death. The matter of the manner of death. Still we must not complain. What does the poet say, Angus, perhaps you remember?'

'What poet?' said Dr Killiecrankie.

'"Never the rose without the thorn",' said the coroner. 'I quote from memory, bitter memory.' (p. 148)

Here what most stands out is the way Beckett sets up the expression 'the matter of the manner', starting with 'the other matter' (the identity of the deceased) to then return to 'the matter of the manner' (the cause of death). The coroner has a habit of repeating things, and Beckett makes sure he repeats this, for this is what so much of his writing is about, the matter (written words, sounds) of the manner (style, thought). The assonance between the two words draws immediate attention to the matter of (or with?) Beckett's manner, and this is underlined then by the pun on 'feature' (of Murphy or of his death?) and then by the comic play with two separate idioms, 'I quote from memory, bitter memory'. The way in which one idiomatic use of the word 'memory' here invites another quite different use in the general compulsion that is human speech looks forward to many other similar gambits in *The Trilogy* ('but I had been under the weather so long; under all weathers ...').[15] Thus Beckett points us to the absurdities of the language at work, its distance from the sad material reality of Murphy's corpse.

Through the French, the Italian becomes:

> 'In questo caso,' disse il coroner, 'mi sarà forse concesso di affrontare la seconda questione, l'identità del ... deceduto. A questo punto, com'è appena il caso di farvi notare, siamo piuttosto turbati da questo preciso aspetto del... del ...'
>
> 'Deplorevole avvenimento,' disse il dottor Killiecrankie.
>
> 'Da questo preciso aspetto del deplorevole avvenimento che ci è stato così utile per quanto concerne la modalità del decesso. La modalità del decesso. Tuttavia non bisogna lamentarsi. Come dice il poeta, Angus, se lo ricorda?'
>
> 'Non ha nessuna importanza,' disse il dottor Killiecrankie. 'Quale poeta?'

---

[15] Samuel Beckett, *Molloy,* Jupiter Books, Calder & Boyars, London, 1971, p.54.

"'Giammai rosa senza spine!'", disse il coroner. 'È' un settenario, mi
pare. Cito a memoria.' (pp. 197-8)

'In that case,' said the coroner, 'I will perhaps be allowed to deal with
the second question, the identity of the ... deceased. At this point, as
it is perhaps worth pointing out, we are rather disturbed by the exact
same aspect of the... of the...'
'Deplorable circumstance,' said Doctor Killiecrankie.
'By the exact same aspect of the deplorable circumstance that was
so useful to us as far as regards the mode of the decease. The mode
of the decease. All the same we must not complain. As the poet says,
Angus, do you remember?'
'It's not important,' said Doctor Killiecrankie. 'Which poet?'
"'Never the rose without the thorn!'" said the coroner. 'It's a seven-
syllable line, I think. I quote from memory.'

Not all is lost (thanks to Beckett's French), but much. The first paragraph is
full of repetitions ('caso' – *case* – 'questo' – *this*) but these seem merely infe-
licitous. Only the ambiguity of 'aspetto' (*aspect*) is kept. The way language
glosses over unpleasant reality with the correct expression (tragic occurrence,
'deplorevole avvenimento' – *deplorable circumstance*) is likewise maintained
and foregrounded, but then in the next paragraph 'the matter of the manner' is
gone, and hence the repetition (which is the matter with the coroner's manner)
loses much of its fun.

To compensate for these losses, in response to the question 'Come dice il
poeta ... ?' (*as the poet says ...?*), we have Dr Killiecrankie's assured 'Non ha
nessuna importanza' – *It's not important* – (from the French, not in the English), before the doctor even knows which poet or which line is being referred
to. It is the kind of provocation that Beckett might well agree with, for he is
hardly one to believe that what poets write can ultimately matter (in his essay
on Proust, Beckett wrote: 'Whatever opinion we may be pleased to hold on
the subject of death, we may be sure that it is meaningless and valueless'[16]
– the opinion, or death?).

But however appropriate and witty this addition might be, it does not draw
our attention to the language in the way the 'matter of the manner' or 'I quote
from memory, bitter memory' do. For this we have to wait for the coroner's
comment, 'È' un settenario, mi pare. Cito a memoria' (*It's a seven syllable
line, I think. I quote from memory*). For this truly does draw our attention to

---

[16] *Proust and Three Dialogues with Georges Duthuit*, cit., p. 6.

the 'matter of the manner', the purely formal aspect of language. What is more, the distance between the level of discourse (literary comment) and the matter in question (Murphy's squalid decease) is part of that long project Beckett has embarked on of highlighting 'the dissonance' between the linguistic 'means and their use'. To make the dissonance scream a little louder, 'Giammai rosa senza spine' (*Never rose without a thorn*) is *not* a 'settenario' (*seven syllable line*). In fact there are eight syllables. (The Italian translator is to be applauded here, the French being 'Jamais de rose sans épines! dit le coroner. C'est un octosyllabe ...' – p. 188 – '*Never rose without a thorn! said the coroner. That is an eight-syllable line...*' whereas here, in the French, there are only seven syllables.) So much for quoting from memory (but how could one, in the circumstances, quote from anything else?).

So far I have suggested that Beckett's writing is concerned with the creation of a deliberate distance between form and content in order to satirize the presence of that distance in all discourse, and above all the extent to which language anaesthetizes an existence which is for the most part unpleasant. I have also suggested that the translation loses much of this effect, particularly in the piece quoted at the opening of the chapter from *Watt*. But advancing this idea in class, students have frequently objected that what is missing in the translation is 'merely' the humour, the element that makes such a pessimistic vision bearable. It is also suggested that for someone determined to state the limits of language in this way, Beckett has a great deal of fun with it. It is time to return for a moment to the discussion of habit in the essay on Proust.

Habit, in whatever form – a room, a house, a hat, a religion, a marriage, a language – is a great deadener. It helps us get through. Without it we will not get through. With it, we will not know very much. 'The only true paradise', Beckett says in his essay on Proust, 'is the paradise that has been lost', i.e., a habit whose loss we are now lamenting, Murphy's cage in the Brompton mew perhaps. In this sense, far from being a negative thing, habit is altogether necessary, even desirable. And in the same essay Beckett goes so far as to insist that 'There is no such thing as a bad habit ...'.

Looked at from this angle, the problem with habit is not so much that it deadens, as that it does not deaden for ever: we are obliged to change. Habits do not last, paradise has a way of getting lost. And here one might quote in full a sentence I elided earlier on: 'The periods of transition that separate consecutive adaptations, *because by no expedient of macabre transubstantiation can the grave-sheets serve as swaddling clothes* [my italics], represent the perilous zones ... etc.'. You cannot get from cradle to grave in the same clothes, or in the same room, with the same words. That is the problem. Beckett's work is a comedy of habits, often linguistic habits, formed and cast off, narrators, voices, invented and tossed away. Each is loved, indeed revelled in for the brief respite it offers, but then sadly understood to be only that. The attitude to language is thus ambiguous: to be criticized for its lack of reality; to be applauded... for its lack of reality.

Watt, hero of the eponymous novel, is a questioner, a philosophical man, constantly seeking to explain the strange phenomena around him. For, once explained, once put into words that is, he can feel happy about those phenomena. The trouble is that words are never quite enough to settle reality. Or never for very long. You can never feel they did the job that Beckett felt Joyce wanted them to do in *Finnegan's Wake*. With the result that one is constantly trying and failing to perform the same impossible task of explaining things to oneself. Quoted below is a moment from the thirty or so pages in which Watt puzzles over the way his master, the mysterious, god-like Mr Knott, has arranged for any food that he leaves to be eaten up by a dog before the day is over. In order to make sure that a dog will always be available for this task an entire family is made responsible for keeping the dog, and, should they be necessary, reserve dogs. Beckett is already two pages into his genealogy of the dog-keeping family, when we have this:

> And then to pass on to the next generation there was Tom's boy young Simon aged twenty, whose it is painful to relate
>
> ?
>
> and his young cousin wife his uncle Sam's girl Ann, aged nineteen, whose it will be learnt with regret beauty and utility were greatly diminished by two withered arms and a game leg of unsuspected tubercular origin, and Sam's two surviving boys Bill and Mat aged eighteen and seventeen respectively, who having come into this world respectively blind and maim were known as Blind Bill and Maim Mat respectively, and Sam's other married daughter Kate aged twenty-one years, a fine girl but a bleeder*, and her young cousin husband her uncle Jack's son Sean aged twenty-one years, a sterling fellow but a bleeder too, and Frank's daughter Bridie aged fifteen years, a prop and a stay to the family, sleeping as she did by day and at night receiving in the toolshed so as not to disturb the family for twopence, or threepence, or fourpence, or sometime's even fivepence a time, that depended, or a bottle of ale, and ... (pp. 99-100)

I break off here at a point about halfway through what is no more than a typical sentence from the central sections of Watt. The footnote indicated in the text reads as follows: 'Haemophilia is, like enlargement of the prostate, an exclusively male disorder. But not in this work' (p. 100). Even the most casual reading of the English transmits a sense of manic compulsion, of a bizarre mismatch between tone and content, of sudden and curious shifts of register in what at first pretends to be the voice of a dry chronicler. To grasp just how much is going on, one need only compare the passage with the Italian, this time translated from the English.

> E poi per passare oltre, alla generazione successiva, c'era il ragazzo di Tom, il giovane Simon di anni venti, di cui è doloroso riferire
> ?
> e la sua giovane moglie cugina, figlia di suo zio Sam, Ann, di anni diciannove, la cui bellezza e vigore fisico, si apprenderà con rammarico, erano menomati gravemente da due braccia avvizzite e una gamba zoppa di indubbia origine tubercolare, e i due ragazzi superstiti di Sam, Bill e Mat rispettivamente di anni diciotto e diciassette, i quali essendo venuti al mondo il primo cieco e il secondo storpio erano conosciuti rispettivamente come Bill il Cieco e Mat lo Storpio, e l'altra figlia maritata di Sam, Kate, di anni ventuno, bella ragazza ma emofiliaca*, e il suo giovane marito cugino, figlio di suo zio Jack, Sean, di anni ventuno, individuo robusto ma emofiliaco pure lui, e la figlia di Frank, Bridie, di anni quindici, aiuto e sostegno della famiglia poiché dormiva di giorno, e di notte riceveva nel ripostiglio degli attrezzi in modo da non disturbare i familiari per due pence, o tre pence, o quattro pence, o talvolta anche cinque pence alla volta il che variava, o una bottiglia di birra, e ... (p. 105)

> And then to pass on, to the following generation, there was Tom's boy, young Simon, twenty years old, of whom it is painful to tell
> ?
> and his young wife and cousin, daughter of his uncle Sam, Ann, nineteen years old, whose beauty and physical strength, it will be learned with regret, were seriously handicapped by two withered arms and a lame leg of undoubted tubercular origin, and Sam's two surviving boys, Bill and Mat, respectively eighteen and seventeen years old, who having come into the world the former blind and the latter lame were known respectively as Blind Bill and Lame Mat, and Sam's other married daughter, Kate, twenty-one years old, a pretty girl but haemophiliac*, and her young husband and cousin, her Uncle Jack's son, Sean, twenty-one years old, and robust fellow but also haemophiliac, and Frank's daughter, Bridie, fifteen years old, help and support of the family since she slept by day and at night received in the toolshed in

such a way as not to disturb the other members of the family for two pence, or three pence, or four pence, or sometimes even five pence at a time, it varied, or a bottle of beer, and…

The footnote this time reads: 'L'emofilia è, come l'ingrossamento della prostata, un disturbo esclusivamente maschile. Ma non in quest'opera' (p. 105) (*Haemophilia is, like enlargement of the prostate, an exclusively male disorder. But not in this work*).

Perhaps the first thing to note is the alterations in sentence structure. The English, apart from the sheer length of the sentence, is highly convoluted: the introduction of a subordinate clause directly after a relative pronoun ('whose it will be learnt with regret beauty and utility') seems particularly unusual, especially given the absence of punctuation. Italian is a language more inclined to a density of subordinate clauses, yet here the translator decides to adopt a more standard structure in, 'la cui bellezza e vigore fisico, si apprenderà con rammarico' (*whose beauty and physical strength, it will be learned with regret*). This is not a necessary change, it would have been perfectly possible to maintain the English ordering and its attendant effects in the Italian, hence one cannot help wondering whether the translator has really appreciated what Beckett is up to.

Other changes are:

- The three English uses of 'respectively' are reduced to two in Italian.
- The alliteration of Blind Bill and Maim Mat is inevitably lost in Bill il Cieco (*Blind Bill*) e Mat lo Storpio (*Lame Mat*).
- The bizarre, repeated, unpunctuated rhythms of 'his young cousin wife his uncle Sam's girl Ann', and then later, 'her young cousin husband her uncle Jack's son Sean', are inevitably diluted in 'la sua giovane moglie cugina, figlia di suo zio Sam, Ann' (*his young wife and cousin, daughter of his uncle Sam, Ann*), and again, 'il suo giovane marito cugino, figlio di suo zio Jack, Sean' (*her young husband and cousin, son of his uncle Jack, Sean*), though Beckett's ever important symmetry is kept.
- 'beauty and utility' were the two criteria by which utilitarian philosophy tended to assess the value of something; this sense of formal measure and system is lost in 'bellezza e vigore fisico' (*beauty and physical strength*).
- 'unsuspected tubercular origin' has been inverted (why?) to 'indubbia origine tubercolare' (*undoubted tubercular origin*).
- The sexual innuendos that Beckett brings out from the idiom 'a prop and a stay' and from 'toolshed' are lost.
- There is the loss of the register shift between 'bleeder' in the text and 'haemophiliac' in the footnote.

The changes will appear slight in a passage so bursting with absurdity as to provoke a sense of hilarity and dismay in any language; nevertheless it seems worth pointing out that they all occur at the cutting edge of Beckett's efficient misuse of language, his revelation of the 'matter of the manner', and in doing so, they blunt it.

The opening line of the passage suggests the authority of chronicle, and, what is more, old chronicle. The tone is almost biblical, certainly dusty. But this authority is then undermined by a gap in the text and a question mark, suggesting that there is something the chronicler does not know, or that the text itself was collected in an imperfect state. In any event, we are made aware of the problem of authority. This comes across well in the translation. But the convoluted word order of the English is an exaggeration of the old-fashioned chronicler's style, and noticeably the convolution takes place at a moment when the reader is invited to respond to the story with sentiment as though it were real ('whose it is painful to relate', 'whose it will be learnt with regret'). But such gestures are formulaic, and, coming as they do in the midst of an immense list of diseases and handicaps they can only have the effect of drawing attention to the mechanical nature of their utterance, indeed to the impossibility of our feeling anything at all for the sufferers described. They are like 'tragic occurrence' in the section quoted from *Murphy*, formulas that help us *not to think* of the significance of what they refer to. Altering the order of these formulas in Italian removes this foregrounding effect and dulls the extent to which we think of them as 'words gone dead' or 'abstracted to death'.

The obsessive repetition of 'respectively' suggests again the chronicler's pedantry. He is determined to get a grip on this hugely extended family. This, then, like the exaggeratedly formal tone, is another aspect that plays off against the hiatus with question mark.

Another thing that contrasts with the texts pedantry and makes us suspicious of its authority is the alliteration of Blind Bill and Maim Mat. Is it really possible that the two boys' handicaps happen to alliterate with their names, that language should offer this bizarre, sub-poetic palliative? From being chronicle, the piece descends to doggerel. Here, Beckett suggests, is another way of language's glossing over something unhappy, through alliteration. It might be objected here that the Italian translator could not have kept the alliteration while translating the illnesses accurately and keeping the names Beckett chose. But since neither the names nor the particular diseases seem important here, but only the ludicrous fact of name-disease alliteration, one can see no reason why the translator should not invent in order to keep faith (having said that, this is one of the few opportunities Beckett himself misses in his French translation).

The rhythms of 'his young cousin wife his uncle Sam's girl Ann' clearly combine once again the fussiness of the chronicler with the way attention is drawn to the formal nature of language, and here one has nothing to object to in the translation except the introduction of the commas. Beckett is clearly removing as many of the commas as possible to increase the humour of the reader's trying to get through these formulations. He does the same in his French translation.

But what are we to make of the shift from 'unsuspected' to 'indubbia' (*undoubted*)? The curiosity of the English (and Beckett's French) is that it suggests that the narrator knows something that the characters do not. From being chronicler he has become omniscient (hence creative) novelist. But if he knows what the characters do not, why did he not know what was in the hiatus? In the Italian everybody knows about the nature of the illness so there is no contradiction. The curiosity in the English is then emphasized by the introduction of the footnote relative to 'bleeder'. While not missing the opportunity to remind us of yet another very real disease (enlargement of the prostate), the footnote nonchalantly reminds us that the whole passage is made up anyway. Yet precisely as it does this, the shift from the old-fashioned, brutal vernacular 'bleeder' (one of the more disturbing shifts of tone in the chronicler's style) to the polite and medical 'haemophilia' suggests another kind of authority, that of the learned scholar making notes on the text. And again we have talked about two painful problems without really thinking about them at all. The shift is here inevitably lost in the Italian, which has only one word for haemophiliac.

Summing up, we can say that while the translation certainly 'works', in that it does carry over many of the passage's devices and is definitely good fun to read, nevertheless it constantly erodes Beckett's comic foregrounding of the formal aspects of language, its tendency to motor on regardless of content, if only to arrive at some appearance of a conclusion. And this, after all, is Beckett's subject. For at the end of this endless passage about the Lynch family and their famished dog that must always be ready to eat the remains of Mr Knott's food, we finally hear that Watt 'had turned, little by little, a disturbance into words, he had made a pillow of old words, for his head. Little by little, and not without labour' (p. 115). Such is the habit-forming power of language, and the keywords here are clearly 'old' and 'not without labour'. At every point of the translation it is the dusty, over-used nature of the words that should be stressed. It takes so much effort to make sense of things. Very soon, those old words will be too old, the pillow will cease to function, and then we will arrive at this kind of passage just a couple of pages further on:

Five generations, twenty-eight souls, nine hundred and eighty years, such was the proud record of the Lynch family, when Watt entered Mr Knott's service.*

Then a moment passed and all was changed. Not that there was death, for there was not. Nor that there was birth, for there was not either. But puff puff breath again they breathed, in and out, the twenty-eight, and all was changed.

As by the clouding the unclouding of the sun the sea, the lake, the ice, the plain, the marsh, the mountain-side, or any other similar natural expanse, be it liquid or be it solid.

Till changing changing in twenty over twenty-eight equals five over seven times twelve equals sixty over seven equals eight months and a half approximately, if none died, if none were born, a thousand years! (p. 101)

Watt has finished his chronicle of the Lynch family, but just when everything seems fixed, everything changes. How? People breathe, people live, people die; statistics do not remain the same for long. And precisely as we appreciate this, the language shifts, the syntax goes to pieces, the text is full of curiosities – 'Nor that there was birth, for there was not either – puff puff breath again they breathed'. But even within change, the language gropes for its lists, its certainties – 'As by the clouding the unclouding of the sun the sea ... or any other similar natural expanse, be it liquid or be it solid' – until finally the mind fastens on the principle of change itself in a sort of mad search for mechanisms to calculate a fixed point in the future: the day, that is, when the sum of the ages of the Lynch family will amount to 1000 years ('Till changing changing ...').

There is a sort of wildness and desperation in the language here that gains from the contrast with the slow labour of old words that has come before. The reader is left, on first reading at least, bewildered. When he understands the section with its mad schoolroom mathematics, the full comedy of 'approximately' will become apparent. All this effort for an 'approximate' calculation of the great day when the Lynches will achieve their collective thousand years!

With just slight losses in the demotic aspect of the syntax of the second paragraph the Italian holds up admirably here.

Cinque generazioni, ventotto anime, novecentottant'anni, tale era il superbo primato della famiglia Lynch, quando Watt entrò al servizio del signor Knott. *

Poi un istante e tutto cambiò. Non una morte, ché morte non ci fu.

Neppure una nascita, ché nascita neppure ci fu. Ma ciuf ciuf un respiro, dentro e fuori, dei ventotto, e al respiro successivo tutto era cambiato.

Come con il coprirsi e scoprirsi del sole il mare, il lago, il ghiaccio, la piana, la palude, il pendio della montagna o altra simile distesa naturale, sia essa liquida, o solida.

Finché cambiando cambiando in venti diviso ventotto è uguale a cinque diviso sette volte dodici è uguale a sessanta diviso sette è uguale a otto mesi e mezzo pressapoco, se non moriva nessuno, se non nasceva nessuno, mille anni! (p. 107)

Five generations, twenty-eight souls, nine-hundred-and-eighty years, such was the proud record of the Lynch family, when Watt entered the service of Mr Knott. *

Then an instant and everything changed. Not a death, for death there was not. Nor a birth, for birth there was not either. But puff puff a breath, in and out, of the twenty-eight, and at the next breath everything had changed.

As with the covering and uncovering of the sun the sea, the lake, the ice, the plain, the march, the mountainside or other similar natural expanses, whether liquid or solid.

Until changing changing in twenty divided by twenty-eight equals five divided by seven times twelve equals sixty divided by seven equals eight and a half months more or less, if no one died, if no one was born, a thousand years!

The footnote below the English text reads: 'The figures given here are incorrect. The consequent calculations are therefore doubly erroneous'. But of course it could hardly have mattered to Watt if his calculations were erroneous, so long as he was not aware of this. What matters for him is getting back to his pillow of old words, 'for to explain had always been to exorcize, for Watt' (p. 75).

With his fascination for the matter of the manner of language one can see how for Beckett translation would have held a particular interest, revealing that such mechanisms were not limited to any particular language but had rather to do with the mind itself, its constant attempts to settle into habits of thought, to gloss over experience. Patrick Bowles, who worked with Beckett on the translation of *Molloy* from French to English, wrote of their collaboration: 'From the outset, he (Beckett) stressed that it shouldn't merely be translated; we should write a new book in the new language. For with the transposition of speech occurs a transposition of thought, and even, at times, of actions.

"You wouldn't say that in English, you'd say something else".[17] The keywords here would seem to be 'you'd say', indicating the extent to which thought is driven by language, or atrophied in it.

In conclusion, Beckett's translation of his own writing shows an author being faithful to the original inspiration of the work, rather than the surface sense of the text at any particular point (though it is remarkable in general how close Beckett does stay to his original). By doing so, he alerts us to the kind of changes that need to be made before a translation can have anything like the integration (or in this case disintegration) of language and content that the original had. If the Italian is slightly less convincing and less pleasurable than either the French or English, it is because it lacks that tight relationship, because there is less of the word play that at once underlines what Beckett is doing and makes his pessimism fun to read, makes it fit, that is, for presentation at a conference on the great comic writers of this century. At which point it would seem appropriate to close with Beckett's own French translation of the quotation from *Watt* which opened our essay. Here everything is changed semantically, in order that it remain the same in its overall effect:

> Personnellement bien sûr je déplore tout. Pas un mot, pas une joie, pas un acte, pas une voix, pas une pensée, pas un pleur, pas un doute, pas une peur, pas un oui, pas un non, pas un cul, pas un con, pas une soif, pas une peine, pas un rire, pas une haine, pas un nom, pas une face, nulle heure, nulle place, que je ne déplore amèrement. Une ordure de bout en bout.[18]

Back-translation cannot illustrate how Beckett changes the semantics to keep rhyme and rhythm. But for the record, here is an English version of this French.

> Personally of course I deplore everything. Not a word, not a joy, not an action, not a voice, not a thought, not a tear, not a doubt, not a fear, not a yes, not a no, not an arse, not a cock, not a thirst, not a pain, not a laugh, not a hate, not a name, not a face, no time, no place, that I do not deplore bitterly. An ordure from beginning to end.

[17] Quoted by Deirdre Bair in her book, *Samuel Beckett: A Biography*, 1978, p.464.
[18] Samuel Beckett, *Watt*, Les Editions de Minuit, Paris, 1968, p. 46.

6. Barbara Pym and the Untranslatable Commonplace

Since the revival of Barbara Pym's fortunes in 1977, it has been generally acknowledged that she was a novelist of some stature, yet a certain unease and confusion remain as to the exact nature of her achievement. Critics, such as Michael Cotsell in his *Barbara Pym* (Macmillan's Modern Novelists series), make a great deal of her rejection of avant-garde experimentalism, her determination to write 'unabashedly romantic' novels,[1] and certainly much of her popularity has depended on the apparently traditional nature of her work. All the same, critics are equally eager to claim for her the serious role of having accurately reflected and interpreted the historical developments of her time, in particular that sense of existential angst typical of the work of many of her contemporaries. One thus arrives at such curious conclusions as: 'Her presentation has nothing in common with that of such a writer as Beckett – she is far too warm and amusing in her appreciation of the texture of ordinary lives – but nevertheless pointlessness and futility are everywhere in her novels ...'.[2] In short, there is some vagueness as to the exact nature of the poetics Pym adopts to link the enthusiastic focus on domestic detail and the painful awareness of futility, to the extent that there are moments when Cotsell betrays a desire that Pym had concentrated on the former and played down the latter.

Apart from this uncertainty as to exactly why and how Pym's works 'work', it may also be interesting to reflect on how they have, or haven't travelled. Since the revival of 1977 and the reissuing of all her novels in paperback, success in the UK has been matched only by success in the USA, while in Europe the translation of her novels has not brought Pym any particular acclaim, or sales, and even less has she entered into the canon of English literary novelists of her time (Graham Greene, Anthony Powell, Elizabeth Bowen, *et al.*). Only when published in the original English, then, have her novels been widely read and loved. And even here there is a distinction to be drawn. For in the USA (and one is thinking not so much of the universities as of the kind of opinions expressed in the literary pages of the 'serious' papers) Pym is seen not as a great novelist, or even a particularly literary novelist, but as

---

[1] Michael Cotsell, *Barbara Pym,* Macmillan, London, 1989, p. 4.
[2] Ibid., p. 3.

an exponent of a special kind of English quaintness, offering a fund of genteel drollery that Americans perhaps love to look back at, enthuse over and define themselves in contrast to.

While I appreciate that such claims are dangerously general in nature, my purpose is to arrive at the following hypothesis: that there may be something in Pym's novels that is not only difficult to convey in translation, but perhaps not even properly understood outside the country (or even the milieu) in which she was writing. The aim of this chapter will be to examine this idea through a close comparison of passages from the original English of *A Few Green Leaves,* the last of Pym's novels, with their translation in Italian.

In a discussion of Henry Green's *Party Going* in his book *The Genesis of Secrecy,* Frank Kermode remarks that 'it belongs to a class of narratives which *have* to mean more, or other than they manifestly say',[3] because, as Kermode goes on to point out, Green's novel so wilfully fails to satisfy our normal expectations while never appearing to be exactly incompetent. Now *A Few Green Leaves* is not on the same level of strangeness as *Party Going,* which we shall be looking at in the next chapter, but it shares with it, more than any other Pym novel, a cheerful willingness to frustrate the expectations it so rapidly and traditionally sets up. The young(ish) Emma Howick comes to live (alone) in a small Oxfordshire village. A variety of possible suitors present themselves: Tom, the clergyman, Adam, a food inspector and journalist, and Graham, an ex-flame and successful anthropologist. The reader is prepared for a series of vicissitudes revolving around the question, will she get the right man, a plot Pym openly nods to by calling her heroine Emma and explicitly mentioning Jane Austen's novel.

It might be objected of course that in modern times such obvious reference back to a traditional kind of story can only mean that the author will be setting out to distort it and/or transform it, and that in this sense Pym does prepare us for what follows. But this is true only to a limited extent. For as *A Few Green Leaves* unfolds it becomes clear that this is not a satire of the romantic novel (the way Austen's own *Northanger Abbey* is), or even a modern recasting of an old story, or cynical denial that romance can happen. What is disconcerting in *A Few Green Leaves* is not the subversion of a traditional plot, but the almost disappearance of any plot at all: every move towards romantic contact dissolves in a mass (or a wealth, if you like) of minor details; so much so, that it is only in the very last pages of the novel that we are given the consolation of a vague allusion to a possible romance that may, or again may not, take

---

[3] Frank Kermode, *The Genesis of Secrecy,* Harvard University Press, Cambridge, Massachusetts, 1979, p. 7.

place after the book is closed.

Inevitably, *A Few Green Leaves* is the novel that critics find hardest to cope with. 'Its weakness', writes Michael Cotsell clearly regretting earlier and more exuberant works, 'is that it does not succeed in greatly interesting us in the lives of its characters. This is partly because, instead of focusing ... on a small group, it employs quite a large cast, some of whom seem merely sketched'.[4] Interestingly enough, in his discussion of *Party Going* Kermode points out that the traditionalist critic's chief objection to that book is its presentation of characters so vacuous that we can take no real interest in them. Green's novel seems to fritter away in a long series of inane conversations while the plot is so breathtakingly inconsequential that nobody could possibly care what happens. In Pym's case, no sooner has she set up what appears to be the traditional romantic story line than this breaks down into insignificant scenes full of quaint minutiae and culture-specific bric-a-brac.

What is it, then, that the book 'means', or that the author hopes will make up for our thwarted expectations (whether of romance or satire)? It is time to examine a first piece of text. Here is the Italian to the second paragraph of the opening page of the book. Emma has decided to join in the annual village walk through the grounds of the local manor house, something permitted, though she doesn't know this, only on the Sunday after Easter. The local clergyman, Tom, explains the tradition (the Italian is, as always followed by a back-translation):

> Quel diritto alla passeggiata annuale risaliva al secolo diciassettesi-
> mo, l'aveva appreso dal parroco Tom Dagnall, uomo alto e di austere
> avvenenza, i cui occhi castani mancavano tuttavia della sfumatura di
> sottomissione canina che si addice a tale colore. Era vedovo e di solito
> non frequentava le nubili, ma Emma era figlia della sua vecchia amica
> Beatrix Howick e sembrava una di quelle donne sul cui aspetto le riviste
> femminili hanno molto da dire, sebbene a Tom questa idea non fosse
> venuta in mente. La vedeva soltanto come una persona di buon senso,
> intorno alla trentina, scura di capelli, magra e forse capace di parlare
> con intelligenza della storia locale, suo grande interesse e addirittura
> la sua passione. Inoltre era venuta da poco ad abitare nel cottage della
> madre e gli pareva di avere, come parroco, il dovere di far sì che si
> sentisse a suo agio nella comunità. (p.5)[5]

---

[4] Michael Cotsell, *Barbara Pym*, Macmillan, London, 1989, p. 132.
[5] All quotations in Italian are taken from *Qualche foglia verde*, La Tartaruga edizioni, Milan, 1989. Translation by Frida Ballini. This is the only translation available in Italian. Page numbers are indicated in brackets at the end of each quotation.

This right to the annual walk went back to the seventeenth century, she had learned from the rector, Tom Dagnall, a tall man of austere good looks, whose brown eyes nevertheless lacked that hint of canine submission that goes well with this colour. He was a widower and did not normally frequent single women, but Emma was the daughter of his old friend Beatrix Howick and seemed to be one of those women whose looks women's magazines have a great deal to say about, though this was not an idea that had occurred to Tom. He just saw her as a sensible person, about thirty years old, thin, with dark hair and perhaps capable of talking intelligently about local history, his great interest and even passion. Besides, she had recently come to live in her mother's cottage and it seemed to him that as rector it was his duty to do what he could to have her feel at home in the community.

Perhaps the first thing that strikes one about Pym, in any language, is how much information she packs into a few sentences, and in what an apparently haphazard way that information is delivered. Almost never does the first sentence of a paragraph lead us to suspect where it will end, almost never is anyone described directly, but always in terms of something else. Here Emma meets one of the prime candidates for romance, but the introduction comes through his pedantic comment on local history, something which we are soon to be told is 'addirittura la sua passione' (*even his passion*). Thus, at the moment he is introduced, the clergyman appears to be excluded from courting Emma because his passion lies elsewhere. The most he hopes for from her is intelligent conversation about what really interests him.

Two of the sentences are quite sibylline in the Italian. The first is the comment on his eyes which 'mancavano tuttavia della sfumatura di sottomissione canina che si addice a tale colore' (*whose brown eyes nevertheless lacked that hint of canine submission that goes well with this colour*). The second is the remark that Emma 'sembrava una di quelle donne sul cui aspetto le riviste femminili hanno molto da dire' (*seemed to be one of those women whose looks women's magazines have a great deal to say about*).

Particularly curious in the first sentence is the 'tuttavia' (*however, nevertheless*). If Tom is a man of 'austera avvenenza' (*austere good looks*), why is it surprising that his brown eyes do not have a look of 'sottomissione canina' (*canine submission*)? We would hardly expect an austere fellow to look submissive. In the second sentence we simply do not understand what kind of 'type' Emma is and what exactly it is that the 'riviste femminili' (*women's magazines*) have to say about her. Is she attractive or isn't she? Here is the English:

> This annual walk was a right dating back from the seventeenth century, Tom Dagnall, the rector, had told her. He was a tall man, austerely good-looking, but his brown eyes lacked the dog-like qualities so often associated with that colour. As a widower he tended not to attach himself to single women, but Emma was the daughter of his old friend Beatrix Howick and rather the type that women's magazines used to make a feature of 'improving', though this thought had not occurred to Tom. He saw her only as a sensible person in her thirties, dark-haired, thin and possibly capable of talking intelligently about local history, his great interest and passion. Besides, she had recently come to live in her mother's cottage and he felt he had a certain duty, as rector, to make her welcome. (p.7)[6]

With regard to the two sentences that appeared curious in the Italian one notes the following differences: that the English does not suggest that 'canine submission' 'goes well with' ('si addice a') brown eyes, merely that 'dog-like qualities' are 'so often associated with that colour'. That is, Pym does not herself endorse the notion that brown eyes and 'dog-likeness' (let alone 'submission') go together, but lets us know that this is a commonly held view. At this point we can begin to attach some sense to the 'but', the mystifying 'tuttavia' (*however/ nevertheless*) in the Italian. Perhaps what Pym is saying is that whereas Tom is conventional, as a clergyman, in his austere good looks, his brown eyes are not entirely conventional, in that they do not have the 'dog-like qualities' brown eyes are often associated with. But the exact nature of the irony is still not clear and likewise, in both languages, Tom's character.

With regard to the other sentence, the divergence is more substantial. Emma is the type 'women's magazines used to make a feature of "improving"'. Thus she is not very attractive, or at least does not dress well (and this partly explains, perhaps, Tom's readiness to waive his rule, or fear, of talking to single women). One notes, however, that the word 'improving', like so many throughout the book, is in inverted commas, suggesting that this is not necessarily the author's opinion.

The other important difference in this sentence is that the English sets this habit of women's magazines in the past. They 'used to' try to 'improve' types like Emma, but now they have given up, or at least turned their attention elsewhere. Types like Emma no longer feature in women's magazines. Yet she is to be the heroine of the book. Much of *A Few Green Leaves* plays

---

[6] All quotations from the original English of *A Few Green Leaves* are taken from the Grafton edition, London, 1981. Page numbers are indicated in brackets at the end of each quotation.

on the idea that its characters have in some way outlived their time: '... all in all Miss Vereker had nothing to complain of in her present life, except that it was not the past' (p. 183).

Two other divergences shout very loud. The Italian eliminates the consequential 'as' in the remark 'As a widower he tended not to attach himself to single women', so that this becomes 'Era vedovo e di solito non frequentava le nubili' (*He was a widower and did not normally frequent single women*). The Italian offers no more than an assembly of facts, the English suggests necessary consequence: apparently there is some kind of convention that says that widowed clergymen do not frequent single women. The result of course is that one part of the reader's mind wants to protest that the opposite should be true. Being a widower he *should* be seeing eligible women. The irony generated here by the gap between polite convention (widowed clergymen do not frequent single women) and what would seem most natural is then continued in the comedy of Tom's elaborate excuses for, on this occasion, not observing his usual habit of steering clear of the girls. Notably, he finds another convention, his duty towards new parishioners, that, together with the excuse that Emma is not attractive (in the women's magazine sense) and is the daughter of an old friend, cancels out, or overrides the first convention.

The other divergence in the translation comes with the announcement that local history is Tom's 'great interest and passion'. The fact that the English does not qualify this, as the Italian does with 'addirittura' (*even*), thus showing surprise and pointing up the comedy, gives us a particularly Pym-like bleakness: in Pym's world it is *not* surprising that local history is Tom's passion. After all, we will soon discover that Adam Prince's passion is good wine, that Emma's is anthropology, that Miss Lickerish spends her time looking after hedgehogs and that Tom's sister becomes obsessed by the idea of possessing a dog (that would have the dog-like qualities which Tom almost has, but not quite). The comedy is certainly there in the English, indeed even more so if one remembers that the English syntax begs the question as to whether the adjective 'great' qualifies both 'interest' and 'passion' ('his great interest and passion'), but it is at once more discreet, and sadder.

Of course we could put all this down to poor translation, rather than any inherent untranslatability in Pym's English, and that is certainly true of divergences such as the absence of the consequential 'as' and the introduction of the unnecessary 'addirittura' (*even*), as well as the difficulty the Italian has here with an exact translation of the reference to Emma's age. But poor translation can in itself be revealing, especially in one so clearly capable, as this translator will show herself to be, of understanding syntactically complex English and presenting it in fairly polished Italian. What I hope to show is that there is a link between these divergences which suggests a particular approach, or vision, that Pym has, that the translator has failed to grasp.

The paragraph begins by referring to an ancient custom that Emma is, unknowingly, following (the annual walk through the manor house grounds). It goes on to say that Tom does not have the quality that his eye colour is so often associated with. Then we learn that Tom generally does follow, though not in this case, some acknowledged convention that deters him from frequenting single women. The woman with whom he is now breaking this habit is then described, not directly, but through reference to what was, in the past, a convention of women's magazines. The paragraph concludes by conceding that a clergyman has a certain duty to make someone from outside the community welcome and that it is this 'duty' which permits Tom to disregard his normal concern (presumably) for the kind of gossip that would be aroused by his talking to unattached women.

One's first impression, then, is of chronic indirectness and an obsessive attention to nuance and etiquette. But the situation becomes clearer if we look at the paragraph in terms of point of view. Essentially, we could say that at least three points of view are established: the first is the point of view of society, or rather the multiplicity of points of view which go to make up social conventions: this is the point of view of women's magazines, of people who associate brown eyes with dog-like qualities, of a community which expects a rector to behave in a certain way, of established customs which permit particular walks on particular days, etc.

The next point of view is Tom's, the view of a man who as it were picks his way through conflicting conventions, or, in the case of the women's magazine, simply does not know of them ('though this thought had not occurred to Tom'), as Emma had not known about the custom behind the walk she was taking.

The third point of view is that of the narrator who makes it clear that it is she describing her characters in relation to conventional points of view, in which she is expert, but to which she does not necessarily subscribe, as is signalled in the use of inverted commas around 'improving'.

All slippages so far noted in the translation have to do with the author's habit of describing her characters in relation to received ideas or conventions: Tom's eyes not having the submissiveness *expected of* brown eyes, Emma the kind of person women's magazines *used to wish to improve,* Tom not frequenting single women *because* single.

The habit of signalling some received idea or piece of jargon by using inverted commas is something Pym does so frequently in *A Few Green Leaves* that it is worth putting a little pressure on the technique. Here are some examples with their respective translations and back-translations:

> All in good time, when she [Emma] had had a chance to study the village, to 'evaluate' whatever material she was able to collect. (p. 14)

> Ogni cosa a suo tempo, non appena avesse avuto l'occasione di studiare il villaggio e valutare il materiale da raccogliere. (p. 11)

> Everything in its own time, as soon as she had had the chance to study the village and assess the material to collect.

Pym's third person narrative moves effortlessly in and out of indirect discourse. Here our attention is drawn to the way Emma's thoughts are conditioned, or coloured, by the jargon of the field she works in (anthropology). 'Evaluate' is a rather technical register to employ alongside more homely expressions, like 'all in good time'. 'Think over' would have been more in line with the tone up to that point. The Italian has difficulty acknowledging this switch since 'valutare' (*assess/evaluate*) does not suggest a particularly technical register in Italian. The elimination of this element also eliminates an intriguing question that the English raises: how far is Emma aware of the slip into jargon? As we shall see, a person's consciousness or otherwise of the conventions driving thought and behaviour is an important factor in the way the novel deals with characterization. The following example refers to Adam Prince, a gourmet food journalist:

> Emma's mother had told her that, before his present job he had been an Anglican priest who had 'gone over to Rome' (p. 15)

> La madre aveva detto a Emma che prima di avere quell'incarico era stato un prete anglicano, poi era passato alla chiesa Cattolica (p. 12)

> Her mother had told Emma that before taking this job he had been an Anglican clergyman, then had passed to the Catholic Church.

'Gone over to Rome' is a dismissive expression, registering an Anglican's disdain for another's betrayal. 'Rome' on its own is, in the context of Anglican-Roman Catholic antagonism, a derogatory way of referring to the Catholic Church (it would hardly be used by a Catholic). In this case the expression both indicates Emma's mother's traditional Anglican position, and gestures to a social and historical context necessarily lost in the straightforward and colourless 'passato alla chiesa Cattolica' (*passed to the Catholic Church*).

The next example is taken from Emma's notes on her fellow villagers; here she is describing the young doctor Shrubsole.

> Nice young man, not particularly bright, but well-meaning, kind and up-to-date – fashionable interest in 'geriatrics'. (p. 40)

> Giovanotto simpatico, non molto brillante, ma premuroso, cortese, aggiornato, interesse di modo per la geriatria. (p. 32)

> Nice young man, not really brilliant, but thoughtful, polite, up-to-date, fashionable interest in geriatrics.

The fact that Emma herself uses inverted commas in her diary suggests her awareness of the extent to which the word 'geriatrics' is fashionable jargon and hence her closeness to the novel's narrator, in that they both have the habit of drawing attention to jargon words. The only difference in the Italian here is the decision not to use inverted commas, thus not to highlight Emma's awareness that the word is jargon. The Italian, that is, fails to indicate Emma's interest in a use of language which she does not necessarily endorse.

In the next example the ageing Doctor Gellibrand has attended a church service at which his brother, Harry, was the priest:

> he had been impressed and a little envious of the 'show' his brother Harry had put on for High Mass (p. 22)

> era rimasto colpito e un pocchino invidioso per lo spettacolo che suo fratello era riuscito a organizzare durante la Messa Alta (p. 18)

> he had been struck and a little envious of the show that his brother had managed to organize during High Mass

Again the Italian loses only the inverted commas and the self-consciousness of the English in its deployment of idiom.

In the next example Emma is thinking about her habit of taking notes on the behaviour of the villagers:

> This hardly counted as 'work', she felt, this idle speculating (p. 42)

> Pensò che non avrebbe potuto considerare un vero lavoro quella vaga riflessione (p. 34)

> She thought that this vague reflection could not be considered a real
> job.

Placing the inverted commas around 'work' draws our attention to the virtue
attached to that word in public debate, and to Emma's sense of what others
would think of her activities. Losing the inverted commas loses this sense of a
public vision of what 'work' is. This comes over even more clearly in the next
example. We are talking about Adam Prince's work as a food journalist:

> but he didn't count as an ordinary man who went out to work and did
> a 'proper' job, as you might say. (p. 43)

> ma Adam non veniva considerato alla stregua di uno che ha un impiego
> oppure un incarico, per così dire, preciso. (p. 35)

> but Adam was not considered in the same league as someone who had
> a, as it might be, precise job or duty.

'Proper' is a key word in Pym's text and very far from the Italian 'preciso'
(*precise*). It suggests the way in which everybody agrees things should be
done. This would have been translatable in Italian with expressions like 'un
lavoro come si deve' (literally: *a job as one must*).

The next example refers to a pair of jeans that Adam Prince brings to the
church jumble sale because too tight for him:

> definitely a 'bad buy', as the fashion writers might say. (p. 44)

> decisamente un acquisto infelice, secondo la definizione dei giornali
> di moda. (p. 35)

> decidedly an unhappy purchase, in the definition of fashion magazines.

The problem here is that 'bad buy' is a standard collocation in English, monosyllabic and alliterative. 'Acquisto infelice' hardly draws our attention to a
jargon expression in the same way.

In the next example we are at a jumble sale; Tom Dagnall's spinster sister
is talking to Adam Prince:

> 'We get very little in the way of men's clothing'.
> Adam smiled at the word 'clothing', feeling that perhaps she had not

intended to use it but had found herself slipping into the jumble sale jargon or vernacular ... (p. 44)

'Riceviamo ben poche offerte di vestiario per uomo'.
Nell'udire quel termine Adam sorrise, ebbe l'impressione che forse Daphne non se ne fosse servita con intenzione, ma solo scivolando per caso nel gergo delle vendite per beneficenza... (p. 36)

'We get very few offers of men's clothing.'
Hearing this term Adam smiled, he had the impression that perhaps Daphne had not used it intentionally, but was merely slipping by chance into the jargon of charity sales...

Pym makes her strategy very clear here as Adam declares his intellectual superiority by recognizing how Daphne's mind is being unconsciously driven by a particular jargon. The success of the passage depends on our recognizing 'clothing' or 'vestiario' (*clothing*) as jargon that *truly is used at jumble sales*.

The next passage refers to the young doctor Martin Shrubsole's attempts to 'improve' his mother-in-law's diet.

Martin had succeeded in 'weaning' her away from sugar in tea (p. 51)

sebbene Martin fosse riuscito a svezzarla dallo zucchero nel tè (p. 42)

although Martin had succeeded in weaning her from sugar in tea

Here the expression 'to wean away from', a standard idiom in English, is translated directly into Italian where it is hardly so common and does not share the same pious overtones. What we understand is Martin's complicity with public language as he assumes an intellectual superiority to his mother-in-law whom he imagines as less 'clued up' (to join in the game) than himself.

Here is a little more of Martin and his mother-in-law:

and the best thing of all was that Martin had agreed that she should come and live with them now that the lease of her flat had run out – 'share their home', was the way people put it. (p. 52)

e la cosa migliore era che Martin avesse accettato, quando era scaduto il periodo di affittanza dell'appartamento, di tenerla in casa con sé. (p. 44)

and the best thing was that Martin had accepted, when her lease on her
flat ran out, to have her at home with them [he and his wife]

Again the Italian loses the commonplace piety ('share their home'). We get
the facts but miss their framing in terms of a conventional, self-righteous
point of view.

In the next example, we go to the house of the other doctor, Dr Gellibrand:

entering the graciously furnished hall of the Gellibrand's house, 'residence' one might almost say (p. 54)

Ma quando entrò nel vestibolo elegantemente ammobiliato di casa Gellibrand (la si sarebbe potuta chiamare quasi una residenza) (p. 45)

But when he entered the elegantly furnished hall of the Gellibrands'
house (you might almost have called it an abode)

Again what is lost is the distinction between Pym's point of view and conventional pretensions. The inverted commas alert us to the way certain people
speak and invite us to ask whether 'residence' does not suggest snobbery. The
Italian has no such nuance here, with the further problem that there is no habit
in Italy of referring to a luxurious home as a 'residenza'. On the contrary, the
word has quite different connotations, usually referring simply to the fact
that one resides in a certain place. Unaware of English idiom the translator is
deceived by a false cognate.

In the next example Emma is entertaining her old lover, the famous anthropologist. He is staying over in her house. It is shortly before bedtime, a
crucial moment:

'Would you like a drink?' Emma had almost said 'nightcap', the kind
of thing associated with milkiness and a generally more cosy atmosphere. (p. 82)

'Vuoi bere qualcosa?' Emma era stata sul punto di offrirgli 'il bicchiere
della buona notte', il tipo di bevanda che richiama il latte e una atmosfera in genere più familiare (p. 70)

'Do you want something to drink?' Emma had been about to offer him
'the goodnight glass,' the kind of drink that made you think of milk
and in general a more homely atmosphere.'

As with 'clothing' and 'residence' the problem here is our recognition or otherwise of 'il bicchiere della buona notte' as appropriate. Of course there is such an expression in Italian, but it is more usually associated with alcohol than milky drinks.

Enough. I deliberately chose such a large number of examples from so few pages to suggest how incessant the technique is, just as the attention to local detail is incessant. We might say that the words and phrases in inverted commas are a verbal equivalent of Pym's famous local detail and equally culture-specific. The problems for the translator are all too clear. Often there is no equivalent jargon term in Italian (as with 'proper job' or 'share their home' or 'nightcap'), or alternatively one feels that the word the translator has been forced to choose is not one an Italian would use in the same situation ('quasi una residenza' – *almost a residence* – for example, or 'vestiario' – *clothing*), or simply has nothing that would place it in a particular lexical field ('valutare' – *assess*). It is for this reason perhaps that the translator decides not to follow Pym's use of inverted commas, since they would only rarely be appropriate (in the examples given above, 'geriatria' – *geriatrics* – might have been given this treatment, but inverted commas would be perplexing if used only very occasionally).

What all this means is that we begin to lose the book's constant distinction between points of view: the stock point of view which invades the characters' minds in the form of a public and largely atrophied language, the private point of view which sometimes resists that, or is at least aware of it, and the narrator's point of view, which places and frames both of the others, but which itself is never fixed.

None of this, as I suggested at the beginning of this essay, would really matter too much if Pym's novel had a traditional and satisfactory plot of the variety that could be enjoyed for its own sake or, again, if the book were exclusively about this social milieu, these people, their way of doing things, if, that is, it were a genuinely anthropological endeavour where what mattered was the presentation of interesting information, since in this case the whole problem could be resolved by using explanatory footnotes. But Pym's achievement lies not just in her description of this very particular world, but in the way she shows how convention and received ideas suffocate personal initiative and smother any possible plot, while at the same time being the source of a great deal of fun and irony. In short, local detail and conventional idiomatic expressions are sources simultaneously of pleasure and frustration. One cannot have Pym's richness of detail without her sense of futility; they operate together in a reciprocally tensing relationship.

Apart from her use of inverted commas, Pym has many ways of revealing how inhibited her characters are by the language of convention. I offer just four examples, though it would not be difficult to find hundreds. Here we are at a village meeting:

> The chairman, a mild man who seemed to be in awe of the sharp-tongued woman participant, was doing his best to see that each of the men got a fair crack of the whip, as he might have put it. (p. 15)

> Il moderatore, che sembrava intimidito dalla lingua tagliente della donna partecipante all'incontro, faceva del suo meglio affinché ciascuno degli uomini avesse la sua parte. (p. 12)

> The moderator, who seemed to be intimidated by woman participant's sharp tongue, did his best to allow each of the men to take part

In this case the idiomatic expression 'fair crack of the whip' is highlighted by the remark 'as he might have put it'. Fascinating here is the fact that nobody has actually said, or thought these words. But Pym lets us know that were the chairman to describe his behaviour, he would doubtless fall back on this commonplace. She reminds us, that is, of the way these things are talked and thought about, even if nobody in the book has talked or thought about them. Again the Italian limits itself to describing what the chairman actually did, losing the sense of a community and the predictability of thought and speech.

In the next example we go back to the jumble sale and Tom's spinster sister, Daphne:

> 'No,' Daphne agreed. 'The village women have such marvellous things now. They wouldn't look at cast-offs – it's we who buy them. Of course it's all to the good,' she added, feeling that she ought to say something on these lines. (p. 47)

> 'No,' convenne Daphne. 'Adesso le donne di qui hanno della roba tanto bella. Loro non guardano i vestiti smessi. Siamo noi che li compriamo. Naturalmente meglio così,' aggiunse. (p. 39)

> 'No,' agreed Daphne. 'Now the women here have such nice things. They don't look at cast-off clothes. It's we who buy them. Of course it's better this way,' she added.

Daphne, Tom's sister, is presented as one of the people least conscious of the way her speech and thought are driven by received ideas. Here she senses what is the correct thing to say and automatically says it. The Italian is defeatist. There would really be no problem in following the English more closely. Either translator or editor has simply misunderstood, or not noticed, Pym's strategy.

Now back to Martin Shrubsole, his wife Avice and his problematic mother-in-law:

> he and Avice had the idea that her mother might be usefully occupied in copying parish registers or something of that nature which, it was thought, might help to keep her brain in good trim, ticking over, as it were, rather than endlessly knitting and watching television. (p. 53)

> lui e Avice pensavano che potesse occuparsi utilmente nel copiare i registri della parrocchia, per mantenere attivo il cervello, farlo funzionare con regolarità, e così allontanarla un po' dall'eterno lavoro a maglia e dall'eterna televisione. (p. 44)

> he and Avice thought she might usefully busy herself copying the parish registers, to keep her brain active, make it work with regularity, and hence bring her away for a little from her eternal knitting and eternal television.

Here the 'as it were' alerts us to the wonderful combination of idiom and piety involved in 'to keep her brain in good trim, ticking over'. The irony here is particularly fine: while Martin, the young doctor, piously wishes to keep his mother-in-law alert and youthful, he himself cannot help expressing his thoughts in the tired language of received commonplace. The Italian offers nothing at the idiomatic level and thus loses much of this.

Now back to the rather more attractive character of Tom Dagnall, the rector:

> Tom ... let his thoughts dwell on various people in the village. This was in its way a kind of prayer, like bringing them into the church which so few of them actually visited, or never darkened its doors, as a more dramatic phrase had it. (p. 60)

> Tom ... lasciava vagare i pensieri su varie persone del villaggio. Era in un certo modo una specie di preghiera, quasi un introdurre in chiesa gente che in realtà la frequentava pochissimo, o per dirla con toni più poetici, mai ne oscurava la soglia. (p. 50)

> Tom … allowed his thoughts to wander over various people in the
> village. It was in a way a type of prayer, almost a way of bringing into
> church people who in reality hardly came at all, or to put it in more
> poetic tones, never darkened the threshold.

Again the job done elsewhere with inverted commas is achieved with a comment from the narrator, 'as a more dramatic phrase had it'. Here the translator
makes the mistake of substituting the stock expression 'darken the door' for
what is in Italian is not an idiom at all, 'oscurare la soglia' (*darkened the
threshold/doorway*), when, at least in this case, there was a perfectly acceptable Italian idiom available in 'varcare la soglia' (*cross the threshold*). One
also wonders about the translation of 'a more dramatic phrase' with 'toni più
poetici' (*more poetic tones*) since poetry, as we shall see, plays a role in the
book which is quite distinct from that of idiom.

As with our first series of examples, then, the translator's difficulties
in these short passages are embarrassingly obvious, while Pym's vision of
people speaking and thinking under the pressure of received ideas loses its
clarity. In passing, it's worth noting that none of these expressions are in any
way unusual in themselves, nor does Pym's prose venture any creative distortion of idiom or even lyrical excursions. Again there is a parallel to be drawn
with the abundant detail in the book, which, though brilliantly observed, is
never extraordinary, even though it may seem so to those not familiar with
the society she describes. Pym never seeks to see objects under an unusual
light or to uncover the exotic in the familiar, typical strategies of modernism.
On the contrary, language and detail stay absolutely with the everyday and
the ordinary.

The problem for the translator is that not only does Pym's detail seem
rather bizarre when transferred into another cultural context, but its attach-
ment to stock phrases is undermined because of the inevitable difficulties
of maintaining the same semantic content while finding equivalent idioms
in Italian. In short, Italian idioms refer to Italian culture, not to English and
hence are not easily used to translate English idioms. What is lost, then, is the
English reader's sense of *immediate recognition*, of a deep harmony between
language and detail, a recognition that validates the humour and irony, but
at the same time calls the reader's own way of thinking into question: if I
recognize this so immediately, do I myself not live in this way? Pym's prose
is challenging.

Two other features of the narrative confirm the way idiomatic specificity is
being used: one is Pym's use of silence and the other her use of poetry. Here
are two examples; in the first we have the threesome, Emma, Tom Dagnall

and his sister, Daphne; in the second we are at Dr Gellibrand's garden party:

> She [Daphne] now joined Emma and her brother and began asking
> Emma whether she had settled down well in the village and whether
> she was going to like living there; impossible questions to answer or
> even speculate on, Emma felt. (p. 8)

> Si affiancò al fratello e a Emma e prese a chiederle se si trovava
> bene nel villaggio e se pensava di stabilirvisi, tutte domande alle quali
> Emma trovò impossibile rispondere, impossibile anche solo prenderle
> in considerazione. (p. 6)

> She joined her brother and Emma and started asking her if she was
> happy in the village and if she was thinking of settling there, all ques-
> tions to which Emma found it impossible to answer, impossible even
> to consider them.

> they were driven on by their hostess ... down a rocky path to a pool
> where a water lily, showing its first bud, demanded to be admired.
> Emma, finding herself unable to comment adequately on this phenom-
> enon, was glad to be diverted by a commotion behind her. (p. 54)

> la padrona di casa li fece scendere per un sentiero sassoso fino a un
> laghetto nel quale il primo bocciolo di una ninfea in procinto di aprirsi
> esigeva di essere ammirato.
> Emma si sentì incapace di formulare un commento adatto a quel fe-
> nomeno e fu lieta di venire distratta da una agitazione alle sue spalle.
> (pp. 45-6)

> the mistress of the house led them down a stony path to a little pond
> where the first water-lily bud on the point of opening demanded to
> be admired.
> Emma felt unable to formulate any suitable comment on this phenom-
> enon and was happy to be distracted by a commotion behind her.

Silence comes when something more than the stock response is called for,
when a genuine moment of reflection is required (will Emma be happy here
in the village?), or perhaps some heartfelt appreciation of beauty (the water
lily). Later on in the book a moment of possible romance prompts a more
embarrassing silence: Graham Pettifer (ex-lover and famous anthropologist),
on arriving quite suddenly at Emma's house, is moodily silent, so that she has

to seek refuge in the 'ritual' of making eggs for him. When the two go to bed the evening finishes thus:

> They were standing together in the spare room, side by side, not touching ... He made no move towards her but stroked the cover of the divan bed admiringly. 'William Morris, isn't it?'
> 'Yes, Golden Lily I think it's called. Goodnight then.'
> 'Goodnight.'
> Nothing more was said and it was only as she lay in bed ... (p. 82)

> Erano nella camera degli ospiti, in piedi e vicini, ma senza toccarsi ... Lui non fece l'atto di avvicinarsi, ma accarezzò con ammirazione il disegno della coperta sul divano letto: 'William Morris, vero?'
> 'Si, credo che il disegno si chiami Giglio d'oro. E allora buona notte.'
> 'Buona notte.'
> Sola a letto, ripensando agli avvenimenti della giornata ... (p. 70)

> They were in the guest room, standing close to each other, but without touching … He made no move to get closer, but stroked the pattern of the bedspread on the divan with admiration: 'William Morris, right?'
> 'Yes, I think the pattern is called Golden Lily. Goodnight then.'
> 'Goodnight.'
> Alone in bed, thinking back over the day's events…

A William Morris design on one's bedspread is an excellent and elegant thing and talking about it (caressing it even!) can gloss over a moment of embarrassment, but the underlying silence is all too evident and finally comes to the fore ('Nothing more was said'). The intriguing thing here is the way the translation decides to leave out this remark. It is not that it can present any problem for the translator, and indeed the previous silences are indicated well enough. What it does suggest is that the translator has not appreciated how such moments fit into the book's overall scheme: these are situations where no stock response is available and the characters are inadequate to think of anything else.

The translator's problems become even greater when Pym introduces poetry, which in *A Few Green Leaves* tends to appear in simple lyric form, a lyricism significantly associated with the past. As such it suggests an intensity, or merely a felicitous directness of expression that is usually lacking in the novel's characters. Poetry is, as it were, what might have been said at those moments of silence. This example, where the two potential suitors Tom (the rector) and Adam (the food journalist) come across Emma working in the garden, brings together both silence and poetry:

> She was just in the act of cutting down some branches of this when she saw Tom approaching with Adam Prince.
> 'What a charming picture you make, with the roses,' said Adam smoothly.
> Emma tried to think of a gracious answer to this rather obvious compliment. Then, before she had been able to produce anything, Tom, suddenly and ridiculously, burst into poetry.
> The two divinest things this world has got
> A lovely woman in a rural spot
> he recited. There was a brief stunned silence, surely one of dismay ... (p. 72)

> Stava appunto per tagliarne qualche ramo, quando vide che Tom si avvicinava insieme con Adam Prince.
> 'Che delizioso quadretto, con tutte quelle rose,' esclamò Adam. Emma cercò di trovare una risposta cortese al complimento un po' banale, ma prima di averne il tempo, in modo un po' comico, Tom proruppe all'improvviso in versi:
> Due cose divine ha questo mondo
> Una bella donna e la natura.
> Seguì un breve silenzio di stupore, anzi di sbigottimento ... (p. 61)

> She was just about to cut off a branch or two, when she saw that Tom was approaching with Adam Prince.
> 'What a splendid little picture, with all those roses,' exclaimed Adam. Emma tried to find a polite response to this rather banal compliment, but before she had time to do so, in a rather comic way Tom suddenly burst out into verse:
> Two divine things has this world
> A beautiful woman and nature.
> There was a brief silence of amazement, or rather of dismay...

Much of the divergence here is due to lazy translation, and in particular a failure to appreciate what it was that should have been translated. The encounter begins with Adam's too obvious and urbane compliment ('"What a charming picture you make, with the roses," said Adam smoothly'), something on the level of a stock remark. The translator's failure to give us the adverb 'smoothly' is an error here, if for no other reason than because it is part of Pym's strategy to have her characters always 'in character', so that if at some point in the book there is some minimal shift, some possible development, however tiny, we will notice it. Here, Tom's spontaneous outburst, in contrast both to Adam's frequently noted smoothness and the clergyman's own habitual cautiousness, is indeed such a development, one of precious few in the book, indeed one of the only occasions where Pym allows herself the shift of register involved in writing, 'Tom, suddenly and ridiculously, burst into poetry'. Here the translator baulks at such a strong word as 'ridiculously', retreating into the qualification of 'un po' comico' (*a bit funny*).

First, then, there is Emma's silence as conventional response fails her, then Tom's outburst. Intriguingly, this cannot come in the form of some natural heartfelt comment of his own, but in 'poetry' (the word is significant and should not have been changed to 'versi' (*lines* [of poetry])). Here what is important is the directness of this poetry, the irony of its not being very good poetry, and above all the plonky, obvious rhyme.

The translation, lazily offering a merely semantic (or not even) transposition of the two lines, makes no attempt to get any of this across.

I suggested in the previous paragraphs that the register of *A Few Green Leaves* almost never changes. There are no moments of great drama, great romance, of horror or joy, no shifts in the evenly polished sentence structures, no sudden speeding of rhythm, deployment of onomatopoeia, of assonance, none, in short, of those stylistic techniques that characterize the great novelists of the earlier part of the century, Joyce and Lawrence and Woolf, and so many of those who followed in their footsteps. This steadiness of register goes together with the fact that there is almost no character development, only the occasional feeble effort to break free from smothering convention (the 'few green leaves' of the title perhaps?).

On the other hand, as indicated in the very first text I quoted, there is a constant play of points of view, a constant placing of jargon, of buzz words, of conventional modes of expression, against the backdrop of Pym's clear and conservative prose. In terms purely of layout, for example, one notes that Pym frequently mixes dialogue, thought and narrative without paragraph breaks and without even indicating the switch from narrative to indirect speech. It is this constant movement forever trapped within certain limits, this business of always having to recognize the shift in and out of received ideas, identifying the source of a word, a thought, an idiom, that offers so much pleasure to the English reader. It is because Emma herself, as we have said, is fascinated by this process of distinction, both of artefacts and idioms, that we tend to see her anthropologist's point of view as closest to the narrator's. Here she is observing one of the villagers at a sherry party:

> She had 'good bones', Emma thought, and had obviously once been beautiful – the worm in the bud, though that wasn't the kind of thought one could put into words at a sherry party. No doubt the mention of flowers had suggested the bud and the worm in it ... (p. 57)

> Ha una buona ossatura, pensò Emma, un tempo doveva essere stata bella ... il verme dentro al bocciolo, ma non era il genere di pensieri da tradurre in parole a un party. L'idea del bocciolo con dentro il verme gliela aveva senza dubbio suggerita l'allusione ai fiori ... (p. 48)

> She had a good bone structure, thought Emma, once she must have been beautiful ... the worm in the bud, but it wasn't the kind of thought to translate into words at a party. The idea of the bud with the worm inside had no doubt been suggested to her by the allusion to flowers ...

Again, though this time the translator cannot be blamed, the Italian is a series of small slippages which detract from that process of recognition and distinction that here Pym, Emma and the reader are to share together. There is the loss of the commonplace expression 'good bones', the reference back to Blake (the worm in the bud) and the precise social context of 'sherry party'. Emma, as always, reveals herself as subject to the pressure of conventional ideas, a conventional education – this is evident from the way her mind bounces back and forth amongst idiom, jargon and poetry – but at the same time aware of that process and taking pleasure in recognizing where the words and thoughts come from. It is Emma, after all, who later in the novel will go so far as to complete a sentence that somebody else begins, thus indicating her familiarity with the conventional thought driving it: '"So *many* delphinium, one hardly knows ..." What on earth to do with them, Emma thought, completing the sentence' (pp. 73-4).

Perhaps it is time to remark on one of the central images of the book. Examining some old church registers Tom, the rector, has discovered that in the seventeenth century the local folk used to be 'buried in woollen'. It is an idea that, on cold days at least, gives Tom 'comfortable feelings' (p. 25). If one has to be buried in a freezing churchyard, one might at least be buried in something nice and warm, though buried, of course, one remains. In August, however, Tom feels that being buried in wool must be 'decidedly stuffy' (p. 25).

The application of this image to the characters in the book and their relation to convention will require no great leap of the imagination. They are buried in the conventional bric-a-brac of their daily lives and mental processes. But at least these are woolly and warm when existential winds blow cold, as Emma so plainly remarks on the evening when she finds herself looking after an unhappy Graham Pettifer, her ex-lover. 'So, after the ritual cup of tea, [came] the ritual comfort of the pub, the drink; the cosy atmosphere, the company' (p. 80). This comfortableness in the banal and woolly minutiae of conventional social life, the daily ritual of things and thoughts and words, is frightening in its nullity and in the absence of drama it implies, but also immensely cosy.

'Ritual', of course, is a word that appears many times in *A Few Green Leaves,* and no doubt justly so, given that two of the protagonists are anthropologists and another a clergyman. Amusingly, though, Pym most frequently uses it when referring to people's obsession with consulting the local doctors, who, in the general retreat from spirituality, have overtaken the clergyman as a possible source of comfort for those suffering from existential ills. Pym speaks of the village folk as leaving the surgery carrying 'ritual scraps' of paper (sadly translated as 'il magico pezzo di carta' – *the magic piece of paper*), and it would be easy to see *A Few Green Leaves* with all its lists of jumble-sale left-overs and interminable social functions where most of the people 'did not betray the fact that they might have led distinguished lives' as a great hoarding of 'ritual scraps' offering the same kind of placebo comfort as the doctor's prescriptions. Consider, for example, the heart-breaking list of objects that Daphne, Tom's spinster sister, sorts through in her search for a decent cast-off skirt among the things people have brought for the jumble sale:

> The clothes in the first box were a disappointing lot – mini, courtelle, Acrilan and other man-made fibres, nothing ample, long or of pure wool or cotton. Daphne turned to a box of oddments – chipped cups and odd saucers suitable for cat dishes, plastic earrings, an old string of pearls with the pearliness pealing off, a tattered paperback novel whose cover portrayed the bare shoulders of a couple in bed, a bundle of knitting needles, a plastic butter-dish split at one corner, an old prayerbook with no cover and pages missing, a rusty nutmeg grater, a wrist-watch not in working order, a china animal of indeterminate sex, lacking an ear, a glass ditto lacking one leg, a cracked handbag mirror, a small transistor radio, a photo-frame with a faded photograph of a person on a beach, a brooch without a pin saying 'MOTHER', an empty tin of hair lacquer, a dried-up pot of foundation cream, a red collar for a small dog or even a cat, a fork with the prongs bent, an old soap dish ... (p. 45)

Perhaps Pym is not, after all, so far away from Eliot's *Wasteland* cry: 'these fragments I have shored against my ruins'. The problem, as far as translating

her is concerned, or even reading her in other cultures, is that when the fragments, the 'ritual scraps', are not just a list of objects but of social situations,
and above all of those endless commonplaces that are, as it were, the reification of a now dead language, then they may not be recognizable and thus lose
their potency, or rather the poignancy of their impotence, cannot perform
even the small act of comfort they should, nor be seen in all their desolate
fragmentariness. Putting it another way, it may be that a proper appreciation
of the extent to which the detail genuinely is suffocating (rather than quaint
and bizarre) coupled with a pleasure in recognizing its authenticity (and
hence a consolation for the bleakness of the vision), depends very much on
the reader's familiarity with the detail described and above all the language
in which it is couched.

In the opening remarks to this chapter, I quoted one critic's difficulty as
he admits that although 'Pym's presentation has nothing in common with a
writer like Beckett', she is nevertheless fascinated by the same themes of
'pointlessness and futility'. One can't help feeling, however, that on one
level the opposite is true. In her presentation of the way the language, public
language, constantly guides thought, rather than being controlled by it, and
thus becomes a trap, an amusing, many-coloured and endlessly fascinating
shroud, Pym is very dose to the Beckett we examined in our previous chapter,
the Beckett who insistently draws attention to the way language atrophies into
comfortable habit. In this sense both writers share with Lawrence a sense of
uneasiness as regards what Steiner referred to as 'being housed' in language.
In all three cases the problems for translation are related to the strategy each
writer adopts to express this uneasiness. The enormous distance between Pym
and Beckett has to do with the radically different exposition of their themes,
rather than with the themes themselves: Beckett constantly causes idiom to
collide with context ('I have no bone to pick with graveyards'[7]) or with other
idioms ('but I had been under the weather so long, under all weathers'[8]) in
order to have the language, as he puts it, 'fall into disrepute'[9]; Pym more quietly
and lightly points up moribund idiomatic expressions with inverted commas,
or 'as it were', or 'as a more dramatic phrase had it'.

The difference in language and style is also reflected in the different
kinds of images each writer draws on to express his or her vision. Pym goes
to historical fact for the picture of people comfortably 'buried in woollen',
Beckett more bizarrely has one of his characters, Molloy, wrapping himself

---

[7] Samuel Beckett, *First Love,* Penguin Syrens, London, 1994, p. 4.
[8] Samuel Beckett, *Molloy,* Calder & Boyars, London, 1966, p. 54.
[9] Samuel Beckett, *Disjecta,* Calder, London, 1983, pp. 171-3.

up against the cold in old copies of *The Times Literary Supplement*.[10] Here, to offer a different kind of example to those quoted in the previous chapter, is Beckett expressing a recognizably Pymian approach to language in a very Beckettian fashion. The speaker is the ancient Malone of *Malone Dies,* determined to pass the time by telling himself stories, in this case about a young boy named Saposcat.

> The market. The inadequacy of the exchanges between rural and urban areas had not escaped the excellent youth. He had mustered, on this subject, the following considerations, some perhaps close to, others no doubt far from, the truth.
> In his country the problem – no, I can't do it.
> The peasants. His visits to. I can't. Assembled in the farmyard they watched him depart, on stumbling, wavering feet, as though they scarcely felt the ground. Often he stopped, stood tottering a moment, then suddenly was off again, in a new direction. So he went, limp, drifting, as though tossed by the earth. And when, after a halt, he started off again, it was like a big thistledown plucked by the wind from the place where it had settled. There is a choice of images.[11]

Malone begins by trying to amuse himself with the deployment of a traditional and jargon-ridden prose, imagining his character as engaged in making fairly obvious sociological distinctions (in this case the analogy with Emma in *A Few Green Leaves* is clear enough). But the consolation of this straightforward language and the sort of knowing, purposeful narrative it implies does not satisfy (as so often in Pym one is aware that for protagonists like Emma the anthropological observations and comfy conversations do not satisfy), upon which Malone, looking for comfort elsewhere, shifts into something far more lyrical (as silence invites poetry in Pym), describing the wanderings of his protagonist, a description that mirrors, we cannot help feeling, the wanderings of his own prose. But even now, Malone is aware that although this is attractive it is only another more accomplished form of literary compulsion and consolation. 'Nice choice of images', he remarks, at once complacent and despondent, again a very Pym-like cocktail of emotions.

As we have seen, studies of Beckett in Italian show some of the same problems as the translation of Pym, particularly when it comes to the commonplace ('I am no enemy of the commonplace', announces Molloy after making the

---

[10] *Molloy,* p. 31.
[11] *Samuel Beckett, Malone Dies,* Calder & Boyars, London, 1975, p. 24.

very Pymian remark 'if only your mother could see you now'[12]). But Beckett himself showed the way his work might be translated by translating himself from French to English or vice versa. And what he does, as we saw in passages from *Murphy* and *Watt,* is to play the same games of punning and alliteration in those places where the language he is working in invites him to, accepting small changes in the semantic content along the way.

Would such a policy be possible when translating Pym? No. For Beckett, the trap, the medium that at once consoles and stifles us, is primarily the language, its vocabulary, syntax, rhythm and so on. His characters and plots, unlike Pym's, are increasingly set, not in any recognizable place, but in the language itself. It is the words and rhetorical surface we recognize, not the physical location and cultural context. Hence there is very little culture-specific detail, almost nothing that refers to real places, people and traditions. The translator can thus play with his own language without the problem one encounters in Pym of a highly specific setting which must be recognized.

This difference between the two writers points to a second: that in moving away from conventional setting and traditional drama between characters, Beckett declares the extremity of his vision quite openly. He, of all people, cannot be mistaken, even by the most workman-like translator, for what he is not. Part of the charm of Pym, on the other hand, is her apparent willingness to be misunderstood, to be seen for what she is not, a traditional writer of genteel, romance fiction, and this in order to remain attached to the one small milieu which happens to be her particular consolation. Hence, even if Pym had had the linguistic competence, it is hard to imagine her wishing to write in another language or translate herself into it, since this would take her away from the English environment she needs.

For Beckett, on the other hand, the experiment of writing in French and translating himself back and forth was an inevitable part of the desire to escape the strictures of his native language, even if that only meant exchanging them for the shackles of another. Ultimately, it is in Pym's apparent closeness to, but crucial distance from, the traditional romantic genre that much of the pleasure of reading her lies. Unfortunately, the distinction is too subtly generated for the Italian translation that we have considered to emulate. But in translating only the plot, only the traditional element of the book, the Italian does show very convincingly that Pym is not a traditional novelist. For in the Italian version the book offers very little pleasure at all.

This brings us to an interesting question: is it possible that a writer might be truly great, but truly untranslatable, un-exportable? If Pym is to be considered

---

[12] *Molloy,* p. 40.

great it is in the way she uses the claustrophobia of a particular milieu and its language to express a common human condition. Her untranslatability lies first in the difficulty of re-creating a convincing wealth of recognizable commonplaces while remaining within the limits of the semantic content, and second in the way unfamiliarity with the milieu Pym describes, and with its idiom, may distract attention from her underlying vision. The question as to greatness and translatability, however, is something we will look at more closely in the next chapter.

7. On the Borders of Comprehensibility: the Challenge of Henry Green

Despite their widely differing visions and styles, the five writers we have considered in the previous chapters, Lawrence, Joyce, Woolf, Beckett and Pym, do have, so far as our own purposes are concerned, one thing in common: their works are all translated into Italian. In each case translation presented considerable problems, yet there was always confidence on the part of the publishers that an Italian edition would be sufficiently effective to be worthwhile. The same cannot be said of Henry Green. Green wrote eight novels, yet despite his considerable following in the UK, the USA and to a certain extent France, and despite the fact that writers as influential and varied as Angus Wilson, Elizabeth Bowen and more recently John Updike have pronounced Green's work among the finest flowers of British modernism, only two of his novels have been translated in Italy, one in 1990 and one in 2006 (indeed as I began revising this book).

It is not that Italian publishers do not share the general admiration for Green's work. The Italian language rights to all his works were purchased many years ago by such reputable houses as Adelphi and Einaudi. It is just that again and again translations are rejected by editors as 'unreadable in Italian'. Here is the opening passage from *Party Going,* considered by many as Green's masterpiece.

> Fog was so dense, bird that had been disturbed went flat into a balustrade and slowly fell, dead at her feet.
> There it lay and Miss Fellowes looked up to where that pall of fog was twenty foot above and out of which it had fallen, turning over once. She bent down and took a wing then entered a tunnel in front of her, and this had DEPARTURES lit up over it, carrying her dead pigeon. (1)[1]

It is not difficult to find plenty that is extraordinary here. Apart from the lack of declared place and time, there is the disorientating absence of any article before the first two nouns ('Fog was so dense, bird ...') coupled with a generally unsettling use of deixis throughout the passage. First we have the

---

[1] All quotations from *Party Going* are from the Vintage Classics edition of 2000. Page numbers are indicated in brackets at the end of each quotation.

possessive 'her' ('dead at her feet'), referring to we do not know whom; then, in the second paragraph, the curious demonstrative in '*that* pall of fog', where 'that' seems extravagantly marked; and finally something similar in 'and *this* had DEPARTURES lit up over it', where 'and this' seems, again, an unnecessarily emphasized substitution for the more obvious 'that', especially when one considers that the clause is to be followed by the participle 'carrying', whose subject, 'she', is way back at the beginning of the sentence, thus: 'She bent down and took a wing then entered a tunnel in front of her, and this had DEPARTURES lit up over it, carrying her dead pigeon'.

Other obvious curiosities are the strongly vernacular forms 'went flat into a balustrade' and 'twenty foot', instead of 'twenty feet', a tendency that suggests that the absent articles in the opening sentence might likewise involve a mimicking of the vernacular where such omissions are common. More generally, Green deploys some very strange focusing and foregrounding. Things rise to prominence that do not seem to deserve it, structures are made more complex than they need be, sometimes the syntax seems discontinuous, even 'wrong'. The effect is to create a powerful sense of disorientation, as if the world Green is talking about were one in which we have yet to be initiated, a place not unlike a fog perhaps, where the reader, like the pigeon, risks running up against unexpected obstacles.

Here is one of the many attempts at an Italian translation of this opening passage, rejected by the publishers, Adelphi:

> Era nebbia così densa, l'uccello che era stato disturbato sbatté contro una balaustrata e cadde lentamente, morto, ai suoi piedi.
> Giaceva lì e Miss Fellowes guardò in alto, dove sei metri più su c'era quel manto di nebbia e da dove l'uccello era caduto, con una capovolta. Si chinò e lo sollevò per un'ala, quindi entrò in un sottopassaggio di fronte a lei, e su questo brillava la scritta PARTENZE, portando il suo piccione morto.[2]

And here the back-translation:

> It was such dense fog, the bird that had been disturbed flew straight into a balustrade and fell slowly, dead, at Miss Fellowes' feet.
> It lay there and Miss Fellowes looked up, where six metres higher up there was that cloak of fog and from where the bird had fallen, turning over once. She bent down and picked it up by a wing, then entered

---

[2] Translation by Flora Bonetti, rejected by Adelphi Edizioni and hence unpublished.

a subway in front of her, and on this shone the sign DEPARTURES, carrying her pigeon with her.

The publishers explained their rejection by saying that the piece 'did not sound like Italian' and this because 'it remained too close to the English'. Now, although it is certainly the case that this is not standard Italian, it is also true that the translator has made all sorts of attempts to transform and as it were domesticate Green's syntax. The opening phrase 'Era nebbia così densa' – (*it was such a thick fog*) looks for some kind of vernacular alternative to 'Fog was so dense'. 'Uccello' (*bird*) is given an article. 'Went flat' is translated with the quite ordinary verb 'sbattere' (*to bang into*). In the first sentence of the second paragraph the word 'uccello' (*bird*) is repeated to avoid a confusion that the English, using only the pronoun, seems to delight in, while the syntax is a little reorganized to avoid the bizarre effect of that 'and' in '... Miss Fellowes looked up to where that pall of fog was twenty foot above *and* out of which it had fallen ...'.

The more one looks at the 'and' in this sentence the more one appreciates that it is grammatically anomalous. At first the reader expects that the 'and' will add another complement to the subject/verb structure 'the fog was ...' (as, for example, that pall of fog was twenty foot above and *very thick*). Or perhaps it could add a second verb to 'Miss Fellowes looked up ...' (as, for example, Miss Fellowes looked up to where that pall of fog was twenty foot above and *saw that it* ...). But instead of such predictable solutions, the syntax deviates into what was perhaps least expected, a relative clause, 'and out of which'.

Not surprisingly, the translator normalizes the syntax a little by eliminating the 'to' before the 'where' and then introducing a second 'where' thus: ... Miss Fellowes guardò in alto, dove sei metri più su c'era quel manto di nebbia e da dove l'uccello era caduto ...' (*Miss Fellowes looked up, where six metres higher up there was that cloak of fog and from where the bird had fallen*).

We also notice that where the English offers 'She bent down and took a wing', the Italian again renders this in a more standard fashion with 'si chinò e lo sollevò per un ala' (*she bent down and picked it up by a wing*).

In short, the translator appears torn between a desire to maintain the peculiar syntax and rhythms of the text and a desire to accommodate them in an Italian that the publisher (and reader) might accept. Certainly she did not take the easy way out that the translator of Lawrence's *Women in Love* took in the passages we examined in the first chapter of this book, transforming every curiosity into standard Italian. Crucially, with Lawrence, it was clear that when he twisted his syntax into such expressions as 'destroyed into perfect consciousness' this was in order to draw attention to an idea that formed an essential part of his thinking. But is there any purpose in Green's odd syntax? Does it mean anything? And if it does not, perhaps the translator would have been wise to render the text in the most ordinary Italian possible. Certainly, considered from the point of view of *information*, these two paragraphs could be offered in quite standard English, thus:

> There was such a dense fog that evening that a bird which had been disturbed flew straight into a balustrade and fell dead at Miss Fellowes' feet.
> The bird lay on the ground and Miss Fellowes looked up twenty feet to the pall of fog from which it had fallen, turning over once as it did so. She bent down and picked the bird up by a wing, then entered a tunnel which had an illuminated DEPARTURES sign over it, carrying her pigeon with her.

It is worth noting that even in carrying out this simple exercise our attention is drawn to one or two other curiosities in the English. For example, I have added 'that evening' in the first sentence (drawing on information available further on in the story) because, as the opening sentence of a novel, some kind of placement in time seems to be required. By the same token, I have removed 'slowly' from 'slowly fell' because in the end any object always falls with an acceleration of exactly 33 feet per second. So it is not just Green's syntax which is disorientating, we realize, but his choice of what information to give, and what not to give. It was ingenuous, then, to imagine that *exactly* the same information could be given in an entirely conventional form, if, that is, by 'conventional' we mean something that, of its nature, is not disorientating: there is a link between the skewed content Green offers and the style.

Ten and more years after rejecting the version quoted above, Adelphi finally found a translation they were happy to publish. Here are the opening lines:

> La nebbia era densa; un uccello che era stato disturbato colpì in pieno una balaustrata e lentamente cadde, morto a pochi passi da lei.
> Lì giaceva e la signorina Fellowes guardò in alto dove a sette metri da terra c'era quel manto di nebbia dal quale era caduto, girandosi una volta. Si chinò e lo prese per un'ala, poi scese in un sottopassaggio davanti a lei, con sopra l'insegna PARTENZE, portando il suo piccione morto. (11)[3]

---

[3] This and all further quotations from the Italian translation of *Party Going* are taken from *Partenza in Gruppo*, translation by Carlo Bay, Adelphi Edizioni, Milan, 2006.

> The fog was thick; a bird that had been disturbed hit a balustrade full on and slowly fell, dead a few steps away from her.
> There it lay and Miss Fellowes looked up where seven metres from the ground there was that cloak of fog from which it had fallen, turning over once. She bent down and picked it up by a wing, then went down into a subway in front of her with the sign DEPARTURES over it, carrying her dead pigeon.

Here it is evident from the first sentence that more concessions have been made to standard Italian. All the same the biggest change seems to have nothing to do with the problems of translation: the consequential 'so' of the first sentence 'fog was so dense, bird that had been disturbed went flat...' has been removed. At this point I, for one, am suddenly made aware that *all the action of the book* appears to have been set off by this consequence in the first sentence: the fog was so dense, Green is telling us that ... all these things happened and that I wrote about them in this foggy way.

Other changes are equally obvious if not quite so damaging. The bird now falls a few steps away from Miss Fellowes, diminishing the drama of the event. The syntax of the opening sentence of the second paragraph has been entirely normalized and likewise the focusing of the following sentence. Nevertheless, all the information Green gave us is there and the portentous discovery of the dead pigeon combined with the 'departures' sign does still deliver its menacing symbolism. So again the question arises, do these changes matter; is there a unity of intention or effect in Green's 'departures' both from ordinary syntax and, more generally, from a traditional narrative style?

Once again we find that in this regard Green differs, or appears to differ, from the writers so far considered. Of Lawrence, Joyce, Woolf, Beckett and Pym, we can establish superstructures of interpretation (often helpfully backed up by the theorizing of the writers themselves), that, while never quite accounting for everything, do offer a satisfactory reading that unites content and method, explaining, as it were, why what was said had to be said in the way it was said. This, after all, is what I have been doing in this book. Indeed what I have been suggesting is that a translation's effectiveness depends on the translator's appreciating the relationship between content and language and maintaining it, thus producing a text that stands in relation to ordinary usage in his own language as the original stood in relation to traditional narrative style, or styles, in English. But to date, so far as I know, no one has established quite what the relationship between Green's prose style and his ultimate 'meaning' might be. This very 'problem' is no doubt what lies behind his never having been properly admitted to the canon, his failure to become, as have Joyce or

Beckett, a common object of study.

In his book *The Genesis of Secrecy,* a discussion of the nature of text interpretation, Frank Kermode mentions *Party Going* as a text that entirely thwarts the interpreter's desire to establish a unity of purpose among all the elements of the text. There is no place here for a summary of the immensely complex plot of Green's novel, but suffice it to say that Kermode sets out to offer a mythological reading of the narrative, in contrast to the more banal, as he sees it, political readings of other critics. Having established the grounds for this new interpretation, however, he admits that he is unable to integrate it with Green's bizarre use of language. He concludes:

> 'The mythological reading I proposed is not only blind and deaf to
> the political reading; it also ignores the whole linguistic and rhetorical
> dimension of the novel. For example: where normal English usage calls
> for definite articles, *Party Going* often uses demonstratives ('those
> two nannies', 'that bird'). This can be very unsettling ... ; it is a kind
> of grammatical assertion of the uniqueness of the text, a hint, perhaps,
> that it is not easily reducible to something else. Thus does a stylistic
> eccentricity hamper the interpreter, one of whose most useful moves
> is to see his text in relation to some larger whole: an oeuvre, a genre,
> some organized corpus like mythology.'[4]

Kermode puts his finger here on the principal problem for a would-be transla-tor of Green. For who is more completely an interpreter than the translator of a work? Who is more concerned in the business of transforming, if not reducing, the original text into something else? Every choice the translator makes involves interpretation, and interpretation involves understanding the relation of part to whole. How can you set about translating Green's strange use of language if you are not sure what purpose it serves? To say, as Kermode does, that 'it is a kind of grammatical assertion of the uniqueness of the text' is unhelpful. Does this mean the translator has *carte-blanche* to invent the 'uniqueness' of his translation as he will, simply in order that uniqueness there shall be? In which case, what exactly is the work of art he is translating? Does a style that is merely, as Kermode suggests, an 'eccentricity' really deserve translating? And isn't this question of uniqueness a red herring, since any uniqueness is always perceived in its peculiar relation to everything else. That

---

[4] Frank Kermode, *The Genesis of Secrecy,* Harvard University Press, Cambridge, Mas-sachusetts, 1979, p. 12.

is, uniqueness in writing will always mean more than mere uniqueness. It is uniqueness in a particular direction away from what is not unique.

Perhaps the difficulty has been exaggerated and Kermode is unnecessarily defeatist. Perhaps it is simply a question of Green's language standing in a *different* relation to his text than any we are so far familiar with. We have already pointed out, for example, that the opening lines of *Party Going* are deliberately disorientating, giving the impression that this world (a railway station), far from being a place the reader is familiar with, is strange, beautiful, menacing. In this sense certain effects are not unlike those used in cubist painting: parts are split off and rearranged, some foregrounded, some understated, in a new and unsettling relation to each other and to the whole. This dislocation largely depends on Green's wayward syntax. Consider the following paragraph where Julia, one of the novel's main characters, walks in the fog through a park towards the railway station:

> Then at another turn she was on more open ground. Headlights of cars above turning into a road as they swept round hooting swept their light above where she walked, illuminating lower branches of trees. As she hurried she started at each blaring horn and each time she would look up to make sure that noise heralded a light and then was reassured to see leaves brilliantly green veined like marble with wet dirt and these veins reflecting each light back for a moment then it would be gone out beyond her and then was altogether gone and there was another. (7)

In Adelphi's recently published version, this is translated thus:

> Poi sbucò in una parte più aperta del parco. Alla curva della strada i fari delle automobili che suonavano il clacson diffondevano la loro luce più in alto rispetto a dove camminava lei, illuminando i rami inferiori degli alberi. Andava di corsa e trasaliva a ogni clacson e ogni volta sollevava lo sguardo per accertarsi che il rumore preannunciasse la luce e poi si sentiva più sicura nel vedere le foglie di un verde brillante venate come marmo per via del terriccio bagnato; e le venature per un momento trattenevano il riflesso di ogni luce, poi il riflesso si allontanava e scompariva del tutto e poi ce n'era un altro. (18-19)

> Then she came out into a more open part of the park. At the bend in the road the headlights of the cars that were sounding their horns spread their light higher up than where she was walking, illuminating the lower branches of the trees. She walked quickly and started at every sound of a horn and each time lifted her eyes to check that the noise

announced the light and then felt more secure in seeing the leaves of
a brilliant green veined like marble because of the wet dirt; and for a
moment the veins held the reflection of each light, then the reflection
moved away and disappeared altogether and then there was another.

The desire for a disorientation that matches that of the character is evident.
The repetition of 'swept', first as intransitive, then transitive ('as they swept
round hooting swept their light'), the different uses of the word 'light', the
switching from large objects to minutiae, from the visual to the audible, all
combine to achieve this effect (the translation is in difficulty and normalizing
radically, as a reading of the back-translation will confirm). There also seems
to be a lyrical delight in multiplicity, in gathering disparate things – 'leaves',
'marble', 'wet dirt' – and doing so in such a way that the syntax is deliberately
tangled, challenging our ability to sort these various things out, but at the same
time pleasing us with what we are now beginning to read as a very powerful,
if decidedly unusual, rhythm.

In a hint at what he is doing, Green describes Julia as constantly checking
that there is a strict relationship between the sound of the horn and the lights
of the cars: 'As she hurried she started at each blaring horn and each time she
would look up to make sure that noise heralded a light…'. We all seek to see
the world as a seamless weave of cause and effect. But what reassures Julia
(the light consequent on the sound) also distracts her as she now observes the
beauty of the leaves, even though their attractive marble-like veining is actually the result of dirt. The reader too looks for confirmation that the syntactical
structures announced are properly completed; but on the way he, like Julia, is
often seriously and pleasantly distracted. Here, for example, Green is talking
about the 'dark flood' of London crowds leaving their offices and walking
through the fog to the station:

> As pavements swelled out under this dark flood so that if you had
> been ensconced in that pall of fog looking down below at twenty foot
> deep of night illuminated by street lamps, these crowded pavements
> would have looked to you as if for all the world they might have been
> conduits. (5)

> Ora, a chi fosse nascosto dentro quel manto di nebbia e avesse guar-
> dato dieci metri più in giù nella notte buia illuminata dai lampioni,
> i marciapiedi gonfi di quella nera marea sarebbero sembrati precisi
> identici a delle fognature. (17)

Now, to someone who was hidden inside that cloak of fog and who looked ten metres down in the dark night lit by the streetlamps, the pavements swollen by that black tide would have looked exactly like drains.

The English begins with an 'As', suggesting an ongoing action within which another action will be announced. But almost immediately a consequential clause is introduced with 'so that' and this interpolation becomes so elaborately bizarre we hardly notice that the opening of the sentence has been forgotten and the action necessary to complete the 'as' clause does not take place. The translation simplifies, cuts and above all returns the sentence to standard grammar, as if the discrepancy were an embarrassment.

Yet, discrepancy, the anxiety and excitement of things not adding up, of parts having an uneasy relation to whole, is a constant feature in Green's work. When he is not presenting us with people groping through fog he loves to have a central character whose senses are impaired; blindness, deafness, shellshock and senility all have prominence in his fiction, and each impairment offers an intensification of what Green seems to be presenting to us as the ordinary human condition, one where expectation is baffled by discrepancy ("life after all is one discrepancy after another", he remarked, defending some of the unexplained twists and turns in his stories).

It's worth noting, however, that this bafflement isn't simply unpleasant in Green. His is not a classic existential pessimism. Discrepancy may be disorientating, but it also seems to let beauty and wonder into his characters' lives, and into Green's texts: freed from a strict correlation of cause and effect, objects, people, parts of speech, colours, sounds and lights are all experienced with new immediacy. Here are another few lines describing Julia's walk in the fog with traffic passing by:

These lights would come like thoughts in darkness, in a stream; a flash and then each was away. Looking round, and she was always glancing back, she would now and then see loving couples dimly two by two; in flashes their faces and anything white in their clothes picked up what light was at moments reflected down on them. (7)

Queste luci arrivavano come pensieri nell'oscurità, in un flusso; un lampo e poi via. Lanciando un'occhiata intorno, e sempre si guardava alle spalle, di tanto in tanto scorgeva nella penombra coppie di amanti a due a due; a ogni lampo i volti e tutto quello che c'era di bianco nei loro vestiti raccoglievano la luce che per un momento gli si rifletteva addosso. (19)

> These lights came like thoughts in the darkness, in a flow; a flash and
> then away. Glancing around, and she was always looking behind her,
> from time to time in the half light she noticed couples of lovers two by
> two; at every flash their faces and everything there was of white in their
> clothes gathered the light that for a moment was reflected on them.

Again there is a tendency to break up the normal sequences with which information is delivered so that isolated elements are seen more clearly, but in
a tenuous relationship with each other and the whole. Again the effect is to
create anxiety, wonder and beauty, simultaneously.

Having established these consistent elements of style, let us turn to the
other novel of Green's that has been translated into Italian. *Doting* was Green's
last work, published in 1952. That it was chosen for translation, when other
more highly praised works were set aside, is perhaps due to the fact that it is
made up almost entirely of dialogue arranged in a series of scenes, each with
only the briefest and simplest of narrative introductions and then only a few
spare comments on gesture, tone of voice and, very rarely, action. The single
exception to this, in *Doting,* is the opening scene, which is elaborate to say the
least. Perhaps it occurred to the publishers that a novel with so much dialogue
would present fewer problems for translation since dialogue tends to follow
more standard forms.

The plot of *Doting* needs to be given so that we have a sense of the larger
structure to which any local curiosities can be related. Like almost all Green's
plots it involves half a dozen characters getting involved in the most complex
conspiratorial relationships.

Arthur and Diana Middleton, a middle-class, middle-aged couple, take
their seventeen-year-old son, Peter, out for an evening on his return from
boarding school for the summer holidays. To keep him company they invite
the nineteen-year-old Annabel, the daughter of old friends. Mr Middleton
shows an excessive interest in Annabel. Following that evening he begins to
take her out to lunch and when Mrs Middleton leaves with the son on holiday,
he invites the girl to his flat to dinner that very evening. On the way to the
station, however, there is a car accident, the boy has to be taken to hospital,
and Mrs Middleton (Diana) returns home unexpectedly to discover Annabel
by the washbasin in the main bedroom trying to remove a coffee stain from
her skirt, while Mr Middleton is on his knees at her feet.

The exact significance of this scene is discussed for the rest of the book.
Diana takes revenge by going out with widower Charles Addinsell, a mutual
friend. But she refuses to go to bed with him. Jealous himself, and accused
of protracting his relationship with Annabel, Arthur decides to kill two birds

with one stone by introducing Charles to the girl. The widower begins to take Annabel out, neglecting the wife. But just as Annabel has refused actually to go to bed with Arthur, she now refuses to go to bed with Charles. As she laments to her confidante, Claire, she is unable to fall in love with anyone.

Jealous now that Annabel has taken her flame away from her, Diana schemes to get Charles along to the dinner party that will mark the end of her son Peter's summer holidays. To do this she has to invite another woman to make up numbers (three men, three women), and chooses Claire, Annabel's confidante. However, on being introduced to each other beforehand, Charles and Claire at once go off together and become lovers to the immense chagrin of all the other players. The end-of-holiday dinner party that closes the book is thus a *tour de force* of ill-concealed rancour as everybody laments the behaviour of everybody else while the young son remains oblivious to everything.

Such a summary is reductive, but suffice it to say that the book has those qualities of 'great formal brilliance' and 'indeterminable purport'[5] that Beckett's Watt observed in the house of Mr Knott, each passage of the novel being infinitely nuanced as the central characters despair not only of getting what they want, but even of deciding what it is they do want. The title *Doting* is helpful here. A dictionary definition of the verb to 'dote' tells us: 'to be stupid or foolish: to be weakly affectionate: to show excessive love', while derivations like 'dotage' and 'dotard' are, of course, associated with the weakness of old age. In short, *Doting* is not a positive-sounding title; it suggests a foolish affection without outcome. The choice, for the Italian title, of *'Passioni'* (Passions) thus seems inappropriate.

As remarked earlier, the action of *Doting* is conducted almost entirely through dialogue in the form of direct speech. There is no indirect discourse and very little narrative prose. The opening scene however is rather different; in particular it includes two descriptions of two artists, or performers. Since Green himself remarked that he always worked and reworked the first twenty pages of a novel endlessly before proceeding, 'because in my idea you have to get everything into them',[6] this is a scene that has to be considered.

Mr and Mrs Middleton are in a restaurant-cum-night-club with son Peter and friend of the family Annabel. As they choose their meal, a number of cabaret acts are performed on a small stage below them. The first is a dancer:

> All she wore was a blue sequin on the point of each breast and a few
> more to cover her sex. As she swayed those hips, sequins caught the

[5] Samuel Beckett, *Watt,* Calder, London, 1963, p. 71.

[6] Henry Green, *Surviving, The Uncollected Writings of Henry Green,* Harville, London, 1993, p. 242.

light to strike off in a blaze of royal blue while the skin stayed moonlit and the palms of her two hands, daubed probably with a darker pigment, made a deeper shadow above raised arms of a red so harsh it was almost black in that space through which she waved her opened fingers in figure of eights before the cut jet of two staring eyes. (p. 172)[7]

Indossava solo una paillette azzurra sulla punta dei seni e qualcuna in più a coprirle il sesso. Dimenava i fianchi e la luce rimbalzava dalle paillettes in una fiammata azzurra mentre la pelle restava lunare e il palmo delle mani, probabilmente scurito, creava sopra le braccia sollevate, una zona d'ombra di un rosso così crudo da sembrare quasi nero nello spazio che le sue dita attraversavano disegnando degli otto di fronte al giaietto intagliato degli occhi sgranati. (p.5)[8]

She wore just one blue sequin on the tips of her breasts and a few more to cover her sex. She shook her hips and the light bounced off the sequins in a blue blaze while her skin stayed moonlike and the palms of her hands, probably darkened, created above her raised arms, an area of darkness of a red so harsh it seemed almost black in the space that her fingers crossed making figures of eight before the cut jet of two wide-open eyes.

Looking for divergences between the two texts, we can see that the deixis is different throughout, unusual in the English and standard in the Italian, as follows:

- 'those hips'(non-standard in English since previously undeclared) – 'i fianchi' (*the hips*, standard Italian usage, hence the back-translation *her hips*)
- 'sequins' (since already declared, the definite article would have been expected) – 'dalle paillettes' (*from the sequins*, standard)
- 'the skin' (a possessive 'her' would have been more common) – 'la pelle' (*the skin*, again standard usage in Italian which does not commonly use possessives with parts of the body)
- 'her two hands' (the 'two' is redundant) – 'delle mani' (*of the hands*, standard)

[7] All quotations from *Doting* are taken from, Henry Green, *Nothing, Doting, Blindness,* Picador, London, 1979. Page numbers are indicated in brackets at the end of each quotation.
[8] All quotations from the Italian translation of *Doting* are taken from Henry Green, *Passioni,* translation by Stefania Bertola, Einaudi, Turin, 1990. Page numbers are indicated in brackets at the end of each quotation.

- 'raised arms' (one would have expected a possessive) – 'le braccia sollevate' (*the raised arms*, standard)
- 'that space' (extravagantly marked) – 'lo spazio' (*the space*, standard)
- 'two staring eyes' (the 'two' is redundant, absence of possessive) – 'degli occhi sgranati' (*of the wide open eyes*, standard)

In general it is easy to note the reifying tendency of the deixis in the English. The parts of the body in particular, usually preceded by a possessive in English, are treated as separate objects (the unnecessary use of number underlines the effect). The opening sentence with its 'on the point of each breast', rather than 'on her nipples', sets the tone for this and establishes that the reification is cool, even clinical, rather than salacious, the tendency then being clinched in the final phrase, 'the cut jet of two staring eyes'.

But the deixis also has the effect of imposing unusual rhythms, since the use of demonstratives introduces heavy stresses that definite or indefinite articles do not, while the absence of articles before plurals eliminates unstressed syllables. The result is the formation of groups of heavy stresses ('skin stayed moonlit' – 'two hands, daubed probably' – 'red so harsh' – 'two staring eyes') which intensify the impression of reification. This effect, occasionally reinforced by alliteration ('daubed probably with a darker pigment, made a deeper shadow'), is absent in the more standard prose of the Italian, and indeed it is difficult to see how it could have been achieved. Not that the Italian is without rhythm (consider, for example: 'di un rosso così crudo da sembrare quasi nero' – *of a red so harsh as to seem almost black*), just that it is not the peculiar, heavily stressed rhythm of the English.

Also worth noting are the two comparatives in the English which are lost in the Italian as follows:

the palms of her two hands, daubed probably with a darker pigment, made a deeper shadow above raised arms

il palmo delle mani, probabilmente scurito, creava sopra le braccia sollevate, una zona d'ombra

the palms of her hands, probably darkened, created above her raised arms, an area of darkness

The curiosity of both of these comparatives is that they are introduced without a term of comparison: a darker pigment than what other pigment; a deeper shadow than which other shadow? As such, they create one of those small, disorientating discrepancies in Green's syntax where an expectation of inner cohesion is not fulfilled.

Finally, one cannot help but note the elimination, in the Italian, of various elements in the English, as follows: 'caught the light' – 'royal blue' – 'darker pigment' – 'opened fingers'. Of course if one sets out to rewrite the Italian in such a way as to include these elements it becomes clear that the translator probably eliminated them to avoid making the central sentence too long, heavy and complex, and in this respect their absence fits in with the decision to cut out the temporal clause introduced in the English with 'as' ('As she swayed those hips ...') replacing it with the simpler solution, more common in Italian, of two verbs connected by a conjunction ('Dimenava i fianchi e la luce ...' *She shook her hips and the light...*). They are changes in the interests of fluency and standard Italian prosody.

What is the overall result? The paragraph in English offers something intentionally virtuoso, a curiously clinical but very rich and colourful description of an artistic performance where sexuality is contained in formal gesture and artifice. The long second sentence describes this artifice and itself deploys artifice, concluding with a sense of mystery as it focuses on what traditionally lies beyond artifice, the eyes, but here instead is presented as the product of the craftsman: 'the cut jet of two staring eyes'.

In Italian the paragraph is not so obviously purposeful. The palette is more watery, the virtuosity almost non-existent. In particular, the different nature of standard deixis in Italian very largely eliminates the reifying effect of the English, for in Italian the use of the article rather than the possessive is standard in descriptions of parts of the body, so no strangeness can be achieved here. The sentence, though in many ways cleverly translated, thus loses much of its power as a preview of the novel's treatment of sexuality.

Green's strategy in these opening pages becomes even clearer when the second artist appears, this time a juggler. Our four characters, ever indecisive, are still fussing over the menu:

> Chattering away, having fun with the Sicilian who, on being asked how their lobster would be cooked, said 'in rice very nice, in the shell very well', they altogether ignored, as they decided against this lobster, miracles of skill spun out a few feet beneath – no less than the balancing of a billiard ivory ball on the juggler's chin, then a pint beer mug on top of that ball at the exact angle needed to cheat gravity, and at last the second ivory sphere which this man placed from a stick, or cue, to top all on the mug's handle – the ball supporting a pint pot, then the pint pot a second ball until, unnoticed by our party, the man removed

his chin and these separate objects fell, balls of ivory each to a hand, and the jug to a toe of his patent leather shoe where he let it hang and shine to a faint look of surprise, the artist. (pp. 175-6)

Although it presents no problem for the translator, it's worth noticing how Green splits his characters off from what he is describing. Instead of the description being used, as in the traditional novel, either to establish a background that affects the drama, or to suggest, as in Conrad, for example, the mode of perception of a character observing the scene, here the characters are oblivious to something that is going on, something, what is more, that in no way affects them, nor plays any part whatsoever in the plot.

Aside from contributing to a general sense of fragmentation, Green thus suggests that the lavish description must have some other meaning. With a hindsight awareness of the plot, its complex permutations achieved with the same few characters, a limited range of themes and limited narrative resources (almost exclusively dialogue from now on), it is hard not to see this as a cheeky description of the juggling Green himself is about to do with his characters. The word 'artist' that closes the sentence makes this more or less explicit.

The description itself presents many of the stylistic elements we saw in the description of the dancer and the passages from *Party Going*. There is so much that is teasing: the introduction of the subordinate clause after 'ignored' which makes a surprise of 'miracles of skill' ('ignored, as they decided against this lobster, miracles of skill'); the use of the verb 'spun out' which of course can refer not only to juggling but to the telling of a story, particularly long stories that, like *Doting*, go nowhere; the inversion of the normal order of adjectives in 'billiard ivory ball' (rather than the standard, ivory billiard ball) which rehearses the incongruity of the juggler's trick; the talk of 'cheating gravity' which suggests the non-realistic nature of Green's art; the redundant 'stick, or cue' which makes us wait for just a moment longer for the image that, to top all, so to speak, tops all ('placed from a stick, or cue, to top all on the mug's handle'). Then, in the last lines of the sentence, all the disparate objects that art has miraculously held together for a moment are allowed to fall apart. The curious use of the verb 'removed' ('the man removed his chin') gives us the now expected reification and dislocation which is at last made explicit with the words 'separate objects'. But even here it should be observed how the whole is held together by rhythm, assonance and alliteration as Green extricates himself from this particularly tangled trick: 'balls of ivory each to a hand, and the jug to a toe of his patent leather shoe where he let it hang and shine to a faint look of surprise, the artist'.

Here is the Italian:

> Parlottando, divertendosi con il siciliano che, alla domanda circa il loro metodo per cuocere l'aragosta, rispose che col riso è buona ma nel suo guscio è meglio ancora, ignorarono completamente, mentre decidevano a sfavore dell'aragosta, i prodigi di abilità che si stavano verificando più in basso: una palla da biliardo tenuta in equilibrio sul mento del giocoliere, e sopra la palla un boccale da birra messo esattamente nell'unico punto che consentisse di beffare la gravità e infine una seconda sfera d'avorio che l'uomo posò sul manico del boccale con l'aiuto di un bastoncino: la prima palla reggeva il boccale e il boccale la seconda palla finché, all'insaputa del nostro gruppetto, l'uomo ritrasse il mento e gli oggetti caddero, le palle ciascuna in una mano, e il boccale sulla punta di una delle sue scarpe di vernice dove lui, l'artista, lo lasciò sospeso e lucente, guardandolo con vaga sorpresa. (p. 10)

> Chatting, enjoying themselves with the Sicilian who, to the question as to their method of cooking the lobster, replied that with rice it is good but in its shell it is still better, they completely ignored, as they decided against the lobster, prodigies of skill that were taking place lower down: a billiard ball balanced on the juggler's chin, and on the ball a beer mug placed exactly in the only point that made it possible to kid gravity and finally a second ivory sphere that the man placed on the handle of the beer mug with the help of a cue: the first ball supported the mug and the mug the second ball until, unknown to our little group, the man withdrew his chin and the objects fell, the balls each to a hand, and the mug onto the point of one of his patent leather shoes where he, the artist, let it hang and shine, looking at it with vague surprise.

So often you think you have seen everything in a text, only to find, on comparing it with a translation, that there were nuances you hadn't realized were there to be lost. Here my attention is drawn for the first time to the showman's rhetorical gesture, 'no less than', to Green's decision to write 'balls of ivory' rather than 'ivory balls' to get the rhythm of 'balls of ivory each to a hand' and his very odd deixis in 'a toe of his patent leather shoe', as if the juggler had only one shoe but with more than one toe. The Italian eliminates 'no less than', eliminates 'ivory', and standardizes the reference to the shoe with 'una delle sue scarpe' (*one of his shoes*). Without wishing to go into too much detail here, we can simply notice:

- the loss of the word 'separate' (so important thematically)
- the re-positioning earlier on in the sentence of the word 'artist' (which thus loses emphasis)
- the loss of the redundant 'cue' which cues up the culminating detail
- the (inevitable) loss of richness delivered by the punning verbs 'to spin out' and 'to top all'.

In each case these losses in the Italian lead us straight to the heart of Green's strategy. Most of all, it is evident that the Italian reads like a translation of a much standardized version of the English, so much so that while one appreciates that this is a miserably difficult sentence to translate, and while admiring (genuinely) many of the translator's solutions, one wonders whether she or her editor were aware of the image's function in the text, otherwise it would surely have been possible to have held that word 'artista', which clinches all, to the end.

How much does this matter in terms of the book as a whole? We have already said that these are anomalous passages in a novel made up almost entirely of dialogue. Even if they do offer a key to understanding the rest, perhaps they are largely irrelevant to the experience of reading the book from start to finish. It is time to turn to the novel's handling of dialogue.

Green, it should be said, was perhaps most famous and certainly most loved for his dialogue. Speaking of the characters in *Living*, Updike remarks on 'the tart comedy of their talk, heard with the startling fidelity that mistakenly is taken as a mere passive gift – for to write how people talk one must know how they think, and an aggressive psychology and sociology inform Green's articulations on behalf of others'.[9]

This remark alerts us to the fact that Green's dialogue might be more dense and rich than one is accustomed to. But it is also worth noting that dialogue, for Green, means above all the dramatization of misunderstanding. And it is here that one can begin to see the link between the supposedly simple language of dialogue and the highly tangled language of Green's prose. One of the most frequently quoted passages in the critical literature on Green is this exchange from a rare interview with Terry Southern.

> Interviewer:
> I've heard it remarked that your work is 'too sophisticated' for American readers, in that it offers no scenes of violence – and 'too subtle',

---

[9] John Updike, in the preface to Henry Green, *Loving, Living, Party Going,* Picador, London, 1978, p. 11.

in that its message is somewhat veiled. What do you say?

Green:

Unlike the wilds of Texas, there is very little violence over here. A bit of child-killing of course, but no straight-shootin' ...

Interviewer:

And how about 'subtle'?

Green:

I don't follow. Suttee, as I understand it, is the suicide – now forbidden – of a Hindu wife on her husband's flaming bier. I don't want my wife to do that when my time comes – and with great respect, as I know her, she won't ...

Interviewer:

I'm sorry, you misheard me; I said 'subtle' – that the message was too subtle.

Green:

Oh, subtle. How dull![10]

The explanation for such an extraordinary misunderstanding lies in Green's deafness ('the very deaf, as I am, hear the most astounding things all round them ...'[11]), but what is more interesting than the misunderstanding is the way Green responds to it. He must be aware that his interviewer could hardly have brought out the word 'suttee' with reference to his work, and yet he seizes on the chance to talk about it, introducing the ironic remark about his wife. The 'subtle/suttee' misunderstanding thus begins to function as one of those discrepancies or sutures in his syntax where one reality shifts, joyfully one feels, into another. This is something that happens frequently in Green's dialogue, and frequently with the same effect, injecting new vitality into proceedings. Life springs, it seems, from misunderstanding. As far as a translation is concerned, if it is a question of a shift in direction generated by a misheard word, the problem will be whether such a misunderstanding would be possible at the same point in the language of translation. More often, Green's creation of such moments is, to risk the word again, more subtle.

In the novel *Back,* confusion and discrepancy are personified in the figure of Nancy Whitmore. Shellshocked and one-legged, Charley returns from the war to discover that his old (adulterous) mistress, Rose Phillips, is dead. But then her father, Mr Grant, gives him an introduction to another young woman, a war widow, Nancy, whom Charley finds to be identical to Rose. In a state of severe trauma, Charley becomes convinced that Rose faked her death to

---

[10] *Surviving: The Uncollected Writings of Henry Green,* cit., pp. 237-8.

[11] Ibid., p. 239.

escape her first husband, Phillips, whom she had been betraying with Charley, to then marry another man who has died in the war. Here is a snippet of conversation between Charley and his womanizing friend Middlewitch who lives in the same boarding house as Nancy. Charley is claiming that Nancy previously went under a different name (Rose's).

> 'Her name was Rose.'
> 'Whose name?'
> 'Rose Phillips.'
> 'You're telling me a lot about this Rose Phillips, old man,' Mr Middlewitch complained, 'but I've never had the honour, have I?' He was continually looking round the luncheon room for acquaintances.
> 'It's Nance Whitmore.'
> 'What was her name, then, before she married Phillips?'
> 'Nancy Whitmore was Rose Grant.'
> 'You're wrong there, old chap. Nance lost her husband in the war. He wasn't called Phillips. Then she changed her name back by deed poll. But her hubby was Phil White. Is that what you were thinking of? Phil and Phillips? He got his at Alamein.'
> This was more than Charley could stomach.
> 'What's the penalty for bigamy, even when the second husband's dead?' he demanded choking.
> 'Bigamy, old boy? Why ask me? Never marry 'em, that's my motto. Best thing too.'[12]

Charley has problems of recognition. Similar names encourage the confusion. The distracted Middlewitch completely misunderstands Charley's remark on bigamy, imagining his friend is planning it, rather than complaining about it. *Back* is full of conversations of this kind. Eventually we will discover that Nancy is Rose's illegitimate half sister. She is also, as so often with the point of incomprehension in Green's novels, extremely beautiful and full of life. For Charley she forms the vital link between his pre-war past and his happy future. At the end of the book they marry, though he is still calling her Rose.

At this point we might remark that rather than merely containing discrepancies, the whole notion of discrepancy or misunderstanding, or tangle, the whole technique of shifts in plot and prose that are credible but inexplicable, is central to Green's work. Rather than being a problem for would-be interpreters, his novels are about the problem of interpreting the world. And his dialogue,

---

[12] Henry Green, *Back,* The Hogarth Press, London, 1979, p. 114.

even in a novel like *Doting* (where unusually no character suffers from any impairment), is always hovering on the edge of incomprehensibility, perhaps because the characters themselves are not sure what they think, their mental life being notoriously discontinuous. Green makes this explicit in the following exchange between the middle-aged Arthur Middleton and the young Annabel whom he is so eager to take to bed. They have been discussing her boyfriend, Campbell, a melancholy, lonely young poet. Arthur is speaking, enviously:

> 'I see. Then has he asked you yet to share his loneliness for good?'
> She frowned. 'I don't think that's very nice at all,' she said. 'It might be almost nasty,' she added in a sad voice, 'or else you're not so understanding as you seem. But of course Campbell would love to live in sin with me and I might adore it too, yet I'm not going to. Although, as I said, he could really be rather wonderful.'
> 'I'm sorry,' Arthur apologized. 'I was confused.'
> 'What about?'
> 'Everything, Ann.'
> 'Who's to blame you,' she suddenly laughed. 'Look at me! I get so tangled up over my own feelings I often don't know where I am myself.' (p. 204)

A few moment's later, the idea of tangle is picked up again, and at once generates a misunderstanding.

> 'Yes, I see. All right. But to go back to what you were saying, Annabel. Aren't you taking things too seriously? Because you needn't think your emotional life will ever not be in a tangle, dear.'
> 'You say I'm so crazy I shan't once be able to snap out of it?' she demanded in what appeared to be humble indignation. (pp. 204-5)

The Italian for the first part of this passage goes as follows:

> 'Vedo. E ti ha già chiesto di dividere per sempre con lui la sua solitudine?'
> Lei si acciglió. 'Non mi sembra un'osservazione simpatica,' disse, 'direi che è proprio maligna, oppure non hai capito bene la situazione. Ma certo che Campbell sarebbe felice di vivere con me nel peccato e potrebbe piacere moltissimo anche a me, solo che non lo farò. Per quanto, come ho detto, lui sa essere davvero meraviglioso.'
> 'Mi spiace,' si scusò Arthur, 'ero un po' confuso.'
> 'A che proposito?'

'A proposito di tutto, Ann.'

'E chi può biasimarti,' rise lei all'improvviso, 'guarda me! I miei sentimenti sono talmente ingarbugliati che certe volte non so proprio a che punto sono.' (p. 51)

'I see. And has he already asked you to share his solitude with him for ever?'

She frowned. 'That doesn't seem a nice remark to me,' she said, ' I'd say it's really mean, or you haven't understood the situation properly. But of course Campbell would be happy to live in sin with me and I could like it a great deal too, only that I won't do it. Even though, as I said, he can be really marvellous.'

'I'm sorry,' Arthur apologized, ' I was a bit confused.'

'About what?'

'About everything, Ann.'

'And who can blame you,' she laughed suddenly, 'look at me! My feelings are so muddled that sometimes I just don't know where I am up to.'

As with Green's prose, what we seem to have is a translation of a standardized version of the original. The dubious and hesitant 'It might be almost nasty' becomes the far more forthright 'direi che è proprio maligna' (*I would say it's really mean*). The 'sad voice' that qualifies this remark in the original, making Annabel's feelings even more unclear, is eliminated. The complex 'or else you're not so understanding as you seem' becomes the banal 'oppure non hai capito bene la situazione' (*or you haven't understood the situation properly*). The typically vague 'he could really be rather wonderful' becomes the· far more positive 'lui sa essere davvero meraviglioso' (*he can be really marvellous*). The complex syntax of 'I get so tangled up over my own feelings', with its implications of a divided ego, is simplified in 'I miei sentimenti sono talmente ingarbugliati' (*My feelings are so muddled*). Only in one place is the Italian more hesitant and qualifying than the English. In Italian Arthur says, 'Ero un po' confuso' (*I was a bit confused*). In English he says more frankly, 'I was confused'.

Such a list of differences need not be considered as a criticism. The translation of dialogue requires great efforts of domestication, since it must appear as natural. Green is a master of those places where English dialogue lends itself to confusion, to extravagant complication (the use of modals and subjunctives is particularly effective here) and such effects may not always be possible in the same place in another language. That said, it is evident that in this translation either translator or editor has decided to favour the fluency of the story over the tangle of Green's delivery. In short, somebody has not understood, or not respected, the author's intentions. The book is about tangle and hesitancy, a dramatization of half-understood emotions that tug the syntax this way and that. The syntax itself tells us that these people are never going to get anywhere. It is in this sense that Updike is right when he remarks on the aggressive psychology of Green's dialogue. Here are a few more examples, with translation. In the first, Annabel is speaking to her friend Claire about her feelings for Arthur.

'Seriously, are we to go round, for ever, just being careful against our truly better feelings, or judgements?' (p. 213)

È davvero possibile che si passi la propria vita a lottare contro i nostri migliori sentimenti o giudizi?' (p. 63)

Is it really possible that we spend our lives struggling against our better feelings or judgements?

The 'going round for ever', the theme of the book, is sacrificed for something much more forthright. 'Lottare' (*struggle*) does not seem justified by the much more nuanced English.

In the next example Annabel phones Arthur to ask if she can see him, but, aware that his wife is keeping him under observation, he refuses:

'Well,' he at last replied. 'I'm not sure that would be an altogether good notion, Ann. Just at the moment,' he added.
'I see,' she said.
A click then told him she had rung off. (p. 224)

'Ecco,' disse alla fine, 'non so se è una buona idea, almeno al mo-mento.'
'Capisco,' disse lei.
E tolse la comunicazione con un clic. (p. 80)

'Well,' he said in the end, ' I don't know if it's a good idea, at least at the moment.
'I understand,' she said.
And she ended the call with a click.

Again, everything becomes more direct. The painstaking carefulness (against his better feelings?) of 'altogether a good notion' is gone, likewise the odd focusing of the line of narrative that closes the piece.

In the next example Arthur is trying to get his wife, Diana, to stop digressing and tell him about a conversation she has had with Annabel's mother.

> 'I won't listen to any more of this nonsense,' Mr Middleton announced, almost with passion. 'Nor have I the leisure, even if you think you have.' (p. 240)

> 'Non ho intenzione di ascoltare altre sciocchezze,' annunciò quasi con ardore il signor Middleton, 'e non ne ho neanche il tempo, checché tu ne pensi.' (p. 103)

> 'I've no intention of listening to any more silliness,' he Mr Middleton announced almost with ardour, 'and I don't even have the time, whatever you might think.'

Mr Middleton at last speaks, with passion, or almost, but ironically not when declaring himself to Annabel, only when responding to his wife's complaints about his philandering (as in Barbara Pym's work, characters are frequently referred to as having 'passions' for everything but each other). The Italian loses the strength of 'I won't', the irony of the word 'passion' (missing a chance to refer to the Italian title), and then the curious confusion of 'even if you think you have', where one surely expected 'even if you think I have'.

In the following example Annabel and Arthur are discussing the unpredictable nature of marriage. The girl is speaking:

> 'Then it must be frightful to be married!'
> 'At times, possibly. Although things can be almost as bad when you're single, you must admit.'
> 'So what ought one to do, Arthur?'
> 'Go on seeing each other.'
> 'No, about marriage I mean, stupid!'
> 'Nothing, darling. Drift.' (p. 244)

> 'E allora dev'essere spaventoso, esser sposati!'
> 'Forse, a volte. Anche se devi ammettere che può essere altrettanto brutto non esserlo.'
> 'E allora che cosa si deve fare, Arthur?'
> 'Continuare a vederci.'
> 'No, riguardo al matrimonio, stupido!'
> 'Niente, tesoro. Tenersi a galla.' (p. 108)

'Well then it must be frightening, to be married!'

'Maybe, sometimes. Even though you must admit that it can be just as bad not to be.'

'So what must one do, Arthur?'

'Go on seeing each other.'

'No, with regard to marriage, stupid!'

'Nothing, darling. Stay afloat.'

Here the Italian smooths out the difficult 'almost as bad', then has no problem with the typical Greenian misunderstanding arising from the question 'So what ought one to do?', only to run into trouble with the word 'drift', which again describes the languid back and forth of the characters throughout the book, so different from the more desperate 'tenersi a galla' (*stay afloat*, in the sense of keep your head above water). However, it is difficult to see what the Italian could have done here. At the most immediate level of reading the expressions are equivalent.

Back with his wife, Arthur is trying to comfort her for what she sees as an empty life. He is speaking:

> 'On the contrary,' he protested, 'if that is so, then everything matters very much. What concerns me is your happiness, your welfare, my dear.'
>
> 'Does it?'
>
> 'How d'you feel in yourself?' he elaborated. 'Every day!' he added. Picking up his hand from off her shoulder, she kissed the wrist. 'Darling, darling,' she said. (p. 259)

> 'Al contrario,' protestò lui, 'se è davvero così allora importa moltissimo. La tua felicità, il tuo benessere mi preoccupano, cara.'
>
> 'Davvero.'
>
> 'Quello che tu provi dentro di te,' ampliò lui, 'ogni giorno!' aggiunse. Lei gli sollevò la mano e gli baciò il polso.
>
> 'Tesoro mio,' disse. (p. 130)

> 'On the contrary,' he protested, 'if it is really like that then it's very important. Your happiness, your well-being worry me, dear.'
>
> 'Really.'
>
> 'What you feel inside yourself,' he expanded, 'every day!' he added. She lifted his hand and kissed his wrist.
>
> 'My darling,' she said.

Green frequently mixes speech acts with apparently inappropriate speech tags to give nuance to the tone and suggest hidden intentions. In this case a question – 'How d'you feel in yourself?' – is followed by 'he elaborated'. The Italian eliminates this discrepancy by removing the interrogative element from Arthur's remark, attaching it, instead, to his previous comment. It then goes on to tone down the elaborately clinical descriptions of physical movement typical of the book ('picking up his hand from off her shoulder').

In the next example, Arthur's friend, Charles Addinsell, is trying to suggest to Annabel that being single as he is does have its advantages:

> 'I told you before there could be consolations, Ann.' (p. 264)

> 'Ti ho detto che ci sono molte consolazioni, Ann.' (p. 137)

> 'I told you that there are lots of consolations, Ann.'

Here the Italian displays an unnecessary loss of nuance. Hesitancy is important in this sentence because what Charles is talking about is the possible consolation of his going to bed with Ann. At the same time he must be careful not to give her the impression that this is a frequent consolation for him, even though it may well be so. The word 'molte' (lots of) marks the point where the translator's desire for clarity leads her to a straightforward error.

Now Annabel is complaining to Charles that his conversation has put her off marriage altogether:

> 'I'm sure I don't know where I'm going to be, now, with my life.'
> (p. 265)

> 'A questo punto non so più che fare della mia vita.' (p. 138)

> 'At this point I no longer know what to do with my life.'

Another unhelpful untangling in the Italian.

In the next example, Charles has explained to Annabel how one tends to invest less in relationships after one has had someone 'die on you'. Speaking of his son, she responds:

> 'Then are you going to love him less for that?'
> 'I am. You see, Ann, on account of if he died.' (p. 266)

'E per questo lo amerai di meno?'
'Sì. Pensando che potrebbe morire.' (p. 266)

'And as a result you'll love him less?'
'Yes. Thinking that he could die.'

'On account of if ...' is so shamefacedly hesitant. The translation smooths out syntax and psychology.

Arthur and his wife are engaged in another of their endless reappraisals of what really happened between him and Annabel that night at the washbasin:

'Oh,' Mrs Middleton commented in a gay bright voice, 'I don't wish, or choose, to go into the whole old business anew. Above all, I wouldn't want you provoked, darling.' (p. 267)

'Oh,' commentò in tono allegro e brillante la signora Middleton, 'non vorrei proprio riprendere quel vecchio discorso. E sopratutto, non voglio provocarti, tesoro.' (p. 141)

'Oh,' Mrs Middleton commented in a happy, brilliant voice, 'I really wouldn't want to start that old discussion again. And above all, I don't want to provoke you, darling.'

'I wouldn't want you provoked ...'. Comparison with the Italian (or the back-translation) again alerts us to Green's, and Diana Middleton's, irony. The next example is taken from a few lines further down. Arthur is speaking:

'Yes, dear,' he replied with patience and what seemed to be humility. (p. 267)

'Sì, cara,' rispose lui con pazienza e addirittura con umiltà. (p. 142)

'Yes, dear,' he replied with patience and even humility.

Seeming is an important concept in this book. The switch from qualifier to emphasizer is inexplicable. Again from the same conversation we have:

'I see, Arthur. So you don't meet Ann, now?'
'No. And do you ever see Charles?'
'No more, no more!' his wife wailed comically. At which they both laughed in a rather shamefaced way at each other. (p. 268)

'Capisco, Arthur. E così adesso non vedi più Ann?'
'No. E tu vedi Charles?'
'Non più, non più!' gemette buffamente la moglie. E tutti e due
scoppiarono a ridere un po' imbarazzati. (p. 143)

'I see, Arthur. And so now you don't see Ann any more?'
'No. And do you see Charles?'
'No more, no more!' his wife moaned comically. And both of them
burst out laughing a little embarrassed.

How much more complicated and complicitous the English is where both
are embarrassed (by their interest in other lovers), but both laughing *at each
other.*
    The same discussion continues. Arthur is speaking.

'But I used to ring Ann first thing, soon as ever I got to the office
after seeing you over breakfast.'
'Oh, Arthur, first thing! What can your telephone girl have thought?
Just warm from our bed!'
'She wasn't.' (p. 269)

'Ma se chiamavo sempre Ann appena arrivato in ufficio, e subito
dopo averti vista a colazione.'
'Oh, Arthur, appena arrivato! Che cosa avrà pensato la tua centralinista? Ancora con l'odore di letto addosso.'
'La centralinista?' (p. 145)

'But I always called Ann as soon as I arrived at the office, and right
after seeing you at breakfast.'
'Oh, Arthur, as soon as you arrived! What must your switchboard
girl have thought? Still with the smell of bed on her.'
'The switchboard girl?'

Surely the important concept to keep was 'our bed' which sets up, even as he
denies it, one of Mr Middleton's fantasies: having other women in his bed. It is
after all what may or may not have happened in 'our bed' that Mrs Middleton
is concerned about.
    A few lines later, Arthur, as so often, plays the card of self-pity:

'If anybody can be said to have learnt a hard lesson, then it's me,' the
man said. (p. 270)

'Se c'è qualcuno che ha imparato la lezione, quello sono io.' (p. 145)

'If there is someone who has learned a lesson, it's me.'

Here we have a loss of Arthur's complex and insecure pomposity.
   In the next example Arthur is talking to Annabel:

'Oh, Ann, I've been so distressed about it all!' he at once pleaded.
(p. 274)

'Oh, Ann, sapessi quanto mi sono tormentato!' subito gemette lui.
(p. 152)

'Oh, Ann, if you knew how much I've tormented myself' he at once
moaned.

Again the discrepancy between speech tag ('pleaded') and speech act (an account of his unhappiness) is ironed out.
   Charles to Annabel now:

'All right. But why do you think it is so necessary to fall in love?'
'Well, mayn't that be so?' (p. 293)

'Benissimo. Ma perché ritieni tanto necessario innamorarsi?'
'Come può non esserlo?' (p. 178)

'Okay. But why do you think it's so necessary to fall in love?'
'How can it not be?'

The uncertainty of 'mayn't' is ignored, indeed reversed.
   Diana Middleton to husband Arthur:

'you're in a way a reasonable sort of husband.' (p. 323)

'ma in un certo senso sei un ottimo marito.' (p.220)

'but in a certain sense you're an excellent husband.

So many qualifications in the English.
   Again Mrs Middleton, this time at the book's final dinner party, speaking
rather drunkenly of Annabel to the rest of the group (Arthur, Claire, Charles
her son).

'Oh my dears, I'd meant to say something to that young woman tonight! ... Yes, I had. But knowing myself as I do, I don't suppose I will ... I have my little plans at times ... And then I so seldom carry them out, which I'm inclined to regret, always.' (p. 333)

'Oh, cari, avevo intenzione di dire qualcosa a quella ragazza, stasera! ... Sì, volevo farlo. Ma conoscendomi, dubito che lo farò ... A volte faccio dei progetti ... ma raramente li metto in pratica, cosa che poi rimpiango sempre.' (p. 234)

'Oh, my dears, I was intending to say something to that girl, this evening! ... Yes, I wanted to. But knowing myself, I doubt that I will ... Sometimes I make plans ... but I rarely put them into practice, something that then I always regret.'

Again the English is intensely nuanced, Green makes such play with the auxiliaries (Yes, I had. But knowing myself as I do, I don't suppose I will). Much of this is clarified in the Italian because of the nature of the Italian syntax, though surely a little more of the meandering waywardness of the last sentence could have been kept.

Such a list of examples, and one can find them on almost every page, should be sufficient to confirm that the problem posed by Green's dialogue is not dissimilar to that presented by his prose. In both cases there is a tendency to slippage, discrepancy, meandering complication. The drift of the translation, in both prose and dialogue, and the consequent nature of the loss in the Italian version, are clear enough. Above all, the Italian, while always competent, displays an inclination to eliminate complication and a disinclination to look for nuance. Naturally, Green exploits English syntax to get his effects. They cannot all be reproduced. Yet one never feels that the translation is exploiting Italian syntax to look for similar effects. One never feels any uncertainty at all in the Italian syntax.

To clinch and conclude the analysis, here is one of the few passages, and they are rare indeed in this novel, where dialogue and prose are presented together, where all Green's techniques are being deployed at once. It is the crucial moment, the only truly dramatic moment in the book, when Arthur Middleton actually dares to make a pass at Annabel. They are sitting on the sofa in the Middleton's home, drinking coffee after dinner. Arthur believes his wife and son to be safely on the train taking them to Scotland.

But when she had drained her cup she reached up to put this away on the trolley and as she leant back once more it was to find that he had put an arm along the back of the sofa and that she was, so to speak, sitting against it. His hand closed on the bare shoulder. Without looking at him she reached her far hand over and put it over his. Then, when she felt him pulling at her she said 'Arthur,' expressionlessly, and half turned her head away.

He was seated beside the girl but rather too far off. Also this trolley, between the two of them and that fire, was hard by his knees. It seemed he could not move over easily. So he went on pulling, and, as she tilted towards him, he put his far hand round her chin to turn this in his direction. She quietly rubbed this chin against his palm. Then she gently subsided on the man's shoulder.

They kissed.

'Darling,' he murmured. 'So beautiful. Delicious.'

'Oh Arthur,' she said in just that expiring sigh she used to bring telephone conversations to an end.

They kissed again.

Then, probably because he was uncomfortable, for by the looks of it he had too far to reach to get at her, he dropped the far hand under her legs to lift these over his knees. He drew them unresisting to him, but must have forgotten the trolley. For the slow sweep he was imposing on her legs engaged her feet with that trolley and the coffee pot came over on to both.

'My dress!' she exclaimed in a loud, despairing voice.

'Damn,' he said.

The girl at once jumped to her feet. The trolley almost went into the fire and that coffee pot rolled off their laps on to the floor.

'Hot boiling water,' she cried out.

'Oh God, and to think Mrs Everett's gone home,' he yelled.

They started together, fast, for the passage. Once outside, he shouted, 'in here' throwing open his and Diana's bedroom. There was a bathroom opened out of this, but, because the space was small, a basin with hot and cold water had been fitted by Diana's bed. It was to this that Miss Paynton ran. Turning the hot tap on, she zipped off her skirt, and stood with her fat legs starting out of lace knickers.

'Here, let me,' he said, and knelt at her side.

She picked the handkerchief out of his breast pocket, drenched it in that basin, and then, putting her hand inside the skirt she had discarded, she began to rub at the stain.

And it was at this moment Diana entered. (pp. 219-20)

At the centre of the book lies a tangle with a trolley, a coffee pot and a pair of legs, a muddled embrace, a piece of clumsiness. With the dialogue now straightforward and irretrievably banal, the prose is at its most clinical and reifying, all the parts of the body being described on the same terms as the surrounding objects, and gestures being presented much as they might be in a technical manual ('the slow sweep he was imposing on her legs engaged her feet with that trolley'). Not once are we allowed directly into a character's mind. Speech, bodies and things are all separate objects for an artist's juggling.

Here is the Italian and the back-translation:

> Ma quando Annabel ebbe vuotato la tazzina, si sporse in avanti per posarla sul carrello e appoggiandosi nuovamente allo schienale del divano scoprì che lui aveva allungato un braccio in modo che lei si ritrovasse, per così dire, a sedercisi contro. La mano di lui si chiuse attorno alla spalla nuda. Senza guardarlo lei allungò una mano e coprì la sua. Poi, quando sentì che lui la tirava a sé, disse 'Arthur' in tono neutro, e scostò appena la testa.
>
> Il signor Middleton era seduto di fianco alla ragazza ma un po' troppo lontano da lei. E poi il carrello, situato tra loro e il camino, gli premeva contro un ginocchio. Aveva l'impressione di non potersi muovere agevolmente. Perciò preferì attirare a sé la ragazza, e quando Annabel gli parve sufficientemente inclinata allungò l'altra mano, le prese il mento e lo girò nella direzione opportuna. Lei strofinò dolcemente il mento in questione contro il palmo della sua mano. E poi si lasciò morbidamente andare sulla spalla dell'uomo.
>
> Si baciarono.
>
> 'Tesoro,' mormorò lui, 'che bello. Che delizia.'
>
> 'Oh Arthur,' disse lei, con quel sospiro declinante di cui si serviva per porre termine a una telefonata.
>
> Si baciarono di nuovo.
>
> Poi Arthur, forse perché era scomodo e gli sembrava di doversi allungare troppo per stringersi a lei, le passò una mano sotto le gambe per tirarsela sulle ginocchia. Non incontrò alcuna resistenza da parte della ragazza, ma si era probabilmente dimenticato il carrello. Infatti la lenta rotazione che impose alle gambe di Annabel causò una collisione fra i piedi di lei e il carrello, e la caffettiera precipitò addosso a entrambi.
>
> 'Il mio vestito!' esclamò lei, con disperata energia.
>
> 'Accidenti,' disse lui.
>
> La ragazza saltò immediatamente in piedi. Il carrello andò a finire quasi dentro il camino e la caffettiera rotolò a terra. 'Dell'acqua bollente,' gridò lei.

'Oh Dio, e pensare che la signora Everett se ne è andata,' strillò lui.

Si precipitarono insieme in corridoio, e lui gridò 'Per di qua!' aprendo la porta della loro camera da letto. La stanza aveva annesso un bagno ma, per mancanza di spazio, il lavandino con acqua calda e fredda era accanto al letto di Diana. E lì si precipitò Miss Paynton. Aprì il rubinetto dell'acqua calda e si tolse la gonna, restando nelle mutandine di pizzo da cui spuntavano due gambe grasse.

'Lascia fare a me,' disse lui, inginocchiandosi accanto a lei.

Lei gli tirò fuori il fazzoletto dal taschino, lo inzuppò d'acqua e poi, infilando una mano nella gonna, cominciò a sfregare la macchia.

E in quel preciso momento entrò Diana. (pp. 73-5)

But when Annabel had emptied her cup, she reached forward to put it on the trolley and leaning back again on the sofa discovered that he had stretched out an arm so that she found herself, so to speak, sitting against it. His hand closed around her bare shoulder. Without looking at him she reached out a hand and covered his. Then, when she felt that he was drawing her towards him, she said 'Arthur' in a neutral voice, and moved her head just a little.

Mr Middleton was sitting beside the girl but a bit too far away from her. And then the trolley, located between them and the fireplace, was pressing against his knee. He had the impression he couldn't easily move. So he preferred to draw the girl to himself, and when Annabel seemed to him to be sufficiently tilted he reached out his other hand, took her chin and turned it in the appropriate direction. She softly rubbed the chin in question against the palm of his hand. And then let herself go softly on the man's shoulder.

They kissed.

'Darling,' he murmured, 'how nice. What a delight.'

'Oh Arthur,' she said, with that falling sigh she used to end telephone conversations.

They kissed again.

Then Arthur, maybe because he was uncomfortable and it seemed to him he had to reach too far to cuddle against her, passed a hand under her legs to pull her onto his knees. He met no resistance on the girl's part, but had probably forgotten the trolley. In fact the slow rotation he imposed on Annabel's legs caused a collision between her feet and the trolley, and the coffee pot fell onto both of them.

'My dress!' she exclaimed, with desperate energy.

'Oh no,' he said.

The girl immediately jumped to her feet. The trolley almost ended up in the fireplace and the coffee pot rolled to the ground. 'Boiling water,' she shouted.

'Oh God, and to think that Mrs Everett has gone,' he cried.

They ran together into the corridor, and he shouted, 'This way!' opening the door to their bedroom. The room had a bathroom en suite but, for lack of space, the washbasin with hot and cold water was beside Diana's bed. And there Miss Paynton ran. She turned on the hot water tap and took off her skirt, standing in her lace knickers from which two fat legs stuck out.

'Leave it to me,' he said, getting on his knees next to her.

She took the handkerchief out of his pocket, dipped it in water and then, putting one hand in the skirt, began to rub at the stain.

And at that very moment Diana came in.

Here the differences are of two kinds, though the overall effect of each is substantially the same: there is the elimination of one type of material present in the original and the introduction of another type of material that is not present in the original. The elimination almost always involves tiny physical details and thus has to do with the whole problem of Green's strange focusing and reification, everywhere evident in this passage. The introduction of extraneous material, on the other hand, is psychological in nature.

The following details have been omitted:

- 'her far hand' (line 5)
- 'the two of them' (line 9)
- 'dropped the far hand' (line 10)
- 'off their laps' (line 17)
- 'Once outside' (line 20)
- 'had been fitted' (line 23)
- 'that basin' (lines 27, 28)
- 'she had discarded' (line 28)

None of these details could be considered of any importance in itself. They are the kind of things that do get eliminated, or added (though nothing is added here), in a translation as the translator seeks to establish a homogeneous style in his own language and above all to identify those elements in the original that are perhaps only there to establish fluency or rhythm and not because they have any semantic importance. However, it is worth noting that in this case all these omissions are of a kind. They all contribute to the clinical, detached vision of the scene. Some of them seem quite deliberately to break up the fluency and standard focusing of the English ('drenched it in that basin'). Their omission thus has the same standardizing effect as a number of other small shifts the translator makes, as for example the translation of 'engaged that trolley' with the more dramatic, less consciously technical 'causò una collisione' (*caused a collision*), or again the rendering of the brutally clinical 'get at her' with the more romantic 'stringersi a lei' (cuddled himself to her).

The desire to standardize, however, is more evident in the additions than in these omissions or alterations. They are:

'It seemed he could not'
'Aveva l'impressione di non potersi'
he had the impression he couldn't

'So he went on pulling'
'Perciò preferì attirare'
So he preferred to draw

'and, as she tilted towards him'
'quando Annabel gli parve sufficientemente inclinata'
when Annabel seemed to him sufficiently tilted

'for by the looks of it'
'gli sembrava'
it seemed to him

One of the peculiarities of *Doting* is its odd authorial point of view. In one sense the author is omniscient. He knows everything that takes place between all the characters and even tells us on the first page that he knows something that will happen at the end.[13] But he never claims to know the thoughts or intentions of his characters. They are simply observed, very much as one might observe an experiment with mice or guinea pigs, occasionally speculating on motive, but never confidently stating it.

Alternatively, one might say that *Doting* is like a play without soliloquy. We watch the characters, but never know their thoughts. It is an approach which goes hand in hand with the description of character almost as object.

---

[13] 'So they were three in full evening dress apart from Peter's tailored pin stripe suit in which, several weeks later, he was to carry a white goose under one arm, its dead beak almost trailing the platform, to catch the last train back to yet another term' (p. 171). This teasingly obscure sentence which appears on the first page of the novel serves notice that the author has complete control of his time frame.

The translation frequently follows the original here. For example, when Green writes 'Then, probably because he was uncomfortable' the translator gives 'Poi Arthur, forse perché era scomodo' (*Then Arthur, perhaps because he was uncomfortable*). The shift from 'probably' to 'perhaps' indicates a desire for fluency ('probabilmente' might seem heavy here), but the speculative point of view is maintained.

However, in the crucial paragraphs where Arthur actually moves in on the girl, the translator gives us four privileged views inside the protagonist's head and thus cuts against the grain of the text, breaking down the distanced point of view more damagingly than with the omission of one or two details (though it is important to note that the omission of detail goes in the same direction, the two changes are complementary).

The question that springs to mind with these additions, which occur sporadically throughout the book, must be: why did such a competent translator make them? And here the answer has to be, again, that the translator has not understood how Green's text works and thus tends to write the kind of thing she is used to writing in descriptions of action, where gestures are frequently explained through privileged visions inside the characters' minds. *Doting*, however, is about confused intentionality, or rather, the comedy of a great deal of scheming but, paradoxically, without clear intention. 'What do we ever really learn about people?' asks Annabel. 'Not to trust the way they look and that's about all' (p. 292).

Doting uses the verb 'seem' quite obsessively in its brief descriptions of its characters. The Italian translation frequently translates with a straightforward 'essere', removing the uncertainty and distancing effect of the original. Returning now to the opening passages, those elaborate descriptions of dancer and juggler, one can see that with their garish colouring and gesturing they are a triumph of semblance, of looking one thing and being another. In the end it is surely impossible to put a pint pot on a billiard ball, another billiard ball on top, and then the whole lot on one's chin! 'Miracles of skill' indeed!

Elizabeth Bowen said of Green that 'His novels reproduce, as few English novels do, the actual sensations of living.'[14] Updike picks up the theme in his introduction of 1978: 'They live ... and like all living feed on air, on the invisible; the spaces between the words are warm and the strangeness is mysteriously exact, the strangeness of the vital'.[15] Such statements are intuitive and describe a response to Green's writing rather than analysing a text;

---

[14] Elizabeth Bowen reviewing Green, quoted on the cover of *Surviving: The Uncollected Writings of Henry Green*, cit.

[15] John Updike in the preface to, Henry Green, *Loving, Living, Party Going*, cit., p. 15.

all the same Updike's remark does suggest where that life might come from: 'the spaces between the words, the strangeness', in short the discrepancies, the slippage we have been talking about, discrepancies emphasized by an apparently clinical approach. For it is the perception of characters as separate objects, denied any sure knowledge of each other (as the reader is denied direct insight into them) that generates the spaces which fizz with incomprehension, beauty and life.

Green himself made so few remarks about his writing that it is worth quoting the two most famous to close our argument. In *Pack my Bag,* his early autobiography, he claims that 'Prose should be a long intimacy between strangers with no direct appeal to what both may have known. It should slowly appeal to feelings unexpressed, it should in the end draw tears from a stone ...'.[16] Many years later, in the previously quoted interview with Terry Southern, remarking on the deafness that caused the subtle/suttee misunderstanding, Green claims that such misunderstandings: ' ... enliven my replies, until, through mishearing, a new level of communication is reached'.[17]

The energy of Green's texts, their sense of mystery, lyricism and menace, is created by their sudden shifts in plot and syntax, their refusal to refer directly to what reader and writer know. A translator must be aware of this, must never undermine this allusiveness with a nervous bias towards a more standard, directly communicative text. Above all the translator must look, as he writes, for those moments when his own language offers the possibility to mimic Green's syntactical and lexical quirks. Only in this way will the translated text have any chance of generating the same life as the original.

---

[16] Henry Green, *Pack my Bag,* The Hogarth Press, London, 1992, p. 84.
[17] *Surviving: The Uncollected Writings of Henry Green,* cit., p. 239.

8. Translating Individualism: Literature and Globalization

Literature is going global. We have considered six writers. Four are widely recognized as 'great'. Two have high reputations and even cult followings in Britain but have not become part of the canon. They are also the two – Green and Pym – who are not widely or successfully translated and whose work is thus little known abroad. Let us leave aside for a moment the question: are they not widely translated because not recognized as great, or not recognized as great because not widely translated, and merely reflect that today literary greatness goes hand in hand with international celebrity. The idea that an author might be 'great', yet known only to one national group, is becoming unthinkable. This is particularly true outside the English-speaking world. It is assumed that literary greatness can and will travel. When a respected author completes a novel it is delivered more or less simultaneously to publishers in at least a dozen countries. Translatability thus becomes a prerequisite of glory.

Meantime, publishers and cultural organizations are busy with the formation of a global community of readers at both popular and literary levels: worldwide, more people must read fewer names (it makes commercial sense); there will be more news from the global village and less exploration of the home metropolis, less meditation on one's own language and literary traditions. To promote such a development, particularly at the literary level, where gripping plot and heavy advertising are not all, the last few decades have seen, in imitation of the Nobel, a proliferation of international literary prizes with judges in a single country reading the works of authors from many others and determining literary merit regardless of their limited knowledge of the languages and cultural contexts in which the books were written. In cases where the judges are not reading in English, some works come to them at two removes, since it is common practice to translate from the less widely-known languages into English, and then from English into other major European languages. In general, although translators are granted occasional lip-service, and in Italy may even receive fulsome praise (Nadia Fusini's version of *Mrs Dalloway* was widely touted as better than the original), a sublime indifference is shown to the problems of translation and the consequent status of the translated as opposed to the original text, since any serious reflection on this subject is likely to undermine the legitimacy of the prize-giving enterprise and deflate the atmosphere of complacency that surrounds such events. Elfriede Jelinek, controversial winner of the 2004 Nobel Prize, remarked that she could not understand how her writing could work in translation, so heavily does it depend on puns and intertextual references that only German speakers could catch;[1] little attention was paid to this assessment and around the world publishers set about having her novels translated before the publicity effect of the award could wear off. Almost no one, it seems, wishes to examine how profoundly the role of literature is transformed, when, at least in the non-English speaking world, most contemporary novels are being read in translation.

Since my experience is that of the Englishman transplanted in Italy, let me take the example of the Mondello International Book Award, sponsored by the Sicilian city of Palermo, and, always bearing in mind the extended analyses conducted in this book, use it to draw out a number of ironies beneath the surface piety of 'global literature'. In particular, I want to suggest that there is often a profound contradiction between the original inspiration of many international literary successes and the ambiguous cultural function they come to perform in their translated manifestations. We are at the point where the craft of translation meshes rather curiously with the rise of individualism.

The Mondello prize was inaugurated in 1975. "The fact that Italy as the fifth largest economy in the world did not have an international literary prize, was certainly a grave shortcoming",[2] remarked the founder, Francesco Lentini. One might ask if attention to local prestige is a promising motive for instituting an international prize, but never mind. Palermo is more or less the same size as Stockholm and Sicily has an enviable literary tradition. Why shouldn't the Italians choose whose heads will wear the laurels? In fact, over the years, the Mondello has frequently been awarded to writers who would later carry off the Nobel, suggesting that, albeit with fewer resources, the judges are on the same wavelength.

In 1978, the choice fell on a still young Milan Kundera. Since, at that point, all Kundera's work was written in Czech, the jury read his books in Italian translation. Kundera, however, was soon to become notorious for his aggressive attacks on translators and his complaints of the harm they had done both to his own work and to literature in general. Ironically, by the time he was making those attacks, he had switched, in Italy, to the publishing house that more than any other has been accused of imposing a uniform, *belle-lettres* style on its translations. I am not able to comment on versions from Kundera's Czech, but Henry James's story, *The Altar of the Dead*, opens thus

---

[1] Elfriede Jelinek in interview with Gitta Honegger in the journal *Theater* 36(2): 20-37 Duke University Press (2006).

[2] *Premio Mondello, Letteratura 1975-1987*, Comune di Palermo, Palermo, 1987 p. 5.

in the Adelphi edition:

> "Lui non le poteva soffrire, povero Stransom, le celebrazioni
> scialbe, e ancor più detestava quelle pretenziose. Le commem-
> orazioni lo affliggevano non meno dell'oblio..." [3]

Back translated, this reads:

> He could not bear, poor Stransom, dull celebrations, and even more
> did he detest pretentious ones. Commemorations afflicted him no less
> than forgetfulness.

The English original is:

> "He had a mortal dislike, poor Stransom, to lean anniversaries, and
> he disliked them still more when they made a pretence of a figure.
> Celebrations and suppressions were equally painful to him."[4]

The Italian is neat and elegant. The English is complex and subtle. There are
important differences. The translation entirely exorcises the ghost that hovers in
the words 'mortal', 'lean' and 'figure'; surely a carefully chosen lexical cluster
in a story entitled *The Altar of the Dead*. There will be more ghostly hints later
in the first paragraph which again the Italian will lose. As so often, the attention
seems to be on writing attractive Italian without a profound 'literary' reading
of the text, a reading attentive to the unity of content and imagery.

On the semantic level too an attention to fluency prevails. James's English
tells us that Stransom dislikes unhappy anniversaries (in this case that of his
fiancée's death), whether openly celebrated or not. In the Italian we find two
different kinds of celebrations (dull and pretentious), both of which Stransom
dislikes. The sentence has a neat rhetorical balance, but since there is no reference to the nature of the event being celebrated we are not introduced to the
dilemma of how to treat an unhappy anniversary (the subject of James's story).
Above all, it's hard to understand, in the second sentence of the Italian, how
in this context one can be afflicted by 'oblio' (forgetfulness); forgetting, as
the next sentence will tell us, is precisely the liberation that has been denied
to Stransom who remains trapped by memories of a girl who died many years
ago: suppression and forgetfulness are not the same thing. "James's prickly

---

[3] Henry James, *L'altare dei morti*, trans. Giulia Arborio Mella, Adelphi, Milan, 1988.
[4] Henry James, *The Altar of the Dead*, BiblioBazaar, 2006, p. 9.

style does not come across well in Italian", an editor at the publishing house explained at a lecture, commenting on this passage of translation.[5]

Kundera would have pounced on such a defence. His argument with translators is precisely that they prefer a conventional style to the author's. He speaks of a tendency of translators to reject repetition, to use literary vocabulary where the original text was spare and simple; in short, to prefer belles lettres to "stylistic transgression".[6] Their "supreme authority", Kundera insists, "should be the author's personal style".[7] 'But most translators obey another authority, that of the conventional version of "good French".[8]

French being his second language, Kundera's criticisms are mainly levelled at French translators, but they are more than borne out by the analyses of Italian translations in this book (with the exception perhaps of the translation of *Ulysses*). More generally, as thesis tutor to students studying translations of such disparate modern masterpieces as Orwell's *1984*, Fitzgerald's The *Great Gatsby*, Faulkner's *Absalom, Absalom*, Phillip Roth's *The Human Stain*, not to mention at least a hundred other works translated from English into Italian and from Italian into English, I have found over the years that the tendency to sacrifice semantic precision and above all stylistic provocation in translation is almost universal and probably inevitable. The phenomenon is bound to make us wonder if reading in translation does not alter the way we read, lowering our expectations of internal linguistic and even semantic cohesion, encouraging concentration on plot and reinforcing conventional usage of the national language regardless of unconventional elements that may remain in the content and structure of the book.

On the other hand, of course, we might also wonder: why does someone like Milan Kundera care so much about this question of style in translation? His international reputation could hardly be more enviable; he has won many international prizes and may one day win the Nobel. He can hardly complain that poor translation has affected his sales. It may even have made his work more accessible, ironing out those aspects that are unconventional and hence challenging in the original Czech, or more recently the French. So what does it matter to him? The answer to both our perplexities, I think, is to be sought in Kundera's use of those rather disturbing words, "supreme authority". There is more at stake here than at first meets the eye.

---

[5] Giulia Arborio Mella chose this passage as one to discuss at a conference on translation at IULM University, 1995

[6] This and other remarks in M. Kundera, *Testaments Betrayed*, trans. L. Asher, Harper Collins, New York, 1995. See in particular the essay on Kafka.

[7] M. Kundera, *Testaments Betrayed*, cit., p. 110

[8] Loc. cit.

Reading through the press coverage of the early editions of the Mondello prize, it is fascinating to see how determinedly the winning authors reject all the labels that the interviewing journalists equally determinedly seek to thrust upon them. Tadeusz Konwickim, in 1981, is clearly hostile to the then government in his native Poland (his winning book *Small Apocalypse* describes a writer who sets fire to himself outside communist party headquarters), but he flatly refuses to be labelled a 'dissident' by his interviewer. "This is just another definition imported from the USSR", he complains, "I refuse to be catalogued in this way". When he speaks for a moment of a tenuous faith in God, referring to it as "a hope that is almost exclusively verbal", the journalist immediately searches for a recognizable formula to present to the newspaper's readers: "So you believe in the power of the word". Konwickim is shocked: "No, it gives me the shivers. Orthodoxies are pure cult of the word".[9]

Dürenmatt in 1986 is even more provocative. His country Switzerland, does not have "a clean conscience". He refuses to speak at a conference on human rights organized by the French government while that government is involved in arms sales. All the same, the interviewing journalist laments, "the author rejects every label. He refuses to consider himself a Green, an ecologist or a pacifist". "It'll be their fault if the Third World War breaks out one day", says Dürenmatt, piling on the irony. More generally, he remarks that: "a father is there to be given a beating". The only thing he is willing to confirm is that all this passionate opposition is undertaken in the name of "truth". But almost immediately truth is construed as a negative concept, not a positive construct: "My work as a writer prompts me to attack false myths".[10] Truth is the destruction of falsehood.

In one form or another, then, and with remarkable consistency across the years, the various prize winners – but this is true of almost all contemporary authors with literary pretensions – tell us that they mustn't be pinned down. After accepting that her winning book, *The Good Terrorist*, deals intensely with socio-political issues, Doris Lessing insists that "I don't feel I'm committed to a cause. I look at what's going on, that's all". And she renounces the idea that her vision is specifically English. "I look at England with an English eye and simultaneously a foreigner's eye too".[11] The 'supreme authority' of the author, it seems, transcends the limitations of national character. This is a crucial claim. The individual writer is his or her unique self, or wishes to be considered such, *regardless of cultural context*. The writer is beyond such

---

[9] *Premio Mondello*, cit. p. 70-71.

[10] *Premio Mondello*, cit. 1975-1987, p. 180-181.

[11] *Premio Mondello*, cit. p. 222-223.

things. Put another way we might say that these authors would not accept that their individual vision exists only in English, or Czech, or Polish. They want to believe that translators can reproduce their unique points of view in other languages.

It would be hard not to see in the positions assumed by these writers at once a version and perversion of one of the most revolutionary aspects of early Christianity, something that lies at the very heart of Western culture. When Christ offers Everyman the possibility of a direct relationship with his Maker, traditional and temporal hierarchies are peremptorily swept aside. Supreme value passes to the immortal individual and his relationship with the divine. Everything else is relative. We know how determinedly the official church stepped in to tame this delirium and keep the sacred texts out of the way of those who might take them at their word. We know too how every attempt to return to that subversive and liberating original vision was always accompanied by a stress on reading. John Wycliffe, in particular, decided that *all* reading, not just of the Bible, was valuable, in that it placed the individual alone in interpretative contemplation away from the control of orthodoxy. So individualism and reading went hand in hand. Since there were not that many texts available for reading in English in the 14th century, Wycliffe encouraged his followers to write as well as read. What they wrote, of course, were their individual experiences of the divine.

Today the metaphysics have gone but the sense that supreme value resides in the individual's unique apprehension of experience, untainted by orthodox society's convenient and self-serving "false myths", remains. Without a positive credo, however, this individual vision is obliged to establish itself by negatives and denials, nuances and disclaimers. Or rather, as far as writers are concerned, we might say that the individual vision only exists in the literary text itself, the words on the page, refusing any positive, binding alliance with an ideology or credo outside the writer's work. A literary reading thus becomes, as Keats would one day so astutely point out, a lesson in "negative capability", and he goes on to explain, "that is when man is capable of being in uncertainties, Mysteries, doubts without any irritable reaching after fact & reason".[12] Hence the prize-winner's uneasiness in interviews when people ask him to explain his ideas.

In his collection of essays *Literature and the Gods* Roberto Calasso presents the situation thus: "Allergic to the idea of belonging to anything, honourable members, no less than Groucho Marx, of the club of those who would never join a club that accepted them as members, they [writers] used that word

---

[12] Keats, letter to George and Thomas Keats dated Sunday, 21 December 1817.

[literature] to refer to the only landscape where they felt they could live: a sort of second reality that opens out beyond the cracks of that other reality where everyone has agreed the conventions that make the world machine go round".[13]

In his 1981 interview, Konwickim confirmed this tendency to cut any descriptive link between ordinary conventions and his writing. He dreams, he says of living in a world where a writer is not obliged to become a saint, a priest or a prophet. Actually he would prefer a society where the citizen was so free from contamination from "public life" that he wouldn't even know the name of the president of the republic in which he lived. When finally Konwickim is lured into describing his writing positively, he uses the word 'play'.[14] His work is playful. Dürenmatt concurs. His novels are games, he says. How many times have we seen writers seeking this refuge from the probing of critics and interviewers. Post-modernism in particular loves to present itself as playful. But it is always understood that this is a corrosive and iconoclastic form of playing. The more dour poet Edoardo Sanguinetti, again interviewed in relation to the Mondello, insists on the word subversion. He is suspicious of "tradition"[15] he tells us, writers should be subverting it. But both play and subversion require material to conjure with, to undermine; both are incomprehensible without a context that is played with, subverted.

At this point, the urgency of Kundera's statements on translation should be understandable. For in what does the authenticating individuality, the supreme authority, of the writer reside if not in his "personal style", in the way he sets forth his own personal 'negative capability', the way he plays with or subverts the conventional language that upholds the establishment or, less polemically, the common view of things? Style is 'the transformation that the author's thought imposes on reality',[16] Proust tells us, more or less equating style and individual vision. We have seen in an earlier chapter how Lawrence insisted that his style was 'natural to the author',[17] the individual, and hence beyond debate. Style is absolute, you take it or leave it. And if it is lost in translation, then, presumably, the author is lost too, the individual vision is lost; we are left with a text that may or may not be successful, that may or may not be full of interesting ideas, but it is Kundera or Lawrence no longer. In urging translators to reproduce his style *exactly*, Kundera is declaring that he wishes to be truly Kundera in whatever part of the globe his books appear,

---

[13] Roberto Calasso, *Literature and the Gods*, trans. Tim Parks, Knopf, New York, 2001.
[14] *Premio Mondello*, cit. p. 71.
[15] *Premio Mondello*, cit. p. 193.
[16] M. Proust, *Contre Sainte-Beuve*, Gallimard, Paris, 1978, p. 225.
[17] D.H. Lawrence, Foreword to *Women in Love*, Thomas Seltzer, 1920.

Kundera in French, Kundera in English, Kundera in Italian, Kundera in Russian, Kundera in Chinese. He is looking for the supreme confirmation of his individuality, unlimited by cultural or linguistic context.

But why do translators fail to deliver "what is natural to the author"? "I work so hard on style", laments Doris Lessing in the same Mondello interview "and then find out that in translation a sentence has become flat and monotonous".[18] Participating in a debate on *Modernity and Literature* in Palermo in 1979, the Argentinian writer Juan Gelman gives us the key to understanding the problem. Most contributors to the debate, he remarks, have concentrated on modernity as content, whereas he prefers to see the problem linguistically: "what is really in a literary work is not the subject it deals with, but the medium it's working in, its language". And language, he goes on to insist, is a social instrument "made of up of centuries upon centuries of deposits, of history",[19] that bind us to society past and present. Modernity and individuality thus have to express themselves in a language that is far from modern and what's more common to everyone. There is bound to be friction between the two, between individual and language. That friction is style.

Time and again, D.H. Lawrence made it clear that his argument was above all with English, the language in which his society's values were enshrined, to the extent, he claims, that he had to invent "a foreign language"[20] to write his first great novel, *The Rainbow*. Kundera is on the same wavelength: "Partisans of flowing translation", he insists, "object to my translators: 'that's not the way to say it in German (in English, in Spanish, etc.)'. I reply, 'It's not the way to say it in Czech either'".[21] Here, in parenthesis, we discover that in his determination to transmit his style beyond the limits of the Czech (and later the French) that it has subverted, Kundera has collected about himself a stable, as it were, of faithful translators, '*my* translators'. He apparently believes in the possibility of a near identity of translation and original, given good disciples.

Can it be done? We know that for the protestant reform translation was at once an urgent imperative and a thorny problem. The individual met his God (but above all escaped from papist orthodoxy) in the pages of the sacred text. The fate of countless souls might hang upon a nuance. The translator had to be wonderfully competent and himself divinely inspired. Luther's defence of his translation of the Bible will remain one of the great statements on translation

---

[18] *Premio Mondello*, cit. p. 222.

[19] Premio Mondello, cit. p. 47.

[20] The Cambridge Edition of the Letters of D. H. Lawrence, ed. James Boulton, Vol. I, Cambridge, 1979, p. 544.

[21] M. Kundera, *The Art of the Novel*, Faber & Faber, London 1990, pp. 129-130.

when many more fashionable recent theories are forgotten. However, with the Bible, *the essential issues were semantic*. Content was supreme. There was a positive message to express, hence Luther's marvellous and marvellously spirited explanation of his introduction of the word *allein* (alone) in the phrase 'saved by faith alone' (Romans III, 28).[22] The modern writer, on the other hand, is working hard, above all, to avoid transmitting any such message. The novel is great, Lawrence reminds us, comparing the form favourably with the sacred texts, the Bible in particular, because "it cannot tell didactic lies".[23] Any dangerous beliefs a writer may have are qualified, if not contradicted, by the contingent world described. It is this tension and, if we like, negative capability, that gives the genre its vitality, a web of images, stylemes and narrative events that avoids any final message or explanation.

Kundera creates his style, he tells us, in part by writing things that are 'not good Czech'. Presumably this is done at special moments when something in those centuries and centuries of deposits that have created the language is not to Kundera's liking, or needs drawing attention to, or simply, when some particular effect that is congenial to Kundera can be achieved and exploited. It is not a random thing; one presumes, that is, that there will be an internal coherence between Kundera's deviations from 'good Czech', a pattern that gradually builds up a consistent and characteristic friction between individual vision and collective consciousness, a pattern that creates a special place for the text in the overall context of Czech language and literature. This is exactly the sort of thing we have seen in the preceding analyses of English modernist texts and their Italian translations.

Such strategies, typical of so much writing in the twentieth century, put the translator in a difficult if not impossible position, since, as Steiner remarked, when literature seeks to break its public linguistic mould and become idiolect", it also necessarily "seeks untranslatability".[24]

"The structure of the Latin language", Luther so memorably wrote, "is a serious obstacle to someone who wants to write good German".[25] But Luther didn't have to deal with a writer subverting the structure of the Latin language and telling us that *precisely that subversion* and not the content, or rather, that pattern of subversion in relation to the content, was the sacred aspect of the text. Subverting Latin and subverting German are two different things. The languages will offer different targets, different opportunities. Speakers will

---

[22] Siri Nergaard, *La teoria della traduzione nella storia*, Bompiani, Milano, 1993, p. 106.

[23] D.H. Lawrence: 'The Novel', in *Phoenix II*, ed. Warren Roberts and Harry T. Moore, Heinemann, London, 1968.

[24] George Steiner, *After Babel*, Oxford University Press, 1975, p. 183.

[25] Siri Nergaard, *La teoria della traduzione nella storia*, cit, p. 107.

be irritated with them and will play with them in different ways. How could one tackle Beckett's sublime "I have no bone to pick with graveyards"[26] in a language that lacks this or any similar idiom? At such moments the translator will often find that normalizing the text is the only way forward. Obsessed with the importance of maintaining his identity across the globe, Kundera, one has to feel, is being ingenuous about the possibilities of translation.

This brings us to the central irony of much modern international literary celebrity. So many of the best writers gain their initial energy and forge their styles from a struggle with their culture and language of origin. We have quoted Samuel Beckett's remark: "It is indeed becoming more and more difficult, even senseless, for me to write an official English ... it seems to have become as irrelevant as a Victorian bathing suit or the imperturbability of a true gentleman".[27] J.M. Coetzee, another prestigious Mondello and Nobel winner, makes great play of the tension between a literary English, now meaningless, he suggests, in black South Africa, and the language of the dominant majority. In the novel Disgrace, the book's protagonist, David Lurie, reflects on the background of his black neighbour, Petrus, as follows:

> He would not mind hearing Petrus's story one day. But preferably not reduced to English. More and more he is convinced that English is an unfit medium for the truth of South Africa. Stretches of English code whole sentences long have thickened, lost their articulations, their articulateness, their articulatedness. Like a dinosaur expiring and settling in the mud, the language has stiffened. Pressed into the mould of English, Petrus's story would come out arthritic, bygone.[28]

There is hence a suggestion that Coetzee's own decidedly lean style is being developed in response to particular circumstances, a particular linguistic context. Removed from that context into another language it will inevitably, and this despite the apparent ease of translation, lose an important layer of meaning (ie. what is happening to English in the ex-colonial world). Opposition, rebellion, *reaction*, do not exist in a vacuum, they are always part of a specific situation. However much the writer may prize his individual identity, his book is not the same book in another context.

Many writers whose work is galvanized by a struggle against their culture of origin choose to leave their countries, or even change languages (as has

[26] Samuel Beckett, *Samuel Beckett, The Complete Short Prose*, 1929-1989, Grove Press, New York, 1995, p. 25.
[27] Samuel Beckett, *Disjecta,* Calder, London, 1983, p. 173.
[28] J.M. Coetzee, *Disgrace*, Vintage, London, 2000, p. 117.

Kundera). Of the six authors examined in this book, three – Lawrence, Joyce and Beckett – lived most of their adult lives outside of their native countries. All three had to deal with critical hostility and censorship. The very notoriety generated by this sort of non-conformism, this assault on received opinion at home, encourages publication in other languages, since nobody is more avidly sought after than a rebel from another land; indeed, this is a crucial factor in the internationalization of literature, going back as far as the exiled Catullus, the exiled Dante. The writer achieves an international stature because of the heightened individuality consequent on his or her quarrel at home.

Yet in translation, the very element that most distinguished these authors, the linguistic individuality ("idiolect", Steiner says) that provoked their critics and electrified their readers, that friction between individual expression and collective language, is, as we have amply seen, largely and inevitably lost. The book becomes something else, something understood within the values and dynamics of another language and culture. Even the best translation is a total transformation. Depending on the content and structure of the book, the author may still appear to the foreign reader as a rebel, but at the linguistic level, the level that, as Juan Gelman claimed, is most determining, the individual element in his work is lost. It threatens no one in the country of consumption.

We thus note that translation can contribute to a disturbing phenomenon in modern culture whereby, in private communion with the written word, or in the anonymous dark of the cinema perhaps, we excite ourselves by identifying with the energy and intensified individuality of another's rebellion against authority, only to return, on closing the book or leaving the cinema for the prosaic light of the street, to the orthodoxies with which we are comfortable. We enjoy vicariously without being challenged or threatened. Needless to say the experience is all the more comfortable when the rebellion in question is set far from home. The translated rebellion, like the dubbed movie, is in danger of becoming just another man's quarrel elsewhere. I identify with the negative energy, I enjoy the plot, while my own language and the values it encodes remain unchallenged.

Certainly, if the Mondello and other international prizes have been able to anticipate many of the choices of the Nobel, it is because winners tend to be rebel voices in cultures undergoing upheaval. Fashions in international literary prizes are embarrassingly evident. We have the period of the Soviet bloc dissidents (despite Konwickim's rejection of the term), we have the South American outlaws, we have the South Africans, the Chinese, the black American woman, the liberal representatives of the Moslem world. It is hard to keep politics out of these events. And overt political rebellion tends to obscure the more profound and creative questioning of the language itself. Jose Saramago used his Nobel acceptance speech to deliver a scathing attack on multi-nationals and international capitalism, the constant objects of contempt in his novels. The audience, many of whom depended for their income on the success of such enterprises, applauded enthusiastically. In this scenario, the writer whose quarrel with the language is not manifested in rebellious and provocative events at the narrative level is almost certain to be passed over.

It would be strange if writers did not adapt their behaviour to changed circumstances. The passage from rebel to international celebrity was hardly sought after by the likes of Lawrence or Joyce. They were not aware of a mechanism at work. But the same cannot be said today, when it will be obvious to many authors that the path to a certain kind of celebrity is now well trodden. In particular, the international market for fiction is altering the attitudes of some authors to their use of language and choice of material. It is commonplace these days for writers from, say, Scandinavia to choose names for their characters that will not challenge readers of a British translation; for the fiction writer a sale of foreign rights, particularly English language rights, can make the difference between making a living and not. More disturbingly, shortly after winning the Booker Prize with a novel that had strong political themes (the importance of not remaining obedient to evil masters), Kazuo Ishiguro, the Anglo-Japanese writer, gave an interview to *Time Magazine* in which he criticized his British contemporaries for writing in ways that made translation difficult. His rigidly austere prose was, he claimed, partly the result of his attentiveness to eventual translations.

Ishiguro is right, of course, that an attentive writer can make it easier to translate his work. Thinking of his translators, Lawrence could have spared them such expressions as, 'destroyed into perfect consciousness', or 'shut himself together'. But while one is ready to accept a loss in translation, the idea of accepting it a priori in the original so as to avoid it in translation is depressing. What was the sense, then, of fighting for freedom of expression? We should remember that any disturbance at the level of language, the very system in which our thinking is woven, is always more powerful than even the most adventurous and aggressive content. It is at the level of the language that a "negative capability" is established. To translate a highly individual piece of literature leaving the translator's language unruffled and bringing across only the content is to offer the reassurance that experience can be safely housed in standard language, exactly the idea that the modernists rebelled against. Indeed one glimpses behind Ishiguro's remark a dangerous willingness to split apart content and style, as though one could retain freedom of speech and individual identity, but renounce freedom of style in order to be able to speak to a wider public. This split is frequent in 'global literature', perhaps characteristic of it. Language aspires to be mere code, instantly translatable. It is a split that ignores, whether out of ingenuousness or commercial convenience, the fact that, as Beckett shows in *Watt*, language that stays still quickly becomes a mental trap. It will shield us from reality in its rigid system, but it will also make it harder for us to adapt when inevitably one day the shield proves inadequate.

There is another school of thought, of course, championed among others by the American critic, Lawrence Venuti, which rejects the hard task of faithfully recreating the writer's style, declares that the original itself, far from embodying any 'supreme authority', has only the status of a translation (in that it is created as a selection from a huge body of thought and memory) and concludes that the translator has a right to impose his own individuality on the text, not by returning it to the conventional idiom of the language he is working in, but, on the contrary, by following his own genius, his own interpretation and finding a unique style of his own. While this position is anathema to Kundera and indeed to publishers, who have much to gain from the idea of the international superstar author and wish readers to believe they are getting the real thing, we should nevertheless note that at a deeper level Kundera and Venuti have much in common. Both of them are chiefly concerned with promoting individual as against conventional usage, only that in Kundera's case it is the writer's, in Venuti's the translator's. Both believe the result should be subversive of establishment language; it is a question of who is doing the subversion and what relation that subversion has to the work's content. Venuti champions Venuti, Kundera Kundera. Of the two Kundera's aspirations seem the nobler and make more sense, in that his approach insists on the unity of style and content in the original, whereas what Venuti proposes is a hybrid. I would rather read the work of a translator who has done everything he can to understand the deeper sense of the author's text and to find a way of recreating that in translation, than that of the translator playing his own variations over what will inevitably remain Kundera's content.

One notes in passing here the gradual disappearance of the figure who was both author and translator. Lawrence and Beckett both translated a great deal. Today it is almost unimaginable that writers of similar stature working in the English language would surrender the authority of their style to seek instead to deliver someone else's. In particular, I cannot think of a single prominent member of the much praised 'empire-writes-back' school taking time to translate works from their cultures of origin. To do so, perhaps, is to drop the mantle of supreme individual, guru even, that the public expects from the author. Ironically, it was precisely when an active writer was also translating that there was the greatest possibility of one culture's language and literature being enriched by another's. Today, the more the author is a global figure, the less he is likely to translate.

To conclude: these reflections are by no means intended as a general criticism of translation, and even less an appeal not to translate, merely an invitation to be alert to what we are reading when we come to literature in translation and aware of what is at stake, aesthetically, intellectually, as we move to a world where the literary giants of each country are made simultaneously available all over the globe, inevitably taking the shelf space once occupied by our less lionized national writers. No one wants to suggest that a dumbing down is involved in reading Dostoevsky or Bernhard or Calvino in English. Many of my own most important reading experiences have been of authors read in translation. All the same, that absolute congruity between language and subject, typical of the work read in the original, is inevitably lacking in the translation, and with it goes a certain intensity of cohesion and the corresponding mental engagement it stimulates. Reading becomes more a question of semantic surface, of plot and intellectually articulated idea.

How should the reader come to the translated text, then, and how should the translator approach his task? The reader with curiosity of course, always remembering that the translated novel comes to him at a remove, enjoying where possible those novelties that translations bring into the language, wondering how far these give the same effect the author intended, or if they might simply be interesting as spin-offs. In general it is foolish, as a reader, to be anxious that you might not be getting the original author as heard in his own language. You are not. But if one thinks of this as no more than a confirmation of the real and unbridgeable difference between one culture and another, the demonstration that languages cannot be reduced to an underlying code, then this distance from the original can become cause for rejoicing. So long as we have different languages, different cultures, the world cannot become the monolithic thing globalization otherwise threatens to make it. Also, as long as there are different languages we will be free to shake off our individual identities, often more a burden than a boast, and reconstruct ourselves in otherness.

The translator on the other hand, once he or she has fully grasped the impossibility of the translator's task, is free to fail gloriously. An important premise to keep in mind is that everything in the translation will tend to be read *as if written in English*, as if planned that way. Hence it is pointless trying to keep vague allusions to foreign texts that the reader cannot know, or indeed as some translators do, trying to retain something of the structure of the original language in the translation. Such strategies can only be read by the uninitiated as deliberate deviations from standard English intended to qualify the content of the work in some way. This is how we read literature. The reader will look for meaning that isn't there, he will grow confused.

But if this book has anything to say to the translator, I hope it has shown how important it is to understand the strategy of the work *as a whole*, its rhythms, its imagery, its stylistic techniques; only then can we reconstruct it as a coherent whole, and thus, as Beckett liked to say, "fail better".[29] Hence my contention, that the translator must read with the sensibility of the very best literary critic to have any chance at all of capturing the essential traits of a complex text. Translating Pym, one cannot back away from her use of inverted commas around jargon phrases; one must understand what she is about. Translating Green, one cannot pretend to leave standard deixis entirely in place, or introduce psychological interpolations absent in the text; one simply has to notice these things, take nothing for granted. Translating Lawrence, one must have a sense of the relationship between his violent juxtapositions and his overall purpose, of the way he deliberately leaves phrases open to a variety of interpretations. If there is one thing that is astonishing in translation studies, it is its tendency to concentrate on linguistic theory or publishing politics, or to focus on single, separate and usually insuperable translation problems, while forgetting how literature works, as a gathering web of implication and suggestion where everything qualifies everything else. Hence every decision must be taken with the whole in mind. Eventually, of course, when the translation is complete, a new web should be established in the new language, hopefully retaining at least some of the original's resistance to certain conventions, ready in any event to capture and enchant the mind of the reader who will bring to it an entirely different linguistic and cultural context. This is the moment – to close on a happy note – when, the 'supreme authority' of the writer's individual style inevitably lost and forgotten, exciting and unexpected things can nevertheless happen in the alien country of another tongue.

---

[29] Samuel Beckett, *Worstward Ho*, Calder, London, 1983, p. 21.

Bibliography

Bair, Deirdre (1978) *Samuel Beckett: A Biography*, New York: Harcourt.

Beckett, Samuel (1962) *Murphy*, Turin: Einaudi, translated by Franco Quadri.

------ (1965) *Murphy*, Paris: Les Editions de Minuit.

------ (1967) *Watt*, Milan: Sugarco Edizioni, translated by Cesare Cristofolini.

------ (1971) *Waiting for Godot*, London: Faber & Faber.

------ (1971) *Molloy*, London: Jupiter Books, Calder & Boyars.

------ (1972) *Watt*, Jupiter Books edition, London: Calder & Boyars.

------ (1973) *Murphy*, London: Picador.

------ (1975) *Malone Dies*, London: Calder & Boyars.

------ (1976) *I can't go on, I'll go on*, New York: Grove Weidenfeld.

------ (1983) *Disjecta*, London: Calder.

------ (1983) *Worstward Ho*, London: Calder.

------ (1987) *Proust and Three Dialogues with Georges Duthuit*, London: Calder.

------ (1994) *First Love*, London: Penguin Syrens.

------ (1995) *Samuel Beckett, The Complete Short Prose, 1929-1989*, New York: Grove Press.

Budge, Frank (1972) *James Joyce and the Making of Ulysses*, Oxford: Oxford University Press.

Calasso, Roberto (2001) *Literature and the Gods*, New York: Knopf, translated by Tim Parks.

Carswell, Catherine (1932) *The Savage Pilgrimage*, London: Chatto.

Clarke, Colin (1969) '*The Rainbow' and 'Women in Love': A Selection of Critical Essays*, London: Macmillan.

Coetzee, J.M. (2000) *Disgrace*, London: Vintage.

Cotsell, Michael (1989) *Barbara Pym*, London: Macmillan.

Green, Henry (1979) *Nothing, Doting, Blindness*, London: Picador.

------ (1979) *Back*, London: The Hogarth Press.

------ (1990) *Passioni*, Turin: Einaudi, translated by Stefania Bertola.

------ (1992) *Pack my Bag*, London: The Hogarth Press.

------ (1993) *Surviving, The Uncollected Writings of Henry Green*, London: Harville.

------ (2000) *Party Going*, London: Vintage Classics.

------ (2006) *Partenza in Gruppo*, Milan: Adelphi Edizioni, translated by Carlo Bay.

Harvey, Lawrence (1970) *Samuel Beckett: Poet and Critic*, Princeton: Princeton University Press, 1970.

James, Henry (1988) *L'altare dei morti*, Milan: Adelphi, translated by Giulia Arborio Mella.

------ (2006) *The Altar of the Dead*, New York: BiblioBazaar.

Jelinek, Elfriede (2006) 'Interview with Gitta Honegger', *Theater* 36(2): 20-37.

Joyce, James (1922/1993) *Ulysses*, Oxford: Oxford University Press (World's Classics).

------ (1924) *A Portrait of the Artist as a Young Man*, London: Jonathan Cape.

------ (1967) *Dubliners*, London: Jonathan Cape.

------ (1976) *Gente di Dublino*, Garzanti, Milan, translated by Marco Papi and Emilio Tadini.

------ (1976) *Dedalus*, Milan: Adelphi, translated by Cesare Pavese.

------ (1978) *Ulisse*, Milan: Oscar Mondadori, Milan, translated by Giulio de Angelis.

Kermode, Frank (1979) *The Genesis of Secrecy*, Cambridge, Mass.: Harvard University Press.

Kundera, Milan (1990) *The Art of the Novel*, London: Faber & Faber.

------ (1995) *Testaments Betrayed*, New York: Harper Collins, translated by L. Asher.

------ (1968) 'The Novel', in *Phoenix II*, edited by Warren Roberts and Harry T. Moore, London: Heinemann.

------ (1979) *The Letters of D. H. Lawrence*, Volume I, edited by James Boulton, Cambridge: Cambridge University Press.

------ (1981) *The Letters of D.H. Lawrence*, vol. 2, edited by George J. Zytaruk and James T. Boulton, Cambridge: Cambridge University Press.

------ (1982) *Women in Love*, London: Penguin.

------ (1989) *Donne innamorate*, Rizzoli, Milan, translation by Adriana dell'Orto.

Murry, John Middleton (1921) 'The Nostalgia of Mr D.H. Lawrence', *Nation and Athenaeum*, 13 August.

Nergaard, Siri (1993) *La teoria della traduzione nella storia*, Milano: Bompiani.

Proust, Marcel (1978) *Contre Sainte-Beuve*, Paris: Gallimard.

Pym, Barbara (1981) *A Few Green Leaves*, London: Grafton.

------ (1989) *Qualche foglia verde*, Milan: La Tartaruga edizioni, translated by Frida Ballini.

Ricks, Christopher (1993) *Beckett's Dying Words*, Oxford: Oxford University Press.

Senn, Fritz (1982) 'Righting Ulysses', in Colin MacCabe (ed.) *James Joyce: New Perspectives*, Brighton: Harvester.

Steiner, George (1975) *After Babel*, Oxford: Oxford University Press.

Updike, John (1978) 'Preface to Henry Green's *Loving, Living, Party Going*', London: Picador.

Woolf, Virginia (1953) *Mrs Dalloway*, New York: Harcourt Brace Jovanovich.

------ (1993) *La Signora Dalloway*, Milan: Feltrinelli Editore, translated by Nadia Fusini.

Index